Critical Bodies

Critical Bodies

Representations, Identities and Practices of Weight and Body Management

Edited by

Sarah Riley, Maree Burns, Hannah Frith, Sally Wiggins and Pirkko Markula

© Sarah Riley, Maree Burns, Hannah Frith, Sally Wiggins and Pirkko Markula 2008
Softcover reprint of the hardcover 1st edition 2008 978-0-230-51773-8

All rights reserved. No reproduction, copy or transmission of this publication may be made without written permission.

No paragraph of this publication may be reproduced, copied or transmitted save with written permission or in accordance with the provisions of the Copyright, Designs and Patents Act 1988, or under the terms of any licence permitting limited copying issued by the Copyright Licensing Agency, 90 Tottenham Court Road, London W1T 4LP.

Any person who does any unauthorised act in relation to this publication may be liable to criminal prosecution and civil claims for damages.

The authors have asserted their rights to be identified as the author of this work in accordance with the Copyright, Designs and Patents Act 1988.

First published 2008 by
PALGRAVE MACMILLAN
Houndmills, Basingstoke, Hampshire RG21 6XS and
175 Fifth Avenue, New York, N.Y. 10010
Companies and representatives throughout the world

PALGRAVE MACMILLAN is the global academic imprint of the Palgrave Macmillan division of St. Martin's Press, LLC and of Palgrave Macmillan Ltd. Macmillan® is a registered trademark in the United States, United Kingdom and other countries. Palgrave is a registered trademark in the European Union and other countries.

ISBN 978-1-349-35543-3   ISBN 978-0-230-59114-1 (eBook)
DOI 10.1057/9780230591141

A catalogue record for this book is available from the British Library.

A catalog record for this book is available from the Library of Congress.

10 9   8   7   6   5   4   3   2   1
17 16 15 14 13 12 11 10 09 08

Transferred to Digital Printing in 2014

Contents

List of Figures vii

Notes on Contributors viii

Introducing Critical Bodies: Representations, Identities and Practices of Weight and Body Management 1
Pirkko Markula, Maree Burns and Sarah Riley

Section I Representations and Constructions of Body Weight and Body Management 23
Sally Wiggins

1 Deconstructing Un/Healthy Body-weight and Weight Management 27
   Helen Malson

2 'I Feel Ridiculous about Having Had It' – Critical Readings of Lived and Mediated Stories on Eating Disorders 43
   Paula Saukko

3 Learning to Be Healthy, Dying to Be Thin: The Representation of Weight via Body Perfection Codes in Schools 60
   Emma Rich and John Evans

Section II Constructing Embodied Identities 77
Hannah Frith

4 Starving in Cyberspace: The Construction of Identity on 'Pro-eating-disorder' Websites 81
   Katy Day and Tammy Keys

5 Body Talk: Negotiating Body Image and Masculinity 101
   Rosalind Gill

6 Feminist Object Relations Theory and Eating 'Disorders' 117
   Colleen Heenan

v

Section III Meanings of Body Management Practices: Women's Experiences
Pirkko Markula
135

7 Dis/Orders of Weight Control: Bulimic and/or 'Healthy Weight' Practices
Maree Burns and Nicola Gavey
139

8 Sustaining Imbalance – Evidence of Neglect in the Pursuit of Nutritional Health
Lucy Aphramor and Jacqui Gingras
155

9 Older and Younger Women's Experiences of Commercial Weight Loss
Debra Gimlin
175

Conclusion
Critical Bodies: Discourses of Health, Gender and Consumption
Sarah Riley, Hannah Frith, Sally Wiggins, Pirkko Markula and Maree Burns
193

Index
204

List of Figures

Figure 8.1 'Size Matters' Leaflet (BDA, 2004)   161

Notes on Contributors

Lucy Aphramor, RD, is a Senior Health-promotion Specialist in diet and cardiovascular health. She is also a senior research assistant at the Applied Research Centre – Health and Lifestyle Interventions, Coventry University, UK. Her current research looks at the impact of size-discrimination on policy, research directions and on people's health and health-seeking behaviour.

Maree Burns is the coordinator of the Eating Difficulties Education Network in Auckland, New Zealand. Her research interests include examining discourses and representations of disordered eating, obesity and weight/body management, and their constitutive impacts on subjectivity and practice. She has published several articles on the social construction of bulimia, bulimic practices and issues of subjectivity/embodiment. Maree is currently co-editing a book with Helen Malson entitled *Critical Feminist Perspectives on Eating Dis/Orders* (Psychology Press, forthcoming).

Katy Day is a Senior Lecturer in Psychology at Leeds Metropolitan University, where she is a founding member of the Feminism & Health Research Group. Her research interests centre on the social construction of femininity, and include women and alcohol; women's aggression and violence; and the body, food and eating.

John Evans is Professor of Sociology of Education and Physical Education in the School of Sport and Exercise Sciences, Loughborough University. His publications include *Teaching in Transition: The Challenge of Mixed Ability Grouping* (Open University Press, 1985); *Politics, Policy and Practice in Physical Education* (with Dawn Penney, F&FH Spon, 1999); *Educational Policy and Social Reproduction* (with John Fitz and Brian Davies, Routledge, 2005); *PE, Sport and Schooling: Studies in the Sociology of PE* (1986); *Teachers, Teaching and Control* (1988); *Equality, Education and Physical Education* (1993); and *Knowledge and Control: Studies in the Sociology of Physical Education and Health* (Routledge, 2004). He is editor of a special edition of the *Curriculum Journal, International Perspectives on Physical Education,* and founding editor of the international journal *Sport, Education and Society*. He has published widely in the sociology of education and physical education. Currently, his research with Dr Emma Rich centres on the relationships between obesity discourse, formal education and the development of eating disorders. Dr Rich and Prof. Evans lead an ESRC-funded research investigation entitled The Impact of Health Imperatives on Schools.

Hannah Frith is a Lecturer in Research with the Bristol Doctorate in Clinical Psychology at the University of Plymouth, UK. Her research explores the intersection between identity processes and physical appearance and embodiment. Her recent projects include a photographic study of women's experiences of chemotherapy, a photographic account of adolescents' experience of cancer treatment, and an exploration of girls' use of clothing in their identity projects using video, photographs and interviews.

Rosalind Gill is Professor of Social Psychology and Cultural Theory at the Open University, UK. Her work is centrally concerned with gender identities and complex inequalities. She is the co-author of *The Gender Technology Relation* (with Keith Grint) and the author of *Gender and the Media* (Polity Press, 2007). She is currently writing a book about narrative analysis and co-editing (with Roisin Ryan Flood) a collection on *Secrecy and Silence in the Research Process* (Routledge, forthcoming).

Debra Gimlin lectures in sociology at the University of Aberdeen, UK. Her first book, *Body Work: Beauty and Self-image in American Culture* (University of California Press, 2002) examined the linguistic identity work performed by women in various sites of body management. Debra's current research, which is funded by the British Academy, focuses on cross-national differences in women's narratives of embodiment.

Jacqui Gingras, Ph.D., RD, is an Assistant Professor at Ryerson University's School of Nutrition in Toronto, Ontario, Canada. Her research programme involves identifying and acknowledging the social, cultural and political determinants of body-weight and health. She has an interest in how food-and-nutrition knowledge is constituted, legitimised and communicated through power and discourse in anticipation of individual/population behaviour change. Her current research engages autoethnographic, phenomenological and arts-informed methods as a means for situated and particular understandings of dietetic theory, education and practice.

Colleen Heenan is a Psychotherapist and University Lecturer. She has worked therapeutically in the field of women's 'eating disorders' since the 1980s, in both the Leeds' Women's Counselling & Therapy Service and in private practice. Colleen's research interests and publications focus on discursive critiques of the relationship between gender and therapy, and she is the co-author of *Challenging Women: Psychology's Exclusions, Feminist Possibilities; and Psychology, Discourse, Practice: From Regulation to Resistance* (Open University Press, 1995); and the co-editor (with I. Seu) of *Feminism & Psychotherapy: Reflections on Contemporary Theories and Practices* (Sage Press, 1998).

Tammy Keys graduated from Leeds Metropolitan University in 2003 with Joint Honours in psychology and sociology. Her interests are in the social construction of femininity and feminist perspectives on women's health.

Helen Malson is a Reader in Social Psychology in the Centre for Appearance Research and the School of Psychology at the University of the West of England, Bristol. Her research interests lie primarily in the area of gendered subjectivity and embodiment with a particular focus on feminist post-structuralist analyses of the discursive production and regulation of 'eating disorders'. Her work includes explorations of girls' and women's accounts about their experiences of 'anorexic' embodiment and body-management practices and, more recently, of both service users' and service providers' accounts about the treatment of 'eating disorders'. Her publications include *The Thin Woman: Feminism, Post-structuralism and the Social Psychology of Anorexia Nervosa* (Routledge, 1998), and she is currently working with Maree Burns, editing a second book *Critical Feminist Perspectives on Eating Dis/Orders* (Psychology Press, forthcoming).

Pirkko Markula is a Professor in the Faculty of Physical Education and Recreation at University of Alberta, Canada. She is the co-author, with Richard Pringle, of *Foucault, Sport and Exercise: Power, Knowledge and Transforming the Self* (Routledge, 2006). She is a co-editor, with Jim Denison, of *Moving Writing: Crafting Movement in Sport Research* (Peter Lang, 2003). She has also edited *Feminist Sport Studies: Sharing Joy, Sharing Pain* (SUNY Press, 2005). As a sport sociologist, her research interests include post-structuralist feminist analyses of the feminine body in dance, fitness and sport. In addition, she is interested in alternative ways of representing social science research, such as dance performance, performance ethnography and autoethnography.

Nicola Gavey is based in the Department of Psychology at the University of Auckland, New Zealand. Her research focuses on the inter-relationships between gender, power and sexuality. Recent projects include a study of rape narratives and contemporary understandings of the impact of rape, and a collaborative project on the sociocultural implications of Viagra. Her recent publications include *Just Sex? The Cultural Scaffolding of Rape* (Routledge, 2004).

Emma Rich is a lecturer in Physical Education, Gender, Identity and Health in the School of Sport and Exercise Sciences at Loughborough University. Her research interests include gender and physical education/sport; social construction of (ill)health; processes of medicalisation; equity, inclusion and identity in PE; health and cyberspace. She has published in refereed journals and books in sociology, education, physical education, sociology of health and illness, and feminist studies. Her work with Professor John Evans and Rachel Allwood exploring the relationship between education, eating disorders and obesity discourse has been published internationally within the sociology of education, PE and health communities. Dr Rich is co-author of the forthcoming books *Medicalisation of Cyberspace* (with Dr Andy Miah) and *Fat Fabrications* (with John Evans), and is the founder of GSSF (International Gender, Sport and Society Forum). She and Professor John Evans are co-investigators on an ESRC-funded project: The Impact of Health Imperatives on Schools.

Paula Saukko is a Senior Lecturer in the ESRC Centre for Genomics in Society, University of Exeter, UK. Her research interests include eating disorders, qualitative methodology and social implications of genomics of common diseases. She is the author of *Doing Research in Cultural Studies* (Sage, 2003), *The Anorexic Self: A Personal, Political Analysis of a Diagnostic Discourse* (State University of New York [SUNY] Press, in press) and co-editor (with L. Reed) of *Governing the Female Body: Gender, Health and Networks of Power* (also forthcoming from SUNY Press).

Sarah Riley is a Lecturer in Psychology at the University of Bath, UK. Her research is concerned with post-structuralist theories of identity negotiation (on the topics of gender, embodiment and youth/club cultures). She has also written on research methods, with a focus on visual methods and reflexivity. She is the principal investigator for an ESRC project – Reverberating Rhythms: Social Identity and Political Participation in Clubland and the British Academy-funded Exploring Dilemmas of Femininity with Co-operative Inquiry.

Sally Wiggins is a Lecturer in Psychology at the University of Strathclyde, Glasgow. Her research interests focus on the examination of everyday talk around food, eating and weight, and the way in which these issues are bound up with identities and accountability. Her current projects include using discursive psychology to analyse weight management groups within the National Health Service and parent–child interaction around mealtimes. She is co-editor (with Alexa Hepburn) of *Discursive Research in Practice: New Directions in Psychology and Everyday Interaction* (Cambridge University Press, 2007).

Introducing Critical Bodies: Representations, Identities and Practices of Weight and Body Management

Pirkko Markula, Maree Burns and Sarah Riley

Context

> Obesity epidemic 'engulfing the entire world'.
> (*New Scientist*, September 2006)

Issues of weight, size and body management have become highly salient for those living in Westernised cultures at the beginning of the 21st century. At this time, one of the most powerful ways in which bodies are given meaning is through the sociocultural significance accorded to body weight. Rather than existing merely as 'undesirable' and 'desirable' aesthetic forms, fatness, thinness and emaciation are imbued with potent cultural meanings, and personal characteristics are attributed to individuals based upon their physical dimensions. At the height of the so-called worldwide obesity epidemic, it is now generally inconceivable to consider that someone with a body considered fat is also healthy (in either mind or body). Furthermore, adiposity has become associated with being 'at risk' for the development of associated health problems regardless of the *actual* health status of fat bodies. Poor health has been added to the collection of negative associations that cohere around large bodies, including laziness, stupidity, unattractiveness, psychopathology, badness and immorality (Campos, 2004; Gard & Wright, 2005; Joannisse & Synnott, 1999). In contrast, and as many commentators have previously discussed, in Westernised societies the (appropriately) slender body continues to be revered as the sign of a well-regulated life reflective of a multiplicity of individual achievements including, among others, health, normality, sex appeal, success, beauty and control (e.g., Bordo, 1993; Burns, 2004; Lupton, 1996; Malson, 1998). Although in this current climate one has to be extremely thin to be regarded as *too* thin, being emaciated in Western societies (like the fat body existing outside of 'normal' limits) also attracts derision and charges of deviance and (psycho)pathology. As a 'hateful parody' (Gordon, 2000, p. 204) of the cultural slender imperative, the disappearing bodies of women (and more rarely men) who self-starve are also taken as signs of being out of control of one's self and life (Malson, 1998).

Within this climate, representations of both psychological and physical health increasingly depend upon the embodiment of certain physical characteristics, central to which is muscularly toned slenderness. This *image* of health (not being visibly 'over- nor under-weight') is meaningful beyond its healthy significations and suggests that care has been taken and effort expended, regardless of any *actual* experience of well-being. Commensurate with these powerful bodily significations, the behaviours or practices thought to shape bodies, for example eating, not eating, exercising, fasting, dieting and purging, are similarly imbued with persuasive meanings bearing implications for the identity of the practising individual.

These meanings and values associated with consumption, body management and body size are also profoundly gendered (Malson, 1998). Women bear 90 per cent of the burden of eating disorder diagnoses (American Psychiatric Association, 2000). Women have also been classified as overweight and obese in greater numbers than men. For example, in the United States, Yancey, Leslie and Abel (2006) observe that obesity rates are 25 per cent higher in women than in men. In addition, they note that a high percentage of women of colour are classified as obese or overweight (citing statistics that classify 82 per cent of African American and 79 per cent of Mexican American women as overweight). However, these figures differ from recent weight statistics for England, where 23 per cent of both men and women were classified as obese and more men than women (44 per cent to 34 per cent) were classified as overweight (www.statistics.gov.uk).

Regardless of the proportion of men and women in these categories, representations of body size and shape continue to differ for men and women. As many have argued, a gendered aesthetic of slimness for women in particular is already strongly entrenched in the Western cultural requirements of heterosexual femininity (Bartky, 1988; Bordo, 1993), while that of toned muscularity is becoming more of an imperative for men (Gill et al., 2005; Grogan & Richards, 1999; Labre, 2002). That is, regardless of health status, Western cultural ideals of women's (and increasingly men's) bodies already idealise and reinforce sinewy (or in the case of men, muscular) slimness and marginalise overweight bodies. Within this gendered aesthetic, the conception of what is an overweight or 'out of shape' body and therefore who needs to contemplate 'slimming' or body shaping is so broad that it includes the majority of female (and increasingly male) bodies.

Taking this context into account, it is obvious that contemporary public health strategies concerned with the promotion of 'healthy weight' land in a cultural domain that is already highly charged with potent values that cohere around gender, food, consumption, body management and body size. Within this sociocultural milieu what are we to make of claims by the World Health Organisation that the Western world is in the grip of an 'obesity epidemic', while at the same time so-called eating disorders, body image concerns and extreme dieting and body management practices are apparently increasing? How are the potent values that gel around gender, thinness and fatness, eating and not eating, body care and weight management implicated in the shaping and regulating of bodies, selves and behaviour as well as our understandings of these, and why should we care?

To engage with such questions *Critical Bodies* presents current analyses of weight and body management that have been produced within the vibrant arena of critical, discursive, social constructionist and poststructuralist work in the social sciences. From a stance that regards issues of weight and its management not as immutable facts, but as thoroughly social and political concerns, the contributors to this volume, who include psychologists, sociologists and dieticians, share as their focus a desire to critique taken-for-granted assumptions and interpretations of body weight and body management. They are interested in deconstructing the meaning-laden representations of weight management, obesity, fatness, thinness, emaciation, and disordered/ordered eating. In doing so, they unpick the commonsense understandings of bodies and body size, how these understandings are socially produced and the intersections and implications of these understandings for individual bodies and selves.

To achieve this, the authors concentrate upon the central role of language and meaning-making as they interrogate the discourses of contemporary Western culture evident at the broader institutional, public and sociocultural level, and in the more localised and relatively privatised accounts of individuals. A key focus is how discourses of body size exemplify and (re)produce particular understandings of weight and body management that make different kinds of selves, and ways of being in the world, possible for people, and which enable and constrain certain actions and behaviours. As such *Critical Bodies* constitutes a significant departure from the majority of empirical and theoretical work in the fields of health and social sciences (and in particular psychology). These are more traditionally characterised by a positivist approach concerned with describing, recording and verifying the ontological reality of weighty issues, while simultaneously denying their own involvement in the construction of these issues.[1]

In the remainder of this chapter we briefly outline how a positivist and objectivist tradition understands weight and body management issues, arguing that they construct individualised and decontextualised accounts of the body and self. We follow this critique by offering an alternative approach, outlining the theoretical concepts and orientations to knowledge that underpin critical, social constructionist and post-structuralist frameworks. The chapter concludes with an outline of the three-part structure of this book: representations, identities and practices of weight and body management.

Traditional medical and psychological approaches to body management

Much of the research on body weight centres on the problems caused by its improper management. Therefore, underweight bodies, disordered eating and 'obesity' have come under the remit of medical research, but psychiatry and psychology also claim expertise in these areas as it is commonly acknowledged that problems related to body weight are deeply embedded in the individual's psychology. All medical research is driven by an elaboration of a pathology – defining causes, symptoms and an appropriate cure – to clearly identify illness and ultimately to distinguish normal (healthy) individuals from pathological (unhealthy) individuals (Bordo, 1993). For example, medical research on anorexia nervosa has aimed to establish the causes for the illness by defining a 'universal prototype of anorexic personality'. In these studies anorexics are described as being dependent on the opinions of others, needing to conform to other people's expectations, lacking a clearly formed identity and striving to be good or socially acceptable by being pretty and successful (Saukko, 2000; Spitzack, 1993). The diagnostic criteria for anorexia include behaviour that results in marked weight loss, psychopathology characterised by a morbid fear of becoming fat and evidence of an endocrine disorder (such as amenorrhea [Garfinkel, 1995]).[2] Finally, the established cure can range from forced feeding to cognitive therapy (see also Malson, this volume). On the other hand, medical research on obesity has focused on establishing a link between an increased prevalence of such illnesses as cardiovascular disease, hypertension, diabetes, and cancer and increased body mass index (BMI) figures. It has discovered that the evidence illustrating the 'links between obesity and adverse health outcomes ... is quite overwhelming' (Kim & Popkin, 2006, p. 63). In addition, Allison et al. (1999) found that in general, health hazard ratios increased as BMI increased beyond about 25–27. For example, individuals with BMIs 30–35 had a 50 per cent higher mortality rate than individuals with BMIs 23–25. While it is still debated whether obesity is an illness by itself or a cause for other illnesses (see, for example, Ross, 2005), the established cure for obesity ranges from dieting to more invasive medical procedures such as gastrointestinal bypass and stapling of the stomach. Similar to obesity, being underweight or suffering from disordered eating has been identified as primarily women's pathology.

While psychiatry plays a major part in the attempts to cure eating disorders, psychology has assumed an increasingly important role in detecting the formation of body/weight mismanagement. Medical theorising identifies body image distortion (BID) as a critical symptom for 'clinical eating disorders' such as anorexia and bulimia nervosa (Malson, 1998). In the early medical theorising, BID was mainly understood as a purely psychological problem: when affected by BID, patients were unable to see their bodies realistically (e.g., Bruch, 1973). Therefore, BID was seen as an individual perceptual defect: an inability to process visual experiences correctly. Related to research on psychiatry and clinical psychology on eating disorders, the majority of the psychological studies of body image have focused on quantitatively measuring the body image dissatisfaction in young women (Grogan, 2006; Tiggemann, 2004). While in some cases body image has been operationally defined in terms of perceptual factors, psychologists have increasingly started to measure the impact of attitudinal, cognitive-behavioural and sociocultural factors on body image (Grogan, 2006). Similarly, the role of society, particularly media, counts more prominently in current medical diagnoses of BID (Thompson, 1990, p. 42). Psychological research on body image now also reiterates that while body image is subjective, it is open to change through social influence. For example, Grogan (2006) writes: 'Models of antecedents of body image have implicated social factors in causation of body dissatisfaction, weight concerns and discrepancy between current and ideal body shape and size' (p. 525). The media is an important sociocultural risk factor as 'media imagery may be important in producing changes in the ways that the body is perceived and evaluated, depending on the viewer's perception of the importance of those cues' (Grogan, 2006, p. 525). However, family and peer influence are also important factors on the formation of body dissatisfaction. Psychological researchers further acknowledge that the sociocultural pressure on women to attain an unrealistically slender body leads to body dissatisfaction, and also call for increased research on how men, children or older women are impacted by body dissatisfaction in today's society.

While sociocultural impact now factors as a part of the diagnosis for (women's) problems with body weight, medical and psychological research tends to attribute the major cause for BID to an individual's psyche. Drawing on Grogan (2006) we note that the formation of body image is based on an individual's perception of the importance of the sociocultural cues, not the sociocultural impact per se. Similarly, medical research postulates that as not all women suffer from BID or develop eating disorders, the individual psyche, not the presence of media images, must ultimately dictate the likelihood of becoming seriously affected by the singular images (see Markula, 2001).

The medical model and the psychological model advocate that the cure for body weight problems can be based on correcting individuals' attitudes towards themselves. By identifying individuals as pathological, this research relegates the responsibility for weight problems to the individuals.[3] In his seminal article Crawford (1980), drawing from Foucault, argues that as medicine shapes our understanding of illness, individualisation also characterises health care practices. In such disciplines as psychiatry and psychology (see also Blood, 2005) individualism is reinforced by 'therapeutic practice which isolates the individual from the social context in which disease is acquired' (p. 372). While the therapists treat individuals' behaviours, attitudes and emotions as symptoms needing attention (see also Malson in this book), they acknowledge that health problems may originate outside the individual (e.g., media, family). Therefore, psychiatrists and psychologists do not entirely deny the social origin of (women's) body image problems, but tend to reduce the social context to the immediate context of interpersonal relations. The solutions to health problems, like problems with body weight, Crawford (1980) continues, 'are seen to lie within the realm of individual choice' (p. 368), and consequently, 'the solution rests within the individual's determination to resist culture' (p. 368). More recently, Rose (1996) has argued that we have an 'individualised, interiorised, totalised and psychologised' way of understanding ourselves in the current neoliberal society (p. 126). These neoliberal selves are considered as illness-free individuals (Crawford, 1980) because they are constructed 'as autonomous, unitary, rational actors with capacities for control and with responsibility for our own destinies' (Stephenson, 2003, p. 138). In the neoliberal society, the dominant way of understanding the self (and hence how the self then relates to the wider world and behaves in particular ways) is one in which the person is understood as 'a bounded sphere of thought, will and emotion; the site of consciousness and judgement; the author of its acts and the bearer of personal responsibility; an individual with a unique biography assembled over the course of a life' (Rose, 1999, p. 221). The individual is thus understood as rational, 'choiceful', responsible, independent and risk managing (Giddens, 1992; Rose, 1999). In this context, then, the body/weight management is interiorised as individual concern.

In conclusion, within the fields of psychology and medicine, eating disorders, obesity and, more mundane, everyday body management practices (such as dieting and body image concerns) are typically examined as distinct phenomena, using quantitative and experimental methodologies within an objectivist and medicalised framework (for review see Blood, 2005). As many have argued (e.g., Bordo, 1992; Heenan, 1996), a biomedical model informed by reductionist (and masculinist) ideas about health and selfhood individualises and decontextualises understandings and practices of body management and body size. It leads to a focus on the interiority of the person and is therefore primarily concerned with individual psychology as the centre of investigation, diagnosis and treatment. It fails to locate people within their specific sociocultural environments and therefore neither considers nor addresses how these cultures enable the conditions of possibility for various types of embodiment and body management practices. This decontextualising effect masks the values and imperatives attached to differently sized bodies and weight practices and demonstrates a disregard for the constructions and lived experiences of gendered, racialised and classed bodies.

Individualist approaches to the study of fat, thin and so-called normal-weight bodies and related body management function to pathologise certain bodies and practices (e.g., being fat or emaciated or engaging in self-induced vomiting), setting them apart from, and simultaneously failing to interrogate, everyday bodily concerns and activities (e.g., 'healthy' weights, dieting and 'normative' body shaping). Within these traditions, identifying and categorising conditions as if they are distinguishable from 'normal' behaviour and thinking becomes the primary concern. As such the overlaps and continuities between the discursive production of both normative and so-called problematic bodies and body management remain obfuscated, unexamined and firmly located within individuals.

Critical, social constructionist and post-structuralist approaches to body management

In contrast to medical and psychological frameworks that decontextualise and individualise weight issues, critical, social constructionist and post-structuralist approaches (what, for parsimonious purposes, we will from now on call 'critical and constructionist' approaches) turn to sociocultural forces as having powerfully constitutive effects on the individual's body and psyche. These approaches constitute a diverse field and are better thought of as a range of applications united by a 'kind of orientation towards psychological knowledge and practice—and to relations of power in general—than any one kind of theory [or] set of concepts' (Hook, 2004, p. 11).[4] In this section we describe some of the shared concerns that bring together the critical and constructionist work showcased in this book, outlining some ideas that present a challenge to the objectivist approaches discussed above.

Critical and constructionist approaches offer a radically different way of theorising experience, subjectivity and the body as socially produced, multiple, precarious, potentially contradictory and shifting (e.g., Burr, 1995; Potter & Wetherell, 1987; Weedon, 1987). While the medical and psychological frameworks we discussed previously considered how sociocultural factors impact on an individual's behaviour, critical and constructionist scholars, in addition, locate this impact within a larger framework of relations of power. Within critical traditions, no knowledge is neutral but is considered to privilege particular ways of understanding phenomena and as such serves particular interests. Since critical and constructionist approaches serve as umbrella terms for a myriad of social theorising, theorists within this orientation also differ in terms of how they understand the workings of power and its impact on the individual, his/her identity and body.

Critical social scientists (such as Lather, 1997) challenge objectivism as a basis of knowledge construction 'to question the individualistic and exploitative ideology' (Gergen, 1997, p. 17) underlying scientific inquiry. Therefore, research is viewed as inherently political, and methodology is assumed to be permeated with 'ideologically resonant assumptions about what the social world is' (Lather, 1997, p. 94). For example, critical feminist research has accused medical science of exploiting women's bodies through the practice of individual pathology. Several feminist scholars have critiqued medicine as a patriarchal institution 'that uses definitions of illness and disease to maintain the relative inequality of women by drawing attention to their weakness and susceptibility to illness' (Lupton, 1997, p. 97). These feminists argue that throughout the history of medicine women's natural conditions – such as childbirth (Treichler, 1990), menstruation (Gottlieb, 1988; Martin, 1987; Shuttleworth, 1990; Zita, 1988) and menopause (Worcester & Whately, 1992) – have been turned into medical issues. Feminist researchers have also analysed a whole range of other body-related female conditions, like anorexia nervosa, that have been generally pathologised as female illnesses. This conceptualisation of illness, these feminists argue, treats individual women as naturally pathological because it ignores the historical, cultural and societal context of women's lives. The medical profession thus contributes to women's subjectivation by supporting the patriarchal domination of women. From the critical perspective, power is seen as emanating from 'the top down': the dominant group (such as the medical profession) oppresses the marginalised groups (such as women) to stay in power. Ideological constructions, such as femininity characterised by weakness and disease, are then used to maintain these power relations. In this volume, Aphramore and Gingras, for example, examine the construction of nutritional knowledge that, similar to medical knowledge, provides ideological means to oppress overweight and obese clients. Rich and Evans explore the ways in which scientific knowledge on obesity is 'manufactured' by the media to ideologically construct young women's understandings of their selves. These researchers focus on how 'healthism' and the need to achieve at school intersect with representations of the healthy, the fat and the thin body to generate severely negative body-self relationships.

From a critical perspective, hegemonic relations are, however, understood as unstable as the subordinated individuals possess agency to change the dominance. For example, feminist researchers urge women to take back control of their bodies by assuming an active role as health care consumers by challenging the medical knowledge or by engaging in preventative health care activities (e.g., Lupton, 1997). From a post-structuralist perspective, these assumptions of power, ideology and the agentic self remain disputed.

Post-structuralism can encompass diverse theoretical traditions such as Derridean deconstruction, Lacanian-derived psychoanalysis and Foucauldian analysis of the power/discourse nexus. However, they all share the idea that language structures reality and thus plays a key role in the production of truth and power relations. Consider the following example: The insurance industry-generated height/weight tables have been widely adopted by the medical establishment as reliable indicators of the mortality risk associated with particular weights. Since their original publication over a century ago, these tables have been altered so that 'average' weights became known as 'ideal' and then 'desirable' weights, and these indicators of well-being have all been regularly adjusted down to keep in line not only with the health orthodoxies of the day, but also with particular trends in body size and shape. As Gaesser (2002) has pointed out, despite a veneer of scientific objectivity, the interests of the weight-loss industry in these (widely used) weight table alterations are difficult to untangle (for an in-depth discussion of this, see Gaesser, 2002). This example demonstrates that exploring the 'production of truth' from a post-structuralist position requires a consideration of power, that is, the social processes that enable the acceptance and validation of some forms of knowledge over others. Power in these terms is the ability to construct what is 'true'; it operates through language and is diffuse and situated. Since language constructs the forms of knowledge available, the focus shifts from trying to identify or discern truths (e.g., what factors cause anorexia? Or at what weight does mortality risk increase?) to exploring how certain understandings come to be accepted as 'truths' (e.g., how is it that there is a specific and identifiable category 'anorexia'? Or how is it that 'healthy weights' have been adjusted down alongside the downward trends for the culturally idealised body?). For example, Heenan (this volume) discusses how psychoanalytical practice is constructed based on certain accepted 'truths' and analyses how these truths have been formed to accompany the consumerist philosophy of today's world. Michel Foucault's concept 'discourse' can help further understand the relationship between truth, power and knowledge.

Foucault (1978) argued that 'it is in discourse that power and knowledge are joined together' (p. 100). For Foucault, discourse referred to a verbal performance but was not limited to conversations between individual actors. Rather, discourses can be understood as providing meanings that define the practices that people engage in everyday life. Discursive practice, then, provides the conditions for the function or meaning of discourse. Furthermore, discursive formations accumulate meaning within a specific cultural and historical context (Markula & Pringle, 2006). All knowledge and discursive practices are inextricably linked: 'knowledge is defined by the possibilities of use and appropriation offered by discourse' (Foucault, 1972, p. 182). Foucauldian-informed researchers therefore engage in an analysis of how knowledge and discourse are intertwined into societal practices as we know them in a particular historical moment and in a particular societal context. As discourses are also understood as practices that have material implications for bodies and embodiment, they are not considered to be simply patterns of meaning but rather to have 'real' effects and to 'systematically form the objects of which they speak' (Foucault, 1978, p.49). So, while discourses provide ways for persons to explain or give meaning to their experiences and to shape possibilities for subjectivity (and while they are only *accessible* via language), they are much more than that which can be said, or ways of thinking and understanding. They also actively shape materiality, providing, enabling and constraining the practices that individuals engage in and which mould fleshy bodies. For example, Gimlin and Gill (this volume) discuss the ways in which normative gendered discourses of appropriate bodies inform physical practices. Gimlin discusses women's participation in a dieting club and 'slimming' activities while Gill examines how discourses that define masculine identity constrain men's body image and inform their body management and presentation practices.

Foucault further asserted that dominant individuals, groups, corporations and states become influential due to the contingent workings and, at times, tactical usages of discourses (Markula & Pringle, 2006). Unlike the critical theorists we discussed before, Foucault assumed that dominant groups do NOT hold power or arrive to their positions because they HAVE power or are given power at the outset, but rather that power is relational: it refers to relations between people. Furthermore, unlike the critical theorists, Foucault did not view power and freedom as mutually exclusive; rather, he saw freedom as a precondition for a relationship of power. Foucault, therefore, conceptualised power as omnipresent in every relationship and working as a capillary-like network. Within this network, there are multiple points of resistance or struggle. While Foucault was concerned with systems of domination and did not deny the existence of inequalities, he saw power relations as productive. Neither essentially positive nor negative, power relations produce subjectivities, economic systems, laws and, more generally, social realities and transformations (Markula & Pringle, 2006). As an example, we can reconsider the production of femininity as frail and ill through medical discourse from a Foucauldian perspective. If feminists critical of the medicalisation of women's lives tended to conceptualise all women as oppressed, and the patriarchal, male-dominated medical profession as the powerful oppressors, Foucauldian feminists avoid such a dualistic notion of power relations. They argue instead that individual women can be seen as dominated by the medical practices, but can simultaneously use their positions to advance different subject positions (Markula, 2001). Although Foucauldian thought problematises the dualistic oppressed–oppressor power relations, it does not imply that systems of domination have disappeared. Rather than trying to reveal how dominating groups rationally plot and design power strategies for their advancement over the powerless dominated groups, Foucauldian feminists aim to demonstrate how power operates through medical discourse that provides knowledge about how women should understand, regulate and experience their bodies (e.g., Davies, 1998; Lupton, 1997). For example, several feminists have examined the formation of eating disorders, specifically anorexia nervosa (e.g., Bordo, 1993; Eckermann, 1997; Gremillion, 2002; Hardin, 2003; Malson, 1998; Saukko, 2000; Spitzack, 1993; Walstrom, 1996) and bulimia nervosa (Beach, 1996; Brooks et al., 1998; Burns, 2004; Squire, 2002, 2003) within the discursive power relations of contemporary society. These accounts demonstrate how medical discourse constructs the anorexic or bulimic as an essentially pathological individual. In this book, Malson and Saukko continue their earlier work on the formation of the eating-disordered subject through contemporary media representation of Princess Diana (see Saukko) and through clinical counselling practices offered for anorectics (see Malson). Both authors also discuss the role of the individual in shaping his/her identity within the discursive production of subjectivity.

Power relations operate through language to constitute the very subjectivity or identity of individuals by offering variously empowered subject positions for people to take up. As such the person and personhood are understood as inseparable from their sociocultural context (Gergen, 1991; Hollway, 1989). This is an understanding that decentres the self, shifting the focus away from a 'coherent' individual and instead regarding identity not as stable, bounded or as coherent, but as multiply constituted in and by the discourses and discursive regimes to which it is exposed (see Henriques et al., 1984; Weedon, 1987). Foucault was intrigued by the individual's possibility to develop new understandings of the self, yet he considered this a difficult challenge in the contemporary world.

Foucault demonstrated that the control of subjects in modern society centred on disciplining the body: docile bodies are economically efficient and politically obedient (Foucault, 1977). Therefore, power is inscribed on the individual body by normalising specific body practices (for example, see Markula & Pringle, 2006). The manner in which the body is shaped and trained through today's numerous body management techniques has also been of considerable interest for the post-structuralist feminists. From this perspective, psychiatric, medical and nutritional discourse define normal attitude to eating behaviour (e.g., Markula, 2001).

As a result, we observe, examine, measure and compare ourselves against the established norms of healthy eating and healthy weight, and discipline ourselves to reach the required level of normalcy. More detailed scientific knowledge has resulted in stricter criteria for normalcy. For example, the BMI or waist measurement now provides a clear and precise criterion for detecting overweightness. Feminist researchers have long pointed to the strict criteria for the ideal feminine body shape (thin, toned and young) in Westernised societies and how this has become the 'norm' to be achieved by all women. The normalisation of this feminine body has led to women's detailed, obsessive surveillance of their bodily defects (e.g., Bartky, 1988; Bordo, 1993; Markula, 1995; Spitzack, 1990). Not only women's physical body shapes, but also their experiences of their bodies are products of discursive control. For example, Burns and Gavey (this volume) demonstrate how women's experiences of purging are created within the discursive climate that encourages the drive for a healthy-looking, thin body. Within this context, purging is constituted as an effective or even healthy weight loss practice. At the same time, however, such practices can be assigned as resistant to the construction of foolish and pathological femininity. Similarly, in this volume, Day and Keys demonstrate how pro-anorexia websites constitute anorexia as a kind of protest thereby offering subject positions or identities of resistance and defiance to the young women who visit them. These identities potentially sit in stark contrast with the 'anorexic' woman as pathological. The same women, however, continue to position extreme thinness as an ideal form of femininity. These examples demonstrate the complications of redefining how one's subjectivity is constituted within the power/knowledge nexus. They also challenge the notion of agency through which an individual consciously can reveal, resist and overturn the effects of dominant ideology.

From a Foucauldian perspective, an individual is always situated within power relations and therefore no human can exist entirely outside these relations. So, to dismantle the process of subjectivation and to construct a 'different' identity, an individual has to confront the power/discourse nexus. Foucault (1988) rejected the humanist notion of the self as a sovereign, essential, founding and universal substance that could be autonomous, agentic and/or resistant. Instead, he understood the self as a form that could be modified under different cultural conditions. It is possible, therefore, for an individual to choose to transform his/her identity by engaging in a process that Foucault labelled as the technologies of the self (Markula & Pringle, 2006). Foucault's treatment of the self mirrors the general post-structuralist understanding that language constitutes 'selves' or identities that are shifting, complex, multiple and thoroughly social (Davies & Harre, 1990).

Potter and Wetherell (1987) explain that available subject positions shape the possibilities for selfhood, enabling and constraining people with regard to speaking, thinking, being or acting in certain ways. These arrangements shore up prevailing systems of power:

> The discursive articulation of certain kinds of selves or human subjects is involved in the reproduction of certain kinds of society. People become fixed in position through the range of linguistic practices available to them to make sense. The use of a particular discourse which contains a particular organisation of the self not only allows one to warrant and justify one's actions, it also maintains power relations and patterns of domination and subordination.
>
> (p. 109)

While people may 'become fixed in position' (ibid.) by discourse in any particular moment, there are always a multiplicity of discourses available. A particular interest for Foucauldian research is to examine how power is exercised in these situations by the different actors and, as a result, what actually happens. However, as Vivian Burr (1995) reminds us, in any situation, the discourse that the person has drawn upon must already be available in his/her milieu. Second, when using this discourse the person becomes subject to it: '[O]nce we take up a position within a discourse ... we then inevitably come to experience the world and ourselves from the vantage point of that perspective' (p. 145). Third, no discourse is produced arbitrarily, but rather is formed from within the already existing discursive context, a context that, as Potter and Wetherell (1987) note, 'also maintains power relations and patterns of domination and subordination' (p. 109).

To conclude, within the discursive cultures of most Western societies at this particular sociohistorical moment, dominant notions of the self cohere around discourses of neoliberal subjectivity. Within this discourse the self is understood to be an individual who is rational and responsible for his/her behaviour (Giddens, 1992; Rose, 1999). As we have mentioned, this prevailing concept of the person is (re)produced within objectivist research concerned with issues of weight and body management such that failing to maintain an (appropriately) slim body can be read as evidence of unsuccessful personhood: of somebody who has either wilfully chosen 'unhealthy' behaviours or who does not have sufficient self-control to conform to norms of appropriate size and shape. Failing to conform to narrowly defined norms of toned slenderness (by being either too thin or too fat) is constructed as not only unhealthy but also failing as a (responsible) person. Furthermore, from this perspective neoliberalism can be understood as an individualist discourse that de-legitimises those discourses or 'explanations' that highlight the impact of social structures in individuals' lives, so that failure to fulfil culturally validated forms of (embodied) personhood are understood only in terms of psychological failure (McRobbie, 2007; Walkerdine, 2003).

Indeed, powerful discourses of appropriate bodies and 'correct' body management infiltrate and inform shared understandings at both an individual and an institutionalised level such that bodily 'norms' are established with regulatory potential for every 'body'. These discourses are constantly contested and continually shaped in relation to a variety of socially significant variables such as ethnicity, sexuality, socio-economic status (among others) and are rendered meaningful within the particular contexts in which they are located and according to the gendered, classed and racialised power relations operating there. As such they will shape bodies, subjectivities and practices in multiple ways. However, the ubiquity of the idealisation of the slender ideal and derogation of 'overweight' at this particular sociocultural and historical moment has powerfully infiltrated cultural sites and institutions in ways that provide 'templates' or norms for ideal embodiment for all. Against and through these, many people will be judged, positioned and regulated both by others and by themselves.

Critical and constructionist approaches, instead of being concerned with defining and measuring so-called pathology and health, focus upon interrogating, for example, the meanings ascribed to the fat body, to starving oneself or to being a 'normal' weight. Analyses concentrate upon how particular meanings about differently sized bodies (fat, thin and emaciated) and their weight management (dieting, purging, exercising, eating and not eating) gain their 'truth status'; how these knowledges circulate; what interests they serve; and how they are taken up and made 'local', 'private' and 'individual' (e.g. Burns, 2004). Those deploying these perspectives problematise the distinctions between the 'orders' and 'disorders' of weight and body management within the particular sites in which they occur. These sites include social institutions (for example, schools, the media, nutrition clinics, psychological health care and public health) and individual subjectivity/identity accessed via individual talk and other personal texts. Bodies, subjectivities and knowledges are viewed not as essential facts, but as constituted by and within the complex and multiply gendered, racialised and classed discursive practices within which they are embedded (Burns, 2006). Rather than searching for 'definitions', 'causes' and 'treatments', this scholarship asks completely different questions of such phenomena. It is interested in challenging taken-for-granted or commonsense ways of understanding weight issues and the power relations imbricated in these. It is interested in exploring the social processes and institutionalised patterns of meaning that maintain particular understandings and constrain others, and in considering alternative ways in which weight and body management may be understood. It is interested in the ways that fatness, thinness and weight management, and the particular identities associated with them, are locatable and (re)produced within the sociocultural contexts in which they arise.

Critical bodies: Representations, identities and practices

This volume is divided into three areas of focus: representations, identities and practices. These three areas provide a framework for examining weighty issues in terms of (1) the symbolism and imagery of differently sized bodies, body management practices and weight, and their inscriptive potential; (2) the possibilities for the constitution of selves/identities that are (re)produced through these meanings; and (3) the activities and body management practices that are enabled by these discourses and how people make sense of, negotiate with, take up or resist these bodily/identity-forming meanings. Each section opens with a short introduction, setting the scene for the reader and highlighting the conceptual and empirical issues of the subsequent three chapters. A concluding chapter draws together the key themes presented throughout the book and focuses on emerging concerns, unresolved tensions and directions of future research.

In approaching weight and body management practices from the three lenses of representations, identity and practices, this book presents innovative work that examines the body in terms of the cultural meanings inscribed upon it, the senses of self (re)produced through these meanings and the behaviours and activities that are designed to shape the individual's body to fulfil normative cultural expectations in regard to body size. In particular, the work showcased in this book analyses the ways in which norms of slenderness construct an umbrella of sense-making that enables a whole range of weight-management practices and evokes discourses around morality, normality, pathology and health which implicitly underpin discussions of weight and weight management that take place in many sites.

By the end of this volume readers will be left with no doubt as to the appropriateness of the title *Critical Bodies* for a book about language, meaning and discourse. As discussed, bodies are produced out of the meanings that describe or represent them. As such bodies are *critical to* (or important for) our interrogations of the ways in which power shapes embodiment and materiality, highlighting and revealing the constitutive effects of language. In other words, bodies can be thought of as culturally intelligible. More than this however, as the fleshy, fat, thin, emaciated, healthy or unwell materialisation of the discourses that shape them, bodies are also potentially *critical of* (evidencing a judgement about) those same patterns of meaning. In this way bodies flag up to us all that might be problematic about the inescapable discourses of embodiment, body weight and body management that circulate in Westernised cultures at any particular historical moment.

Acknowledgements

This book has its origins in a seminar series entitled Weighty Issues: Representation, Identity and Practice in the Areas of Eating Disorders, Obesity and Body Management, which was funded by the British Psychological Society and the Department of Psychology, University of Bath University (UK). The seminars were held in Bristol and Bath in England in mid-2005. The aim of these seminars, which were convened by the editorial team, was to provide a forum in which researchers using critical psychological, anthropological and sociological approaches to the study of weight, body management, obesity and eating disorders (and their intersections) could come together to discuss developments in the field. Sadly, opportunities for this kind of interdisciplinary dialogue continue to be rare. We would like to thank the funders and all those who gave presentations and otherwise participated in these lively and productive meetings. Our thanks also go to Drs Karen Rodham and Helen Malson, who were involved in the organisation and running of the seminars. At the time, and as prospective editors, we decided that a collection showcasing the exciting work underway in this field would make a useful contribution to the growing literature on qualitative, interpretive, critical and social approaches to weight management, fatness, thinness and the categories of health and illness derived from these. We are delighted that this has resulted in an edited volume, and we are grateful to the authors whose innovative contributions appear here. We are also grateful to our colleague June Hill, whose proofreading assisted the editorial process. Most of the chapters in this volume began as talks at the seminars, with two additional contributions invited to ensure coverage of the key themes. The interweaving of theoretical concepts and empirical examples has hopefully contributed to a volume that will appeal to a wide readership and be useful to an academic audience in a range of social sciences as well as to health practitioners (and the lay public) interested in innovative and critical approaches to the study of weight.

Notes

1. There have been several important edited works on the sociology of fatness and thinness: for example, *Interpreting Weight: The Social Management of Fatness and Thinness* (Sobal & Maurer, 1999a); *Weighty Issues: Fatness and Thinness as Social Problems* (Sobal & Maurer, 1999b); *Food, the Body and the Self* (Lupton, 1996). However these anthologies were published prior to the elevation of concerns about 'overweight' (in both public health and the popular imagination) to 'epidemic' proportions in the Western world.
2. This refers to Russell's (1970) criteria for anorexia nervosa that has been elaborated regularly by the American Psychiatric Association in the *Diagnostic and Statistical Manual of Mental Disorders*.
3. Although within health circles the notion of the 'obesogenic' environment (e.g., Swinburn et al., 1997) is gaining currency, examinations of its influence continue to rest upon notions of individual 'responses' to the environment rather than the constitutive effects of this environment for identity and behaviour.
4. Burr (1995) observes that the term social constructionism is almost exclusively used by psychologists who are 'only just discovering' the ideas already embedded in sociology. She further notes that there is no single definition for social constructionism, but locates the following 'kinds of psychology' under its umbrella: critical psychology (e.g., Fox & Prilleltensky, 1997), critical social psychology (e.g., Gough & McFadden, 2001), discursive psychology (e.g., Edley & Wetherell, 1995; Edwards & Potter, 1992; Harre & Stearns, 1995), deconstructionism and Foucaudian discourse analysis (e.g., Parker et al., 1995) and constructivisms (Crossley, 2000; Gergen & Gergen, 1986; Kelly, 1955).

References

Allison, D. B., Fontaine, K. R., Manson, J. E., Stevens, J. & VanItallie, T. B. (1999). Annual deaths attributable to obesity in the United States. *Journal of American Medical Association*, 282, 1530–8.
American Psychiatric Association. (2000). *Diagnostic and statistical manual of mental disorders* (4th edn revised). Washington, DC: APA.
Bartky, S. (1988). Foucault, femininity, and the modernization of patriarchal power. In I. Diamond & L. Quinby (Eds), *Feminism and Foucault: Reflections on resistance* (pp. 61–86). Boston: Northeastern University Press.
Beach, W. (1996). *Conversations about illness: Family preoccupations with bulimia*. New Jersey: Lawrence Erlbaum Associates.

Blood, S. (2005). *Body work: The social construction of women's body image*. London: Routledge.
Bordo, S. (1992). Eating disorders: The feminist challenge to the concept of pathology. In D. Leder (Ed.), *The body in medical thought and practice* (pp. 197–214). Boston: Kluwer Academic.
Bordo, S. (1993). *Unbearable weight: Weight, feminism, Western culture, and the body*. Los Angeles: University of California Press.
Brooks, A., LeCouteur, A. & Hepworth, J. (1998). Accounts of experiences of bulimia: A discourse analytic study. *International Journal of Eating Disorders*, 24(2), 193–205.
Bruch, H. (1973). *Eating disorders*. New York: Basic Books.
Burns, M. (2004). Eating like an ox: Femininity and dualistic constructions of bulimia and anorexia. *Feminism & Psychology*, 14(2), 269–95.
Burns, M. (2006). Bodies that speak: Examining the dialogues in research interactions. *Qualitative Research in Psychology*, 3(1), 3–18.
Burr, V. (1995). *Social constructionism*. Sussex: Routledge.
Campos, P. (2004). *The obesity myth: Why America's obsession with weight is dangerous to your health*. New York: Gotham Books.
Crawford, R. (1980). Healthism and the medicalization of everyday life. *International Journal of Health Service*, 10, 365–88.
Crossley, M. L. (2000). *Introducing narrative psychology: Self, trauma and the construction of meaning*. Buckingham: Open University Press.
Davies, B. & Harre, R. (1990). Positioning: The discursive production of selves. *Journal for the Theory of Social behaviour*, 20(1), 43–63.
Davies, D. (1998). Health and the discourse of weight control. In A. Petersen & C. Waddell (Eds), *Health matters: A sociology of illness, prevention and care* (pp. 141–55). St Leonards, Australia: Allen & Unwin.
Eckermann, L. (1997). Foucault, embodiment and gendered subjectivities: The case of voluntary self-starvation. In A. Petersen & R. Bunton (Eds), *Foucault, health and medicine* (pp. 151–69). London: Routledge.
Edley, N. & Wetherell, M. (1995). *Men in perspective*. Hemel Hemstead: Harvester Wheatsheaf.
Edwards, D. & Potter, J. (1992). *Discursive psychology*. London: Sage.
Foucault, M. (1972). *The archaeology of knowledge and discourse on language*. New York: Pantheon Books.
Foucault, M. (1977). *Discipline and punish: The birth of the prison*. London: Penguin Books.
Foucault, M. (1978). *The history of sexuality, volume 1: An introduction*. London: Penguin Books.
Foucault, M. (1988). An aesthetics of existence. In L. D. Kritzman (Ed.), *Michel Foucault: Politics, philosophy, culture: Interviews and other writings 1977–1984* (pp. 47–53). London: Routledge.
Fox, D. & Prilleltensky, I. (1997). *Critical psychology: An introduction*. London: Sage.
Gaesser, G. (2002). *Big, fat lies: The truth about your weight and your health*. California: Gurze Books.
Gard, M. & Wright, J. (2005). *The obesity epidemic: Science, morality and ideology*. London: Routledge.
Garfinkel, P. E. (1995). Classification and diagnosis of eating disorders. In Brownell, K. D. & Fairburn, C. G. (Eds), *Eating disorders and obesity: A comprehensive handbook* (pp. 125–34). New York, NY: Guildford.

Gergen, K. J. (1997). Toward a postmodern psychology. In S. Kvale (Ed.), *Psychology and postmodernism* (pp. 17–30). London: Sage.

Gergen, K. J. (1991). *The saturated self: Dilemmas of identity in contemporary life*. New York: Basic Books.

Gergen, K. L. & Gergen, M. M. (1986). Narrative form and the construction of psychological science. In T. R. Sarbin (Ed.), *Narrative psychology: The storied nature of human conduct* (pp. 22–24). New York: Praeger.

Giddens, A. (1992). *Modernity and self-identity*. Cambridge, UK: Polity Press.

Gill, R., Henwood, K. & McLean, C. (2005). Body projects and the regulation of normative masculinity. *Body & Society*. 11, 37–62.

Gordon, R. A. (2000). *Eating disorders: Anatomy of a social epidemic* (2nd edn). Oxford: Blackwell.

Gottlieb, A. (1988). American premenstrual syndrome: A mute voice. *Anthropology Today*, 4(6), 10–12.

Gough, B. & McFadden, M. (2001). *Critical social psychology: An introduction*. Basingstoke: Palgrave Macmillan.

Gremillion, H. (2002). In fitness and health: Crafting bodies in the treatment of anorexia nervosa. *Signs*, 27(2), 381–414.

Grogan, S. (2006). Body image and health: Contemporary perspective. *Journal of Health Psychology*, 11, 523–30.

Grogan, S. & Richards, H. (1999). Body image: Focus groups with boys and men. *Men & Masculinities*, 4(3), 219–32.

Hardin, P. K. (2003). Social and cultural considerations in recovery from anorexia nervosa: A critical poststructuralist analysis. *Advances in nursing science*, 26(1), 5–16.

Harre, R. & Stearns, P. (1995). *Discursive psychology in practice*. London: Sage.

Heenan, C. (1996). Women, food and fat: Too many cooks in the kitchen? In E. Burman, P. Alldred, C. Bewley, B. Goldberg, C. Heenan & D. Marks (Eds), *Challenging women: Psychology's exclusions, feminist possibilities* (pp. 19–35). Buckingham, UK: Open University Press.

Henriques, J., Hollway, W., Urwin, C., Venn, C. & Walkerdine, V. (1984). *Changing the subject: Psychology, social regulation and subjectivity*. London: Methuen.

Hollway, W. (1989). *Subjectivity and method in psychology: Gender, meaning and science*. London: Sage.

Hook, D. (2004). Critical Psychology: The basic co-ordinates. In D. Hook, N. Mkhize, P. Kiguwa, A. Collins, E. Burnman & I. Parker (Eds), *Critical Psychology* (pp. 10–23). Landsdowne, South Africa: UCT Press.

Joannisse, L. & Synnott, A. (1999). Fighting back: Reactions and resistance to the stigma of obesity. In J. Sobal & D. Maurer (Eds), *Interpreting weight: The social management of fatness and thinness* (pp. 49–70). New York: Walter de Gruyter.

Kelly, G. (1955). *The psychology of personal constructs*. New York: W.W. Norton.

Kim, S. & Popkin, B. (2006). Commentary: Understanding the epidemiology of overweight and obesity – a real global public health concern. *International Journal of Epidemiology*, 35, 60–7.

Labre, M. P. (2002). Adolescent body and the muscular male body ideal. *Journal of Adolescent Health*, 30(4), 233–42.

Lather, P. (1997). Postmodernism and the human sciences. In S. Kvale (Ed.), *Psychology and postmodernism* (pp. 88–109). London: Sage.

Lupton, D. (1997). Foucault and the medicalisation critique. In A. Petersen & R. Bunton (Eds), *Foucault, health and medicine* (pp. 94–110). London: Routledge.
Lupton, D. (1996). *Food, the body and the self*. London: Sage Publications.
Malson, H. (1998). *The thin woman: Feminism, post-structuralism and the social psychology of anorexia nervosa*. London: Routledge.
Markula, P. (1995). Firm but shapely, fit but sexy, strong but thin: The postmodern aerobicizing female bodies. *Sociology of Sport Journal*, 12, 424–53.
Markula, P. (2001). Beyond the perfect body: Women's body image distortion in fitness magazine discourse. *Journal of Sport & Social Issues*, 25, 158–79.
Markula, P. & Pringle, R. (2006). *Foucault, sport and exercise: Power, knowledge and transforming the self*. London: Routledge.
Martin, E. (1987). *The women in the body: Cultural analysis of reproduction*. Boston: Beacon.
McRobbie, (2007). *Illegible rage: Young women's post-feminist disorders*. http://www.lse.ac.uk/collections/newFemininities/
Parker, I., Georgaca, E., Harper, D., McLaughlin, T. & Stowell-Smith, M. (1995). *Deconstructing psychopathology*. London: Sage.
Potter, J. & Wetherell. M. (1987). *Discourse and social psychology: Beyond attitudes and behaviour*. London: Sage.
Rose, N. (1996). *Inventing our selves: Psychology, power and personhood*. Cambridge: Cambridge University Press.
Rose, N. (1999). *Governing the soul: The shaping of the private self* (2nd edn). London: Free Association Books.
Ross, B. (2005). Fat or fiction: Weighing the 'obesity epidemic'. In M. Gard & J. Wright (Eds), *The obesity epidemic: Science, morality and ideology* (pp. 86–106). London: Routledge.
Saukko, P. (2000). Between voice and discourse: Quilting interviews on anorexia. *Qualitative Inquiry*, 3, 299–317.
Shuttleworth, S. (1990). Female circulation: Medical discourse and popular advertising in the mid-Victorian era. In M. Jacobus, E. Fox Keller & S. Shuttleworth (Eds), *Body/politics: Women and the discourse of science* (pp. 47–67). New York: Routledge.
Sobal, J. & Maurer. D. (1999a). *Interpreting weight: The social management of fatness and thinness*. New York: Walter de Gruyter.
Sobal, J. & Maurer. D. (1999b). *Weighty issues: Fatness and thinness as social problems*. New York: Walter de Gruyter.
Spitzack, C. (1990). *Confessing excess: Women and the politics of body reduction*. Albany, NY: State University of New York Press.
Spitzack, C. (1993). The spectacle of anorexia nervosa. *Text and Performance Quarterly*, 12, 1–20.
Squire, S. (2002). Anorexia and bulimia: Purity and danger. *Australian Journal of Feminist Studies*, 18(40), 17–26.
Squire, S. (2003). The personal and the political: Writing the theorist's body. *Australian Journal of Feminist Studies*, 17(37), 55–64.
Stephenson, N. (2003). Interrupting neo-liberal subjectivities. *Continuum: Journal of Media & Cultural Studies*, 17(2), 135–45.
Swinburn, B., Ashton, T., Gillespie, J., Cox, B., Menon, A. & Simmons, D. (1997). Health care costs of obesity in New Zealand. *International Journal of Obesity*, 21, 891–6.

Thompson, J. K. (1990). *Body image disturbances: Assessment and treatment.* New York: Pergamon.
Tiggemann, M. (2004). Body image across the adult lifespan: Stability and change. *Body Image: An International Journal of Research,* 1, 29–41.
Treichler, P. (1990). Feminism, medicine, and the meaning of childbirth. In M. Jacobus, E. Fox Keller & S. Shuttleworth (Eds), *Body/politics: Women and the discourse of science* (pp. 113–38). New York: Routledge.
Walkerdine, V. (2003). Reclassifying upward mobility: Femininity and the neoliberal subject. *Gender & Education,* 15(3), 237–48.
Walstrom, M. (1996). 'Mystory' of anorexia nervosa: New discourses for change and recovery. *Cultural Studies,* 1, 67–99.
Weedon, C. (1987). *Feminist practice and poststructuralist theory.* Oxford: Blackwell.
Worcester, N. & Whately, M. (1992). The selling of HRT: Playing on the fear factor. *Feminist Review,* 41, 1–26.
Yancey, A. K., Leslie, J. & Abel, E. K. (2006). Obesity at the crossroads: Feminist and public health perspectives. *Signs,* 31, 425–43.
Zita, J. (1988). The pre-menstrual syndrome: Dis-easing the female cycle. *Hypatia,* 3(1), 157–68.

Section I Representations and Constructions of Body Weight and Body Management

Sally Wiggins

The first section of the book considers the various mundane – yet highly consequential – discursive practices through which body weight and body management practices are represented in Western societies. By representation, we mean the construction, constitution and reification of bodies in discursive and everyday practices; this being an active, rather than a passive process. This process of representation is a cornerstone of social constructionist and post-modernist/structuralist accounts of bodies. It directly challenges notions of the body as separable to mind/society and argues against essentialist accounts of embodiment as fixed, unmediated and as having some bedrock status.

The three chapters in this section take this position in varying forms. Malson uses a feminist Foucauldian approach to analyse the accounts of (mostly female) in-patients in an eating disorders clinic. Her discussion illustrates the way in which representations of thin or 'anorexic' bodies are circular in their production: they are used to pathologise individuals, who then take up these representations and re-present them as ways of accounting for their resistance to treatment. In this way, an 'anorexification' of weight management is produced. In the next chapter, Saukko similarly points to the problems inherent in discourses around eating disorders.[1] Drawing on Foucault and Volosinov, she argues that such discourses, like those of the thin ideal, are themselves damaging in the way they represent the 'victims' of eating disorders as disempowered. Thus to critique representations of weight in terms of eating disorders we may be colluding in a process of moral judgement of individuals. Finally, Rich and Evans pick up this moral thread and demonstrate how discourses of 'health as thinness' pervade schools and become a means by which young women justify their eating practices. They use a sociological framework, drawing heavily on Bernstein's notion of educational codes, to examine accounts of those based in an eating disorders clinic. Again, these young women's accounts demonstrate the ways in which representations of bodies and weight are bound up with institutional practices (those of education, rather than those of the clinic itself, as in Malson's chapter) in a subtle and consequential way. In the introduction to this section, I draw out some themes and issues raised by the chapters, and point forward to how these are taken up in sections two and three.

The power of representations of bodies and weight is in how these become commonsensical ways of understanding and relating to ourselves as embodied beings. This is neither a neutral nor a benign process. In particular, constructions are used to pathologise, marginalise and otherwise hold people accountable for their everyday practices (whether these are around food, exercise or health, for example). Both fatness and thinness, in their varying degrees, are simultaneously produced even in the absence of explicit references to the other – each exists as a category against which the other is defined. For instance, talk about being *over*weight implies that there is some 'ideal' weight which has not been adhered to, and that one can presumably also be *under*weight. To strive to be thin is also to avoid being fat. Thus a dichotomy can be produced in representations of body–weight (in addition to those of mind–body and individual–society that are often reified in weight discourse) and this wields a certain rhetorical force when used to hold others accountable for their weight management practices (cf. Jacques Derrida's notion of binary opposites). Therefore, while the chapters in this section focus in particular on constructions of *thinness*, there is a sense in which fatness is indirectly marked out as problematic.

As the chapter authors note, a pervading theme in the contemporary literature on bodies is that thinness is now often conflated with a healthy ideal; to be thin is to be in optimum health (and in control of this health, e.g., Blood, 2005; Malson, 1998). So not only does thinness constitute femininity in many practices, but this can be subverted by a focus on health, and thus constructions of feminine beauty are smuggled in through the back door. One of the consequences of this, the chapter authors here argue, is that women are often complicit in these practices of representation. Discourses of 'thin equals health' are often used in a non-problematic way, without question or challenge, by the young women in these studies. For instance, participants in Rich and Evans's study learnt weight management in terms of 'body perfection codes', defining what the ideal body shape/weight should be, and how to achieve it. These codes were produced through teachers' talk, through a focus on fitness and 'excellence' in the school curriculum and in pedagogical practices such as the weighing sessions in physical education (PE) classes. In Saukko's chapter, representations of eating disorders construct women as needing to be strong and invulnerable, both mentally and physically; hence health is implicated even in *critiques* of 'thin ideal' representations. Similarly, Malson demonstrates how therapeutic practices for eating disorders rely heavily on weight gain as a means to counteract the health complications that can result in seriously low body weights. Weight (and therefore the body) is thus a matter of quantification and body mass index (BMI); bodies become de-contextualised and removed from class, ethnicity, age and ability. Weight, and the gaining of it, is stripped of all its other meanings and subsumed under health rhetoric.

Another key theme underlying these chapters is the question of how power is implicated in the construction and representation of weight. Who has the *right* to represent bodies in a particular way? How is this representation then taken up and re/used by others? Weight thus becomes a negotiable entity, and its construction can result in the wielding of control over another. The implications of this can themselves be problematic. As Malson notes, constructions of 'normal' weight management practices are the very means by which pathologised weight management is produced. 'Normal' weight management and embodiment set the standards against which 'other' practices can be categorised as deviant or pathological. In the data presented in this section, those who represent body weight and body management are those in authority of some kind: schools and the education system (Rich and Evans), eating-disorder clinicians (Malson) and the media (Saukko). However, this does not necessarily mean that such authority is pervasive; each of the authors works with a different notion of how control and power operate through discourses of weight/bodies and how it can be challenged or resisted. The fluidity and multiplicity of discourse and the process of their negotiation – whether in talk, text or other social practices – means that representations are never fixed but are always, already being re-presented. Hence this is a cyclical process and one that is open to change. What is at stake, perhaps, is neither so much in how weight is represented nor so much of establishing the 'rightness' or 'wrongness' of this, but in how re/presentations are used to hold different practices accountable or normative. At stake is the baggage and effects that come with particular representations.

Each chapter in this section makes use of interview data as the basis of analysis, and thus the chapters are grounded in personal narratives and individually re/presented accounts. There is also a double layer of representation here: first, in the situations which the participants are talking about and secondly, in the production of the participants' accounts themselves. Each of these chapters refers to these two levels to a greater or lesser degree, and this is evident in the status that is given to the interviewee's accounts. Malson uses a feminist/Foucauldian discursive approach and so concentrates on the effects of the technologies or practices of weight management as much as the discourse of 'normal' v. 'pathologised' weight that the participants themselves draw upon. These 'anorexogenic' regimes become bound up with those which are intended to 'cure' or care for eating-disordered patients. Representation is hereby analysed at both levels and – as also seen in Saukko's and Rich & Evans's chapter – Malson is keen to point out the intertextuality of the participants' accounts, each account drawing on discourses from within the clinic setting itself. Saukko's use of Foucault and Volosinov also points to the multiplicity of voices and discourses that are used to construct the neoliberal self. Here, narratives are an important feature and these serve as threads of meaning that are picked up and woven into participants' stories of their own experiences of eating disorders. Finally, in Rich and Evans's chapter there is more of a focus on the representations attended to *within* participants' accounts (i.e., the body perfection codes produced by the school), and here they provide a critical analysis of the implications of these representations on the participants themselves.

As we see in the following chapters as well as in later sections in this volume, representations are just the starting point. Once produced, they can be taken up or challenged as part of the process of negotiating identities and weight management practices. They have consequences. One of the aims of this section is to unpack the means by which representations are produced, and thus to understand how re/presentations may be produced in alternative and less pathologised ways.

Notes

1. In a similar way, Blood (2005) argued that experimental psychological research on body image has contributed to a discourse of 'body image dissatisfaction' that women now use themselves to make sense of and represent their bodies and their relationships with them.

References

Blood, S. (2005). *Body work: The social construction of women's body image.* Hove: Routledge.

Malson, H. (1998). *The thin woman: Feminism, post-structuralism and the social psychology of anorexia nervosa.* London: Routledge.

1
Deconstructing Un/Healthy Body-weight and Weight Management

Helen Malson

Introduction

The practices of body-weight management and the normative corporeal ideals embedded therein occupy a pivotal place in the discursive regulation of bodies in contemporary Western/global cultures (Bordo, 1993). As numerous authors (Bordo, 1993; Burns, 2004; Malson, 1998; Orbach, 1993) have illustrated, the corpo/hyper-real ideal of thinness that is inscribed upon female bodies can be understood as one of the principal 'conditions of possibility' (Foucault, 1972) of those subjectivities and practices of weight management that might be termed 'eating disordered'. From a feminist post-structuralist perspective it is the analyses of these conditions of possibility, the multiple and shifting production and regulation of our always-already discursively constituted embodied subjectivities that are crucial in understanding both pathologised and normalised experiences of body-weight and practices of body management. As outlined below, a growing body of critical feminist analyses have already elucidated how fat and thin bodies are saturated with a multiplicity of gendered meanings and moral connotations, and have identified a considerable array of discursive contexts which are constitutive of 'anorexic' subjectivities, bodies and body-management practices (e.g. Bordo, 1993; Malson, 1998, 1999; Probyn, 1987). In doing so, these analyses have thereby exposed the profoundly regulatory and gendered operations of discourse upon the body, elucidated its multiple and socio-historically shifting meanings, deconstructed the seemingly categorical division between the normal and the pathological, and thus located pathologised disorders of eating firmly in the context of normative orders of body-weight and its management. My aim in this chapter is to build on this work through an exploration of some of the representations of pathologised, therapeutically intended and normative weight-management practices in the specific discursive context of late twentieth and early twenty-first century re-configurations of body-weight and its management. While those culturally constituted normative ideals which regulate female bodies were not so long ago framed, particularly within the realms of popular culture and predominantly in terms of feminine heterosexualised beauty, they are today increasingly likely to be presented as also a matter of health.

Indeed, notions of health and beauty have become increasingly conflated (Lupton, 1996) such that, particularly (though not exclusively) for women, the pursuit of culturally dominant beauty ideals is often presented as a pursuit of health while health is, in turn, often constituted as a matter of achieving an ideal body-weight and shape. In the early twenty-first century, it might be argued, 'being healthy' is largely about *'looking* healthy' (Lupton, 1996; Markula, Burns & Riley, this volume; Rice, in press): a look which is heavily prescribed by the gendered dictates regarding hetero-normatively attractive bodies and the idealisation of thin female bodies entailed therein. That is, contemporary discourses in which idealised female bodies are constituted now borrow substantially not only from discourses of gender and feminised beautification (Bordo, 1993; Burns, 2004; Malson, 1998; Orbach, 1993) but also from discourses of health promotion (Murray, 2005; Shaw, 2005a): discourses which increasingly presume normative body-weight and shape to be not only a central criterion of culturally dominant notions of beauty but also *the* proof of health and healthy body management. Within this discursive context the possibilities of problematising normalised body-weight and normative/normalising weight management practices are, I would suggest, increasingly occluded. Practices such as 'dieting', which only a short time ago were almost always presented as gendered practices of beautification (Ferguson, 1983; Woolf, 1990), are today frequently re-packaged as seemingly less gendered practices of health maximisation.

Representations of thinness as beauty and of dieting as appearance enhancing clearly continue. On the front cover of *Weight Watchers Magazine* (December 2006), for example, is the headline 'Kirsty's a Xmas cracker: From tubby to telly star!' accompanying a full-page photo of a slim, smiling and carefully made-up woman in a strappy satin party dress who, we are told, has become a TV weather forecast presenter after having lost 3st 5lb: 'I would never have applied before I lost weight and I'm not sure I'd have passed the screen test if I had ... it was lovely to be admired, and getting to goal [*sic*] just before Christmas meant I could finally wear the slinky frocks of my dreams' (The forecast is fair, pp. 10–11). This more-than-familiar weight-loss script of femininity is re-produced throughout this and countless other magazines. 'It's time to party: Vicky, Zoë and Angela show off their new slim figures in glamorous outfits' (ibid., p. 4). In the early twenty-first century, however, the construction of thinness as feminine beauty jostles with an increasingly prominent re-presentation of weight and its management as a health issue. For example,

> Never before has there been a year quite like it. Rarely has a week passed without the issue of weight and obesity appearing in the news. Headline after shocking headline has told of how we are gaining weight at an alarming rate – and still ignoring the huge health risks those extra pounds carry.
> (Obesity hits the headlines, 2006, p. 8)

> ... the rapid increase in child and adult obesity over the past decade is storing up very serious health problems for the future if it is not addressed effectively now. Effective action on diet and exercise now will help to tackle heart disease, cancer, diabetes, stroke, high blood pressure, high cholesterol and a range of factors critical to our health.
> (DoH, 2004a, p. 4)

The pursuit of slenderness is thus re-presented – with government endorsement (see also chapters by Riley & Burns and Rich & Evans, this volume) – as achieving or maintaining a 'healthy weight' and, authoritatively formulated as a health issue, this newly prominent construction of body-weight and weight management often appears to nullify feminist and other critiques of 'the tyrann[ies] of slenderness' (Chernin, 1983). Oft-repeated assertions about an alleged 'epidemic of obesity' and about 'excess' body-weight being a major cause of poor health (DoH, 2004a) appear to be occluding arguments that dieting is patriarchally oppressive and potentially physically and psychologically damaging (e.g. Orbach, 1979, 1993) and marginalising concerns about potentially 'anorexia-inducing' effects of idealised hyper-thin models (see Halliwell, Dittmar & Howe, 2005). Reformulated today as health maximising, weight-loss practices, particularly dieting, have now been made to appear necessary, beneficial and hence seemingly above reproach.

It is, of course, extremely well documented that thinness has been idealised and fatness vilified since the 1960s; and claims that 'obesity' is related to poor health are not new (see e.g. Turner, 1987). However, the promotion of weight-loss practices as national and global health priorities is certainly a recent phenomenon: it represents a significant shift in the construction and regulation of body-weight which works to seemingly justify the now-virtually hegemonic assumption that promoting weight-loss practices is to be equated with promoting health. Despite the somewhat dubious quality of much of the evidence upon which such assumptions are based (see Aphramor & Gingras, this volume), the pursuit of ideal body-weight has become an even more intensely fetishised and seemingly unassailable cultural concern than it was before the current 'war against obesity' emerged as a central focus of early twenty-first century healthcare policies.

In 1992 Susan Bordo described anorexia as a 'crystallization of culture', elucidating some of the key ways in which anorexic subjectivities, bodies and practices are constituted within and by the normative discourses of contemporary Western societies. Of course, feminists, since the 1970s, had already explored in various ways how anorexia could be understood as a consequence and as an expression of patriarchal gender relations (Boskind-Lohdahl, 1976; Chernin, 1983; Fallon et al., 1994; Orbach, 1979, 1993). A range of mainstream as well as feminist researchers had also pointed to the ubiquity of idealised thin models and the promotion of dieting in popular media as 'factors' in its aetiology (e.g. Polivy & Herman, 1987). Bordo's work (1990, 1993), however, went further than arguing that anorexia has social causes. Her analyses and those of other critical feminist theorists (Eckerman, 1997; Hepworth, 1999; Malson, 1998, 2000; Probyn, 1987) elucidate anorexia and other eating disorders as discursively constituted. These analyses thus not only explicated a multiplicity of culturally located meanings of eating disorders but, further, deconstructed the seemingly categorical division between the normal and the pathological, and troubled the status of eating disorders as individual psychopathologies.

From this perspective anorexia and other eating disorders are understood then not as (socially caused) aberrations from (that which is constituted and regulated as) healthy normality but, rather, as integral to those culturally dominant, gendered norms. Eating disorders are located firmly *within* a range of normative discursive practices of contemporary Western/global cultures. As a 'crystallization of culture', an intensifying amalgam of certain dimensions of the norm, they are re-theorised as expressions of a range of cultural issues arising in the contexts in which they are embodied. Cultural contexts which have shifted during the early twenty-first century in numerous ways including, as briefly outlined above, the ways in which body-weight and its management is discursively constituted and regulated.

My aim in this chapter is therefore to explore from a feminist poststructuralist perspective how body-weight and technologies of weight management are discursively produced within this shifting cultural context. My exploration draws primarily on a Foucauldian feminist discourse analysis of the accounts of 38 young women and 1 young man about their experiences as in-patients of eating disorder treatment programmes[1]. It is concerned in particular with (1) explicating the ways in which the therapeutically intended weight management practices of these treatment programmes are articulated and (2) exploring the discursive relationships which emerge within these accounts and the inter-textuality between these constructions and those of pathologised and normative body-weights/weight management. In these accounts treatment is frequently constituted as solely a weight management regime aimed at weight-gain and this therapeutically intended regime is frequently construed in negative terms: firstly, because in the focus on weight-gain the patient appears only as a passive body to be 'fattened up', and secondly, because the therapeutically intended technologies of weight monitoring and management are constituted as anorexogenic rather than curative and as themselves re-producing the pathologised values and practices they are intended to ameliorate.

In these accounts, pathologised and therapeutically intended practices of weight management appear inextricably entwined with each other. As I illustrate below, not only can both be understood as re-articulating each other and as normative cultural values and practices but, further, normative values and practices of weight management in the early twenty-first century can in turn be understood as increasingly anorexified. If anorexia represents a 'crystallization of culture' then these recent cultural shifts can be read, I would suggest, as a normalisation of that intensified amalgam.

Prioritising weight management

One of the primary aims of hospital-based interventions for eating disorders is, not surprisingly, weight management: 'ideally' the restoration of a normal(ised) weight. Given the often-very-low BMIs and sometimes very serious health complications of in-patients at admission, such a focus seems virtually inevitable and is apparent in participants' accounts of their treatment experiences. What is perhaps rather less inevitable is a construction, illustrated below, of treatment as being entirely about weight-gain (see also Gremillion, 2002).

> Clare (UK2) I feel all what's happening is I'm just being fattened up.
>
> Georgina (UK12) Um I think you can use the place to get your weight up. Use it as a food house. I mean that. This is what it is.

It's a case of you eat your way out of here. Everyone does it. /Int: mm/ That was all you will gain.

In these interview extracts treatment for eating disorders is equated with a process of weight-gain to the exclusion of all else. For Clare and Georgina being 'fattened up' is *all* there is to it. In the following extract, where Alice discusses both past and present treatment episodes, treatment is similarly construed as a process in which it is only her body-weight that is changed.

> Alice (Aus12) And then I got out and I was fine for a while and then things just went back down hill again 'cos I s'pose all I'd done was put on weight. I didn't actually feel any better. ... like they could put me on supplements [high-calorie canned drinks] and yeah I'd put on weight /Int: mm/ but that's only 'cos they'd be packing me full of food. And then as soon as they'd stop that I'd just be like: I still don't want to eat. /Int: yeah/ That did nothing for me.

Alice asserts that 'supplements' do nothing except increase her weight and she construes her previous treatment episode as having resulted *only* in her gaining weight. 'All [she] 'd done was put on weight'. While treatment appears only as weight-gain, Alice's eating disorder is thus constituted implicitly as more than a problem of body-weight or weight management. Hence, because she 'didn't actually feel any better' she lost weight again once she was discharged. Noticeably too, Alice construes being 'put on' supplements as 'packing me full of food' while Clare similarly talks about 'being fattened up' and Georgina portrays the hospital ward as 'a food house'. Their phrasing suggests, I would argue, a production and regulation of patients as passive bodies (see also Gremillion, 2002) caught in a mechanised, factory-farming-type process from which the only means of escape is to 'eat your way out of [t]here'.

Weight management and the normativity of factory-farmed bodies

In the interview extracts below this metaphoric representation of therapeutically intended weight management as a mechanised processing of bodies is again apparent.

> Liam (UK20) ... the issue here is putting weight on at the moment. It's the re-feeding. It's a factory-feeding farm.

Julie (Aus7) And so I'm just constantly just eating and eating. All I hear is the trolley coming round every five minutes with food.

Barbara (UK12) It seems to be a constant round of eating here /Int: yeah/ so the only time you're free is at night and then you're thinking about tomorrow

The construction of treatment as solely a programme of weight management is thus intensified here in the vivid image of a 'food house' or 'factory feeding farm' where patients are 'just constantly just eating and eating'. While this was not always construed in entirely negative terms (Georgina talks about *using* it to gain weight[2]), it is, nevertheless, a particularly stark image in which treatment appears *only* as a programme of enforced weight-gain, where eating appears ever present and inescapable and where patients appear as passive bodies to be packed full of food.

Justine (Aus11) One girl ... comes up to me and she goes: All I've got to say to you is eat because if you don't they'll give you cans [of supplements]. If you don't have the cans you'll get the [naso-gastric] tube. So eat.

Kate (Aus10) I hated being forced to eat. I hated it so much. /Int: mm/ I used to just cry and cry and cry after every meal because they'd made me eat so much food. /Int: right/ It was very food, like everything was revolved around the food /Int: mm/ and what you ate and how much you ate.

In addition to this construction of treatment, participants did also articulate other accounts in which treatment appears more positively, as more than an issue of weight-gain.[3] The construction of treatment as solely a programme of enforced weight gain is, however, particularly noteworthy, firstly, because of its prominence and vivid articulation in participants' accounts and, secondly, because of the way in which its metaphoric representation as a factory-farming-type process constitutes patients as passive bodies caught in a mechanised, inescapable or enforced 'fattening up' process.

Factory-farmed fit femininity

In her analyses of treatments for eating disorders, Gremillion (2002) has similarly elucidated how the bodies of young women diagnosed as anorexic are constituted as a resource that is to be made fit. She thus highlights a production and regulation of patients as passive bodies, which resonates with this construction of hospital weight management articulated here and, further, illustrates how this discursive process can be understood as re-articulating normative discourses of contemporary Western cultures. Similarly, in the extract below, taken from a popular women's magazine, the female body is constituted as an object to be worked upon.

> These girls look fantastic – and its their muscle tone that does it. Having an incredible body doesn't have to mean looking like you missed breakfast, lunch and dinner. You can't simply starve yourself into a great body anymore. The look these days is more toned, more shapely, healthier and more, well, muscular.... Think about Madonna in her *American Pie* video clip. She's over 40 and looks fabulous. Would she look that great if she wasn't toned? Uh, no. She'd look like an older woman with saggy skin and floppy upper arms.
> (*Cosmopolitan*, 2000, p. 167)

It could be thought that copy such as this indicates a critical re-appraisal of and move away from a long-dominant cultural fetishisation of thinness as a hallmark of feminine physical perfection. '[A]n incredible body', it might seem, is no longer one that has regularly 'missed breakfast, lunch and dinner' and can no longer therefore be viewed as 'anorexia-inducing'. This promotion of a new look that is 'more toned, more shapely, healthier and more, well, muscular' does not, however, represent any loosening of a regulatory stranglehold of the thin ideal and the culturally dominant gendered values entailed therein.[4] Rather, to 'simply starve yourself' is no longer sufficient. Muscle tone is *also* required if the unthinkable fate of becoming 'an older woman with saggy skin and floppy upper arms' is to be avoided. This 'more toned ... healthier' body ideal can be read then not so much as a diminishing of cultural pre-occupations with eliminating body fat but as an intensified emphasis on controlling the body. As Bordo (1990, p. 90) has argued,

> The ideal here is of a body that is absolutely tight, contained, 'bolted down,' firm (in other words, a body that is protected against eruption from within, whose internal processes are under control). Areas that are soft, loose or 'wiggly' are unacceptable, even on extremely thin bodies.

The culturally normative ideal for (women's) bodies thus remains firmly rooted in a discourse of Cartesian dualism in which mind and body are hierarchically opposed such that the body must therefore be 'bolted down' by a self-directing mind/self (Bordo, 1990; Malson, 1998). The female body ideal peddled by the fashion/beauty industries is thus constituted as an object again divorced from any concept of embodied personhood. Like the body in participants' accounts above, the normative female body is constituted here as 'a resource' (Gremillion, 2002), a mere passive object to be worked upon, controlled and made 'fit' – in both senses of the word.

This body, moreover, epitomises the denaturalised body of hyper/postmodernity: the body as sign-commodity (Featherstone, 1982), as 'second order simulacra ... a floating sign-system' (Kroker and Kroker, 1987, pp. 21–3) to be experienced and managed as surface *image* (Malson, 1999). Despite its being marketed as 'healthier', it is a healthier *look* rather than organic functioning or sensate experience that is required here[5] (see also Lupton, 1996). Representations of health and beauty are thus conflated such that 'health' in this context becomes just yet another signifier of a culturally dominant corporeal aesthetic ideal, a look to be acquired primarily – though not entirely – through weight management. The copy quoted above can thus be read in the context of early twenty-first century Western/global cultures as illustrative of a cultural/discursive shift whereby 'health' is now frequently equated with beauty, with (only) a picture of health that is in turn constituted primarily in terms of 'correct' body-weight.

Body-weight has thus, I would argue, become elevated to the status of a convenient master signifier of health. In this post-Thatcher/Reagan context where health has also been made a matter of individual rather than a natural occurrence and State responsibility (see Ogden, 1995, 2002; Willig, 2000; DoH, 2004a/b), the 'obsessive' focus on *individualised* body-weight regulation also becomes evermore intensified. Thus, for example,

> We need to understand the psychology of obesity, take control of our own minds, change our habits, lose the weight and stay slim ... we all must take responsibility for our own choices.
> (Obesity hits the headlines, 2006, p. 8)

With this neoliberalisation of health and healthcare comes a subjectification of individuals who are *made to* choose (see Rose, 1996, p. 17) to monitor and regulate their own health/body-weight[6] with increasing fervour. Anorexia, I would suggest, already enacts *par excellence* this individualised and hyper-disciplined micro-management of the body (Gremillion, 2002; Malson, 1998), such that the neoliberalisation of health care and the intensification of cultural concerns about weight management can be understood both as part of the conditions of possibility of anorexic subjectivity and practice *and* as an anorexification of normative weight management. Anorexic, therapeutically intended and normative practices of weight management thus collide in their individualised and meticulously detailed control over the body constituted as an object or resource to be made good.

Iatrogenic and normative technologies of (anorexic) weight management

In accounts of treatment as exclusively a weight-gain regime, anorexia and its treatment converge with each other and normative technologies of weight management in various ways. This convergence is similarly apparent in the accounts below where treatment is construed as productive of precisely the pathologised bodies and practices they aim to 'cure' (see also Gremillion, 2002). Cas, for example, represents the hospital ward as somewhere where she has learnt more about anorexic practices.

> Cas (Aus8) Everything becomes all about weight, /Int: mm/ numbers, um and calories and kilojoules. I had no idea before I came in here what they were. Came out of here and I knew it pretty well. /Int: mm/ Um and weighing things, stuff like that. /Int: You mean food?/ All that, yep, /Int: right/ I learnt in here./Int: right/ Didn't know it before.

As with some of the patients in the clinic where Gremillion (2002) conducted her research, the ward appears to provide Cas with additional knowledge with which she can hone her anorexic skills. Treatment is thus constituted as iatrogenic and more precisely as anorexogenic in that it appears as training in anorexic/therapeutic technologies of monitoring and regulating food and body-weight. Hence treatment is constituted not only as productive of 'eating disordered' practices but also *as* anorexia-like itself: 'pathology' and 'cure' share their technologies of weight management.

In the accounts below, this construction of treatment as re-articulating anorexic subjectivities and practices is further elaborated where, for example, Amalia and Justine constitute both in terms of an 'obsession' with food and body-weight.

> Amalia (Aus2) There's so many things to change. It's my obsession with my image, my own image. But I'm coming to a clinic that's making me constantly obsessed with my body-weight, /Int: right/

my food ... Everywhere I go I can't get away from it. I wake up and immediately think about food. I'd fall asleep thinking about food /Int: right/ and exercise and what's it gunna do.

Justine (Aus11) I just don't want to be weighed. /Int: mm/ It's not a, if anything, weighing three times a week. I mean the whole point is you know anorexics generally are so ritualistic and so rigid in everything. I mean you're just doing exactly the same thing by weighing three times a week. /Int: mm/ You're getting obsessed with putting on. You're still obsessing. /Int: yeah/ It's obsessive.

In these examples, treatment is explicitly constituted as a re-articulation of an eating disorder. Therapeutic and anorexic weight management regimes differ from each other, as Justine points out, in terms of their aims: weight-gain versus weight-loss. But there is in both cases the obsession with body-weight, the seeming necessity of frequent weighing, the 'ritualistic' and 'rigid' nature of the regime and, as Amalia's extract suggests, the seemingly inescapable nature of anorexia/the treatment programme: '[e]verywhere I go I can't get away from it'. Yet whether she is referring to her own anorexic obsessions or those of the treatment programme, or both, is hard to tell. Pathologised and therapeutically intended regimes of weight management appear here to be indistinguishable. Indeed both Amalia and Cas imply that treatment is more anorexic – more obsessed with body-weight – than *they* are, or at least than they were before their hospital admissions. Hence, while therapeutically intended weight management stands in notable contrast to both anorexic and normative weight management in that it aims at weight-gain rather than loss, it can also be read as re-articulating, even 'refining' and intensifying, both an anorexic 'obsession' with body-weight and the technologies with which that obsession is constituted and enacted upon the body. Indeed, this therapeutically intended/anorexic 'obsession' with body-weight appears at times to be intensified so much so that body-weight becomes metonymic of everything.

Melissa (UK 4) Yeah you have to put on weight to gain privileges ... I mean weight, *everything depends on your weight*. /Int: right/ I mean it doesn't depend on how clearly or how mentally alert you are, or how much you want to get better. It depends on your weight. ... if I want to do cooking it depends on my weight.

Viv (Aus 16) 'Cos then that [her body-weight] determines like the rest, like your progress and what /Int: right/ they're going to do.

Like if they're going to give you the [naso-gastric] tube or if they're going to up your cans.

Cas (Aus 8) Where's the socialising and the normal scenes going on in here? I mean who gets up every morning at six o'clock or every second /Int: yeah/ day to get on some scales? And your whole week or your whole day is gunna be stuffed or it's gunna be good because of one set of scales. I don't think that's normal.

As discussed above (see also Gremillion, 2002), in-patients of eating disorder treatment programmes often appear to be produced within the treatment context as bodies to be fattened up. The body as it is constituted in the process of treatment appears as mere passive object or resource to be controlled, worked on and made fit much as it does in the technologies of anorexia and in the pages of popular women's magazines. At the same time, however, this intense focus on weight management appears to load such significance onto body-weight that, as the above extracts illustrate, body-weight becomes metonymic of everything. Just as anorexia has been defined in terms of an *'over*concern with body size and shape' (DSM-III-R cited in Halmi, 1995), so body-weight is constituted here as *the* signifier of patients' well-being or progress and as that which therefore determines everything. It determines what '[the staff] 're going to do', how many 'cans' a patient will be expected to consume, whether she will or will not be given 'the tube', which activities she will or will not be allowed to do, whether she is allowed 'privileges', including whether or not she will be allowed home for the weekend. It might be hard to imagine how body-weight could be made to signify more if it were not for the fact that, as has been elucidated elsewhere (Bordo, 1993; Malson, 1998; Shaw, 2005b and throughout this volume), in contemporary Western/global culture it is already more than familiar as a fictive index of one's personality, moral character and aesthetic value; one's un/successful embodiment of femininity (or, increasingly, masculinity) and one's ability to properly conduct a self-directed life; one's health[7] and, as a consequence of all this one might imagine, one's entire life.

Conclusions

In this chapter I have sought to explore the representations of therapeutically intended, anorexic and normative technologies of weight management through a feminist Foucauldian analysis of 38 women's and

1 young man's accounts of their experiences as in-patients in eating disorder treatment programmes. In analysing these accounts and their intertextual relationships to a wider body of both popular and official discourse about bodies, body-weight and weight management I have sought to illustrate how the pathologised, the therapeutically intended and the normative are profoundly and inextricably entwined; how representations of body-weight and practices of weight management in eating-disorder treatment programmes can be understood as re-articulating many of the pathologised values, ideas and practices they are intended to cure or ameliorate. This, I have suggested, is because both anorexic and therapeutically intended representations are constituted within and by the culturally dominant discourses and discursive practices surrounding body-weight and its management (see also Gremillion, 2002, 2003).

These representations appear to converge with each other and with culturally dominant, always-gendered constructions of personhood, bodies and body-weight and with normative technologies of body management in a number of ways. They converge in terms of the construction of the body as a passive object or 'resource' to be controlled, worked on and made good (see also Gremillion, 2002); the prioritisation and obsessive focus on body-weight; the technologies of monitoring and regulating body-weight; the intensity of that meticulous scrutiny and management; and the vast significance and determining power accorded to body-weight. Recent cultural shifts in the discursive production of bodies and body-weight including (i) conflations of health with beauty (ii) the production and regulation of the body as a denaturalised and plastic image (iii) the neoliberal individualisation of responsibility for health and (iv) the 'war against obesity' where health and body-weight are conflated, can be understood, I suggest, as simultaneously exacerbating and occluding this anorexic/therapeutic/normative nexus. The responsibility for improving eating-disorder treatment programmes treatment cannot therefore, I would argue, be laid only at the feet of healthcare professionals as if this were only a therapeutic (or anorexic) issue. The folding into each other of pathologised, therapeutically intended and normative constructions and practices suggests instead the need to disrupt the normative more than scapegoat the therapeutically intended. The participants' critiques, discussed above, of therapeutic regimes of weight management which, I would argue, apply equally to anorexic regimes can also be read as much-needed critiques of early twenty-first century normative approaches to regulating body-weight.

Notes

1. In the interview extracts that follow, all names and identifying details have been changed. See Malson et al. (2004) for details of the methodology of the study from which these accounts are drawn. These accounts inevitably raise a range of pressing issues about the nature and experience of treatment. My concern with the accounts in this chapter, however, is not so much with producing an analysis that leads to a critique of and/or recommendations for treatment *per se* (see, however, Burns, 2004; Gremillion, 2002, 2003; Maisel et al., 2004; Malson et al., 2004) but, rather, with exploring the imbrications of 'anorexic', normative and therapeutically intended weight management practices as they are constituted within the shifting discursive contexts of contemporary Western cultures.
2. Georgina's comment here suggests an active agency in *using* the treatment programme much as many of the participants' critical comments can be read as active or agentic in their resistance to the treatment programme. In neither their engagements with nor their resistances against the programmes in which they find themselves can participants be viewed as passively determined by their discursive contexts, but neither can they be understood as autonomously agentic. Just as 'resistance is a matter of perspective' (Rose, 1996) so I would argue are questions of active/passive or agentic/determined use of discourse.
3. Accounts of treatment as solely weight-gain regimes tended to be given in response to questions about participants' general experience of in-patient treatment. Alternative more positive accounts tended to be given in response to being asked about what participants had found helpful in their treatment experiences and/or requests for more detail about their day-to-day activities where participants then talked about specific aspects of their experience such as attending counselling or occupation therapy sessions or, for example, a particular nurse they found it helpful to talk with.
4. The apologetic framing of the exhortation to become 'more, well, muscular' similarly indicates, I would argue, a continuing stranglehold of heteropatriarchal values in this 'new' regulation of female bodies – suggesting perhaps that considerable caution is required here so as to ensure traditional feminine 'ideals' are not breached.
5. The construction of health as surface-image is clearly not re-produced in the context of treatment for eating disorders which must aim to prevent death and conditions such as osteoporosis and where a range of tests are regularly conducted in addition to monitoring body-weight. It is however a normative construction which can be understood as being articulated in anorexic subjectivities and practices (see Malson, 1999) and it clearly consolidates a construction of body-weight (insofar as body-weight is imagistic) as *the* index of health, well-being or self-worth which is articulated in both anorexic and therapeutically intended contexts.
6. This is a focus of neoliberal regulation which can, moreover, be understood in terms of a Cartesian dualist fantasy of controlling 'the body' expressed here as a culturally dominant assumption that we can will our bodies to weigh what we want them to weigh (see Bordo, 1990, p. 90; Gremillion, 2002).
7. Including 'heart disease, cancer, diabetes, stroke, high blood pressure, high cholesterol and a range of factors critical to our health' (DoH, 2004, p. 4).

References

Aphramor, L. & Gingras, J. (this volume). Body management practices and implications. In S. Riley, M. Burns, H. Frith, S. Wiggins & P. Markula (Eds), *Critical bodies: Representations, identities and practices of weight and body management*. Basingstoke: Palgrave Macmillan.
Bordo, S. (1990). Reading the slender body. In M. Jacobus, E. Fox Keller & S. Shuttleworth (Eds), *Body/politics*. London: Routledge.
Bordo, S. (1992). Anorexia nervosa: Psychopathology as the crystallization of culture. In H. Crowley & S. Himmelweit (Eds), *Knowing women: Feminism and knowledge*. Cambridge and Oxford: Polity Press in association with Open University Press.
Bordo, S. (1993). *Unbearable weight*. Berkeley, CA: University of California Press.
Boskind-Lodahl, M. (1976). Cinderella's step-sisters: A feminist perspective on anorexia nervosa and bulimia. *Signs*, 2(2), 342–56.
Burns, M. (2004). Constructing bulimia: Implications for subjectivity and practice. Unpublished Ph.D. Thesis, University of Auckland.
Chernin, K. (1983). *Womansize: The tyranny of slenderness*. London: Women's Press.
Cosmopolitan, Australian edition, (October 2000) p. 167.
Department of Health (DoH) (2004a). Choosing health: Making healthy choices easier: Executive summary. Retrieved October 2006 from http://www.mlanortheast.org.uk/documents/ChoosingHealthExecSummary.pdf
Department of Health (DoH) (2004b). *Choosing health? A consultation on improving people's health*. Retrieved October 2006 from http://www.dh.gov.uk/Consultations/ClosedConsultations/closedConsultationsArticle/fs/en?CONTENT_ID=4084418&chk=u9aLWB
Eckerman, L. (1997). Foucault, embodiment and gendered subjectivies: The case of voluntary self-starvation. In A. Peterson & R. Bunton (Eds), *Foucault, health and medicine*. London: Routledge.
Fallon, P., Katzman, M. A. & Wooley, S. C. (1994) (Eds), *Feminist perspectives on eating disorders*. London: Guilford.
Featherstone, M. (1982). The body in consumer culture. In M. Featherstone, M. Hepworth & B. S.Turner (1991) (Eds), *The body: Social process and cultural theory*. London: Sage.
Ferguson, M. (1983). *Forever feminine*. London: Heinemann.
Foucault, M. (1972). *The Archaeology of Knowledge*. New York: Pantheon Books.
Gremillion, H. (2002). In fitness and in health: Crafting bodies in the treatment of anorexia nervosa. *Signs*, 27(2), 381–596.
Gremillion, H. (2003). *Feeding anorexia: Gender and power at a treatment center*. Durham: Duke University Press.
Halliwell, E., Dittmar, H. & Howe, J. (2005). The impact of advertisements featuring ultra-thin or average-size models on women with a history of eating disorders. *Journal of Community and Applied Social Psychology*, 15, 406–13.
Halmi, K. (1995). Current concepts and definitions. In G. Szmukler, C. Dare & J. Treasure (Eds), *Handbook of eating disorders*. Chichester: Wiley.
Hepworth, J. (1999). *The social construction of anorexia nervosa*. London: Sage.
Kroker, A. & Kroker, M. (1987). Thesis on the disappearing body in the hypermodern condition. In A. Kroker & M. Kroker (Eds), *Panic sex in America*. New York: St Martins Press.

Lupton, D. (1996). *Food, the body and the self*. London: Sage.
Maisel, R., Epston, D. & Borden, A. (2004). *Biting the hand that starves you: Inspiring resistance to anorexia/bulimia*. New York: W.W. Norton and Co.
Malson, H. (1998). *The thin woman: Feminism, post-structuralism and the social psychology of anorexia nervosa*. London: Routledge.
Malson, H. (1999). Women under erasure: Anorexic bodies in postmodern context. *Journal of Community and Applied Social Psychology*, 9, 137–53.
Malson, H. (2000). Discursive constructions of anorexic bodies and the fictioning of gendered beauty. *Psychology, Evolution and Gender*, 1(3), 297–320.
Malson, H., Finn, D.M., Treasure, J., Clarke, S. & Anderson, G. (2004). Constructing 'the eating disordered patient': A discourse analysis of accounts of treatment experiences. *Journal of Community and Applied Social Psychology*, 14(6), 473–89.
Markula, P., Burns, M. & Riley, S. (this volume). Introducing critical bodies: Representations, identities and practices of weight and body management. In S. Riley, M. Burns, H. Frith, S. Wiggins & P. Markula (Eds), *Critical bodies: Representations, identities and practices of weight and body management*. Basingstoke: Palgrave Macmillan.
Murray, S. (2005). Introduction to 'thinking fat'. Special Issue of Social Semiotics, *Social Semiotics*, 15(2), 111–12.
Obesity hits the headlines (2006, November/December), *Lighter Life*, p. 8.
Ogden, J. (1995). Changing the subject of health psychology. *Psychology and Health*, 10, 257–65.
Ogden, J. (2002). *Health and the construction of the individual*. London: Routledge.
Orbach, S. (1979). *Fat is a feminist issue*. Feltham: Hamlyn.
Orbach, S. (1993). *Hunger strike*. Hammondsworth: Penguin.
Polivy, J. & Herman, C. P. (1987). Diagnosis and treatment of normal eating: Special issue: Eating disorders. *Journal of Consulting and Clinical Psychology*, 55(5), 635–44.
Probyn, E. (1987). The anorexic body. In A. Kroker & M. Kroker (Eds), *Panic sex in America*. New York: St Martins Press.
Rice, C. (2007). Becoming 'the fat girl': Acquisition of an unfit identity. *Women's Studies International Forum*, 30(2), 158–74.
Rich, E. & Evans, J. (this volume). Obesity discourse, education and identity. In S. Riley, M. Burns, H. Frith, S. Wiggins & P. Markula (Eds), *Critical bodies: Representations, identities and practices of weight and body management*. Palgrave Macmillan.
Rose, N. (1996). *Inventing ourselves*. Cambridge: Cambridge University Press.
Shaw, A. (2005a). The other side of the looking glass: The marginalisation of fatness and blackness in the construction of gender identity. *Social Semiotics*, 15(2), 143–52.
Shaw, J. (2005b). Effects of fashion magazines on body dissatisfaction and eating psychopathology in adolescent and adult females. *European Eating Disorders Review*, 3(1), 15–23.
The forecast is fair. (2006, December). *Weight Watchers Magazine*, pp. 10–11.
Turner, B. S. (1987). *Medical power and social knowledge*. London: Sage.
Willig, C. (2000). A discourse-dynamic approach to the study of subjectivity in health psychology. *Theory and Psychology*, 10(4), 547–70.
Woolf, N. (1990). *The beauty myth*. London: Chatto and Windus.

2
'I Feel Ridiculous about Having Had It' – Critical Readings of Lived and Mediated Stories on Eating Disorders

Paula Saukko

Eating disorders are commonly perceived to be informed by media images idealising thinness. Research in this area has encompassed both experimental studies on whether exposure to 'thinness-depicting-and-promoting' images predicts anorexia and bulimia (Harrison, 2000), and critical feminist studies on the multifarious meanings associated with the slender body (Bordo, 1993). These studies are often predicated on the assumption that while images of thinness have deleterious effects on individual women's psyche, discussion on eating disorders is emancipatory, pointing towards healthier ways of being a woman.

In this chapter I problematise the idea that while media images of thinness are harmful, images of eating disorders are helpful. I will do this by contrasting the personal stories of two women, whom I call Jeanne and Crystal, with the media representation of Karen Carpenter's anorexia and Princess Diana's bulimia. The personal stories relate to an interview study, which has been discussed elsewhere (Saukko, 2000, in press). The celebrity stories relate to a media analysis, which has also been reported elsewhere (Saukko, 2006). By bringing the two studies together, I illustrate how both personal and public stories of eating disorders reinforce similar normative notions of a healthy psyche in terms of either masculine autonomy or feminine flexibility. This chapter seeks to challenge the taken-for-granted nature of these normative notions of health by exploring their personally and politically both empowering and disempowering implications that come to the fore in the stories that I investigate.

I argue that representations of weight and eating too often repeat Althusserian (1971) notions of false or inauthentic discourses and consciousness as opposed to true, authentic or healthy discourses and psyches. Drawing on Volosinov (1973) and Foucault (1982) I argue that psychological states and public discourses are more contradictory and multifaceted than that. For example, ideas about women's lack of autonomy and vulnerability to beauty ideals can be both politically progressive and psychologically healing *and* blatantly sexist and humiliating. Glossing over these contradictions consolidates problematic normative notions of what women are like and what they should be like, which often underlie eating disorders. This chapter hopes to advance more nuanced forms of critical analysis of eating disorders.

Cultural discourses and eating disorders

Both popular culture and academic scholarship on eating disorders understand the conditions to be influenced by harmful media messages propagating dangerously thin body ideals. Studies on media effects have, for example, measured how exposure to images of thinness produces body dissatisfaction and eating disorders in young women (e.g. Harrison, 2000; for an overview see Wykes & Gunther, 2005).

Feminist scholarship has investigated the symbolism associated with slender bodies that arguably drives women to starve. For example, Bordo (1993) has pointed out that advertisements in the 1980s and 1990s often portrayed slim women doing 'manly' activities, such as wearing pin-striped business suits or engaging in weightlifting, associating an androgynous body-shape with the liberal feminist promise that women can do whatever men can do. At the same time, Bordo argues, a slender body communicates quintessential feminine frailty, accounting for its contradictory appeal as a symbol of both bold masculinity and ethereal femininity.

While the scholarship criticising discourses on thinness is extensive, little has been written about discourses on eating disorders themselves. This indicates that discussion on the conditions is presumed to be on the side of health and emancipation, or at least not problematic enough to warrant further inquiry.

Probyn (1987) was the first to criticise popular, clinical and even feminist discourses on anorexia for framing the anorexic woman as a 'bimbo' who has fallen victim of beauty ideals, affluence and women's liberation. Recent feminist work has argued that clinical theories and treatment regimes (with their fixed-calorie intakes and 'target weights') surrounding anorexia fuel the same normative ideal 'fit' and controlled self and body, which the anorexic is trying to pursue with her starving in the first place (Gremillion, 2003; Malson, this volume). Health-care professionals' understanding of the conditions has also been observed to reproduce similar gendered familiar ideas and practices (patients infantilised as 'children' and staff imagined as 'parents', and eating disorders attributed to female irrationality) that underlie anorexia (Hepworth, 1999; Malson et al., 2004; Moulding, 2003).

In communication studies, Grey (2006) has recently analysed the popular series *Ally McBeal* and the associated media speculation about the main actor Calista Flockhart's anorexia. She argues that both the character McBeal and the actor Flockhart were framed as the skinny, neurotic, anti-feminist, 'inauthentic' woman, who were juxtaposed to a stereotypical large bodied, butch-type 'authentic' feminist woman.

Sociological literature has brought into relief that anorexic women are often acutely aware of the disparaging nature of discourses on anorexia. They may see diagnostic discourses framing them as 'vain' or 'spoilt brats' (Malson, 1998). Anorexic women have also been found to be critical of theories on the conditions that attribute it to 'superficial' reasons, such as media influences, without exploring what they perceive as the 'in-depth' psychological issues underlying eating disorders. This sense of being misunderstood has been observed to fuel distrust among women with eating disorders towards professionals, relatives and friends, and to resort to controversial 'pro-ana' websites, where they feel understood (Fox, Ward & O'Rourke, 2005; Rich, 2006).

All in all, the early critical and feminist literature on eating disorders focused on slender beauty ideals, but recently the discussion has moved to addressing the problematic gendered assumptions embedded in discourses on eating disorders themselves. The recent literature does not merely fill up an empirical gap but also pinpoints to theoretical problems in the previous discussions on eating disorders and body ideals.

From domination to struggle

The trouble with research on slenderness and eating disorders is that it is predicated on a kind of Althusserian understanding, which views discourses or ideologies as creating an 'imaginary' relation between ourselves and the 'real' conditions of our existence (Althusser, 1971). So, the anorexic is seen as 'really' oppressed by sexism, and her dieting is viewed as providing an 'imaginary' solution to the real problem. While this interpretation is not without its merits (and I strongly believe that sexism is a real problem), it oversimplifies the issue.

Categorising discourses as real versus imaginary becomes blind to the empowering aspects of discourses defined as inauthentic and to the disempowering aspects of discourses defined as authentic. This has happened in research on eating disorders when critical efforts were focused on analysing discourses on thinness but discourses on eating disorders were left unscrutinised (e.g. Wykes & Gunter, 2005). Many works criticising the slender body would deny charges of presuming an authentic space or body 'outside of discourse' (e.g. Bordo, 1997), yet this idea creeps into the work. For example, Bordo suggests that the piglet Babe in the children's movie acts as a metaphor for a 'transformative self practice' in that Babe dared to herd sheep in a (gentle) piglet style rather than emulate the ferocious sheep dogs (Bordo, 1997). This metaphor implies that women who embrace their female selves and bodies (like Babe) are authentic as opposed to inauthentic anorexics, who deny their body and gender. Such an idea, however, sets up a normative notion of an authentic female, feminist body or disposition.

The trouble with dichotomous discourses is that they become blind to their own stereotypical and sexist undercurrents. The anorexic may be represented as an unconscious victim of patriarchal ideologies, which, even if supposedly empathising with her plight, constructs the anorexic as a dupe. Alternatively, the anorexic can be understood as a perpetrator, who viciously propagates her sick ideology, while she remains under false consciousness or in denial. These representations are present in the public discussion on pro-ana websites (Pollack, 2003; also Day and Keys, this volume) and Calista Flockhart (Grey, 2006), which set up theoretically indefensible dichotomies of 'strict interpellation or full human agency' (Probyn, 1987, p. 206).

In this chapter I start from the premise that discourses or ideologies are never simply dominating or liberating, but usually an amalgam of contradictory social accents (Volosinov, 1973). Volosinov argues that social voices, which permeate public life and individual consciousness, never simply reiterate a dominant ideology but rather echo the complex social struggles of their time. This maps onto Foucault's (1982) idea of the always double-sided nature of discourses, which produce us both as active subjects, capable of acting on our own behalf (as gays, anorexics and so on), and as passive objects, constrained by the legacy of the discourse (which has defined homosexuality and anorexia as pathologies). Thus, discourses are neither free nor unfree, but they have a history. Translating this into Volosinov's terms (1973), voices always emanate from specific social struggles, being marked by their historical legacy that accounts for their empowering and disempowering dimensions.

In this chapter I explore the historical/political contestations that structure discourses on eating disorders and their personal implications for women who have had an eating disorder.

The lived and the mediated: Two duos

My analysis focuses on two personal and two media stories on eating disorders. The personal stories are based on two interviews I conducted as part of a larger project in the late 1990s (Saukko, 2000, in press). The interviews consisted of two parts: in the first part the women were asked to tell their story of having an eating disorder, and in the second part they were asked about their views on the ways in which women with eating disorders are described. The idea was to invite the interviewees both to tell and to critically reflect on their story of having an eating disorder.

The media stories focus on the news coverage between 1982 and 2004 of Karen Carpenter's anorexia and Princess Diana's bulimia. The details of the methods used in the analysis and the main findings are reported elsewhere (Saukko, 2006). Suffice it to say that all news articles on Carpenter's and Princess Diana's eating disorders were first analysed using the LexisNexis database, peaks in the coverage were identified, and closer qualitative analysis focused on the peaks, such as the deaths of the two celebrities.

I decided to analyse the personal and public stories together, because I was struck by how they repeated similar themes. In this chapter I explore the thematic resonances between the news coverage on Karen Carpenter and the personal story of an American woman 'Jeanne', and the media reporting on Princess Diana and the personal story of another American woman 'Crystal'. I argue that the stories of Carpenter and Jeanne, both reiterate the notion of a healthy self as autonomous and implicitly, masculine. The stories on Princess Diana and Crystal imagine the ideal self as feminine and flexible. I explore the historical and political contradictions of these two different ideals and their personal implications for two 'real' women's lives.

At a theoretical level my exploration of the intertwining of the public and personal stories was informed by Volosinov's (1973) idea of how social struggles translate into intrapersonal contestations through the mediation of social discourses. My reading was also influenced by Foucault's (1982) notion of discourses as often simultaneously empowering and disempowering. In more practical terms I borrowed from Ronai's (1998) notion of 'layered accounts' as well as Denzin's (2002) notion of cinematic interviews. Both of these methodologies outline a mode of analysis and writing that juxtaposes lived and media stories about a specific lived experience with the intention of unsettling their truth value by bringing to the surface their social and historical contingency and investments.

Victim of an ideology

The story of Jeanne and the media stories on Karen Carpenter both echo the idea that the anorexic is a victim of a dominant ideology demanding women to be beautiful and successful. This theory articulates a high modernist ideal of personal autonomy and defines the anorexic as succumbing to a lack of clearly defined self, which becomes vulnerable to harmful social influences, including media messages and parental and peer pressures to be thin (e.g. Bruch, 1978).

At the beginning of the interview, before I asked any questions, Jeanne related her experience of anorexia to a vulnerability to cultural norms:

> I said to [my housemate last night] it doesn't bother me to talk about [anorexia]; it's a positive thing that reminds me, how far I've come. Also kind of reminds me of my vulnerability to cultural norms, and stereotypes, even when I feel invincible about that now. I realize how easily I could be swayed. ... There was such an emphasis in the media on thin women.

The media reporting a few days after Karen Carpenter's death from anorexia told a similar story about why she and other women succumb to starving, emphasising how media images distort their victims' sense of their body and self.

> A researcher in Chicago showed recently that *Playboy* centerfold models had become thinner, year by year, since the magazine's inception ... Victims of anorexia or bulimia share a phobia about being fat, have seriously distorted perceptions of body image and low self-esteem, even though a typical victim is usually bright and often successful. Many anorexics start their compulsive diets after someone's casual reference to 'chubbiness' or 'pudginess' or 'baby fat'. It has been suggested that just such a passing comment in a concert review precipitated Karen Carpenter's problem.
>
> (Rovner, 1983)

While progressing to tell her story of anorexia, Jeanne not only associated it with media messages but a wider political landscape, seeing it as symptomatic of the 'Reagan years' and its ideology of superwoman:

> This was when women were supposed to have it all, be extremely successful in all realms and be extremely thin and good-looking, and

I took that to heart in a really dangerous way. So, I found myself more and more obsessed with eating less and less, and I exercised a lot too. I would make myself run and run and run and run, and even though I felt like shit and had no energy, you know, I'd force myself to do this.

Media also associated Carpenter's anorexia with the US political conservatism, which was supported by the conservative associations of her soft rock music and her personal history of having performed in the Nixon White House and having been briefly married to Thomas Burris, who had been Reagan's financial aid. A particularly strong example of such framing was a Barbie animation, *Superstar: The Karen Carpenter Story*, directed by Todd Haynes a few years after the death of Carpenter, which staged the trademark wholesomeness of Carpenter as the symbol for the psychological and political pathology of the Nixon era. The film received enthusiastic reviews:

> Who could imagine feeling empathy for Barbie or finding depth in the Carpenters' 'Rainy days and Mondays'? ... The coarse grain of the film and the rigidity of the Barbies impugn the popsicle optimism of the Carpenters' soundtrack, just as Karen's anorexia nervosa destroyed her image as the girl in the split-level next door. And beyond all this, Haynes would show us a pop culture of American Clean that cloaked the corruption of the period. As the Barbie Karen coos 'We've only just begun', bombs fall on Cambodia on the television news, part of a series of montage interspersed into the doll docudrama.
>
> (Kempley, 1989)

Jeanne also associated her anorexia with her middle-class family background. When asked whether she thought she matched the general description of anorexia, she answered in the affirmative, particularly with reference to her family:

> [I am] extremely competitive, with parents, who push, even when it's subtle. My parents were very careful not to be overt in their pushing, but they did. It was pretty clear what they wanted, what we were supposed to do. And the better we did it, the more worthy we were. You know, middle-class white girl from an affluent community, mm, well-educated parents, the whole stitch. ... I had a lot of the textbook qualities.

Talking about her family Jeanne also referred to her father, who did not understand why someone would not want to eat, as he had originally grown up in a poor family with ten children competing for food. 'For him food was survival,' Jeanne noted, 'whereas to me it was a way of becoming undesirable.'

The idea of a privileged but pushy family background was also frequently repeated in media coverage of Carpenter. This was particularly evident in the reviews of the TV-movie produced by Richard Carpenter:

> Their parents kept buying them whatever musical instruments they wanted – flute, accordion, drums. They could be whoever they wanted, go as far as their dreams and talent would take them. ... They were as wholesome as their music in that drug-crazed, politically unrestful time – something you could count on, and stand up and salute. And behind the scenes they were popping pills and starving themselves to death.
>
> (Kitman, 1988)

In concluding what she thought of her experience and its description Jeanne stated that she 'struggled' with the fact of having had anorexia, trying to feel sympathy for herself and others who have experienced eating disorders. Yet Jeanne had a hard time acknowledging anorexia was a 'real' problem and felt stupid about it with hindsight:

> I know that people, who suffer, deserve some sympathy. On the other hand ... It's really hard to figure out why people do that kind of thing. It's really easy to shake your head and walk away, than dig deeper. I don't know, because I felt like sort of ashamed to have had the whining ... the whining girls' disease. I felt it was a stupid episode in my life, that it was not a real problem.

The analysis above highlights contradictions embedded in three themes that repeat in Jeanne's personal story and the news coverage of Karen Carpenter: (i) that the anorexic is influenced by the media, (ii) that anorexia is fuelled by a reactionary, conservative political environment and (iii) that anorexia highlights the pathological nature of middle-class families.

Jeanne's remarks about having been swayed by cultural and media images and, afterwards, acquiring a critical or feminist consciousness and 'feeling better' confirms the emancipatory potential of media criticism and conforms to a classical consciousness-raising story. Still, her emancipation story is undercut with references to herself in terms of being 'easily swayed', 'vulnerable' and taking things 'to heart' in a 'dangerous way. These remarks affirm the classical notion of anorexics as easily wooed by social influences in a decidedly gendered way. The process of influencing also appears distinctly irrational; Jeanne's account represents being in disbelief that she could be fooled that way. The irrationality of anorexia is reinforced in the media coverage of Carpenter's death, which associates it with the increasing media portrayal of thin women but emphasises the delusional way in which anorexics become victims of 'seriously distorted' self-images of themselves as too fat.

The stories of Jeanne and Carpenter are also united by a critical reference to the same historical time period: the rise of neoconservatism in the US of the 1970s and 1980s. Particularly left-of-centre US media, as well as the Todd Haynes' film, framed Carpenter's anorexia as a sign of the sickness of the masculine, patriotic militarism and feminine neo-traditionalist notion of family values characteristic of the Nixon and Reagan eras. This commentary is crystallised by Haynes' juxtaposition of Carpenter as a Barbie doll dressed in a frilly outfit and singing softly with shots of bombings of Cambodia. Jeanne's lived story brings into relief the other accent of neoconservative ideology, which emphasised both traditional female qualities of beauty and cut-throat individual competitiveness and success. Regardless of the social critique embedded in these descriptions they also conflate femininity and being politically reactionary, much the same way as the post-war mass culture debates, which framed the domesticated, consuming, suburban women as the harbingers of fascism or communism of sorts (Huyssen, 1986). In the case of Carpenter, the association with femininity and political conservatism is emphasised by gendered references to 'cooing', 'popsicle optimism' and being 'lighthearted'. Carpenter provided an ideal case for emphasising the connection between social conformism and anorexia, because her soft rock music seemed to epitomise the feminine, bland, unoriginal mass culture. The personal articulations of this double-edged critique are echoed in Jeanne's way of looking back to her anorexia as something that was 'stupid', 'sick' and 'ridiculous', illustrating the troubled nature of adapting a feminist left-of-centre identity, which is empowering but is also founded on a masculinist and intellectualist disdain for petty bourgeoisie disposition conflated with superficial or silly femininity.

The idea that anorexics come from affluent middle-class families is equally contradictory. In Jeanne's personal account and in media coverage of Carpenter this is mobilised to testify for the competitive and pressurising or 'pushy' style of middle-class parenting, which involves measuring children's worth based on their achievements. The association between anorexia and the middle class is also frequently used to draw attention to the privileged nature of the women with eating disorders, who 'had everything' and came from an 'affluent' background. Descriptive or critical remarks about socioeconomic privilege, however, easily get translated into framing anorexic women as 'spoilt brats' (Malson, 1998). This is evident in Jeanne's account of how for her father food had been a noble question of 'survival', whereas for her it was a vanity-based issue of 'becoming undesirable'.

Jeanne's concluding remarks epitomise the contradictions of the idea of the anorexic as lacking in personal autonomy and falling victim of media, the political culture and her own family. Jeanne wavers between feeling 'sympathy' for herself and others with anorexia and being 'ashamed' for having had an eating disorder and feeling 'stupid' about it now. This double-edged talk illustrates the simultaneously healing and humiliating sexist nature of the classic definition of the anorexic as non-autonomous.

The adaptable woman

The stories of Crystal and Princess Diana provide an interesting contrast to the notion that the anorexic suffers from lack of an autonomous self, usually imagined as masculine. Crystal's story and Princess Diana's media coverage idealise as well as problematise the feminine self, understood to be adaptable or fluid and open to and caring for others.

The idealisation of a self that exists in interaction with the environment is articulated in Crystal's story of how she became bulimic. She related it to her vegetarianism, which reflected not only her distaste for meat but also a desire to alleviate world hunger and ecological problems:

> I guess I always was a weird eater, 'cause I never liked the taste of meat. So pretty young, like 13 I started cooking for myself, because I didn't like meat. And I started going to the health food stores, because, I needed to find out how to feed myself without getting weak. When I first started out, I would eat noodles, that's all I would eat for weeks, pretty unbalanced. To eat probably. But then I also learnt about economic, and political and other good reasons to be vegetarian, so it became a little bit more politicized.

Crystal relates that she 'used to be completely obsessed' with food. 'And for better or worse, I was interested in food from all different levels, not just the taste of it, but the nutrition, then the economics, I took courses and all that.' Crystal says that 'anxiety was [also] a huge part of it'. She relates that she binge-ate to 'bottle up' and 'numb' her anxiety with performing as an undergraduate at Yale and then applying for medical schools.

It was rumoured that Princess Diana had an eating disorder soon after the birth of Prince William, but the Princess notoriously confessed her bulimia in the 1995 *Panorama* interview, where she also confirmed Charles's unfaithfulness. Her condition became, therefore, associated with the stresses of her life just like in Crystal's case. The media reported her confessing how 'the oppression of the news media and the animosity of "people in my environment" sent her into depression and years of "rampant bulimia"' (Goodman, 1995).

In Princess Diana's case the openness to the world was articulated in the news, media's mostly positive coverage of her extensive charitable work with sick children, people with HIV and victims of landmines:

> The princess was launching a £1.5m building appeal for the residential and support centre for HIV and Aids sufferers and their families. ... Yesterday Princess Diana ... comforted Aids sufferers on a visit to London Lighthouse. She cradled a baby in her arms, played with young children and shared in the sadness of their parents struggling to live with HIV and Aids.
>
> (*The Herald*, 9th October 1996)

Crystal's story also has a slight feminist spin and she was grateful for a self-help group organised by a feminist, 'Mary', for helping her to recover from bulimia. Crystal related that Mary later became famous but at that time was 'offering her stories' for free and identified Crystal being under 'enormous pressure' and bulimia as a way 'to get rid of some of that pressure". However, after her problematic experience of politicising her food habits, Crystal did not want to politicise her bulimia:

> I never got much of a political or feminist awareness [from bulimia]. It was always very humiliating or secretive, and I never really became a political activist. Not like Mary, she took her things and questions out there and turned it into a political statement, made a career out of it. I don't think I will. For myself, the lessons, food is not all that

important. Taking it from the opposite perspective, there are so many other things more important than body shape or food, it's just too limited.

In both similar and different ways, Princess Diana's story articulates the classical feminist idea of connecting the personal and the emotional to the wider political world and causes. This angle was emphasised in the media coverage of how Princess Diana had been treated by the feminist psychotherapist Susie Orbach. At the time of the *Panorama* interview it was claimed that the 'self-belief Diana had gained under [Orbach] gave her the courage to be open with the nation' (Dennis, 1995). The media coverage, particularly after her death, emphasised her ability to change from a virgin princess to a worldly woman of her own right:

> The world had watched her blossom from a demure, shy 19-year-old into an icon to women everywhere. Diana transformed herself into the most modern, popular and dynamic royal ever. She developed fantastic style, and split her time between the young sons she idolized and the charities and humanitarian issues she dedicated her life to.
> (Drury & Nairn, 1997)

Crystal's story also both repeats and challenges the narrative of self-transformation. She emphasises that to recover from bulimia and depression she needed to transform her life and, most of all, how she thought about it. But this transformation does not follow the linear narrative progressing from a state of ignorance to an Enlightenment and emancipation. Rather, Crystal counts how a therapy that used a narrative approach was decisive in helping her to recover by enabling her to come to terms with the different sides of her personality:

> You give the different people in yourself, voices, and names and colors, and personalities. I've got eight of them; one of them is Larry, he is a 40- to 50-year-old man, who's fat, on the couch, probably drinking beer, eating popcorn or something. He's a real downer, very cynical, ooh, very depressed. And his wife is Liz, and she is young, she's like in her twenties. And she's really energetic and bubbling and enthusiastic, and she is almost always on her bike, driving away into the distance. And these different people are ... having these different agendas, but if you can give them voice and hash it out, you can begin to make them interact.

Crystal's personal story and Princess Diana's media image do not idealise a masculine autonomous self. Rather, their stories articulate a feminine, emotional and adaptable or flexible self, which interacts with the world. Three themes repeat in Crystal's personal story and the news coverage of Princess Diana: (i) that letting out emotions is psychologically and politically cathartic and alleviates bulimia, (ii) that the world can be changed through personal actions and (iii) that recovery from bulimia requires self-transformation.

In the stories of Jeanne and Karen Carpenter, emotions are derided as 'popsicle optimism' or 'whining'. In Crystal's and Princess Diana's narratives, emotions are embraced; 'bottling' them up is seen as detrimental and bringing them up or to the public, as in the *Panorama* interview, is viewed as personally and politically cathartic. Braidotti has indeed argued that Diana brought feminine values to the public life, attending to 'desires, aspirations and emotions' which exceeded and expanded what is allowed in politics (1997, p. 4).

Whereas the stories of Jeanne and Karen Carpenter emphasised the detrimental effects of social influences, the stories of Crystal and Princess Diana highlight the positive effects of influencing the social environment through politicising personal issues, such as food habits or bulimia. Crystal's story, however, is ambivalent towards changing the political through the personal. Even if she does not denounce the politics behind her vegetarianism or her therapist Mary's efforts to treat and politicise bulimia, she states that she does not want to get political about her eating disorder. Having learnt from her experience of becoming bulimic as a vegetarian, she concludes that politics around food is 'limiting'. This draws attention to the psychological burden, which in Crystal's case developed into an obsession, associated with imagining politics in terms of controlling everyday behaviours, such as eating. It has long been argued that imagining politics in terms of individual choice, such as consumer choice, leads to an atomised view of politics where, for example, environmental destruction is seen as down to individuals rather than global and national policies. Blackman (1999) and Walkerdine (1999) have observed that representations of Princess Diana epitomised this ideology of changing oneself as a solution to political and psychological problems. While the media coverage of Princess Diana appears positive about femininity and the female quality of caring, it is underpinned by a hard-nosed neoliberal ideology according to which 'failure and psychopathology can be overcome and transformed en route to self-development' (Blackman, 1999, p. 114). Crystal's interview brings to the fore the contradictory personal implications of this idea in terms of both having a political purpose and becoming obsessed with feelings of control and responsibility in relation to global politics.

Even if there are differences between the personal story of Jeanne and the mediated stories of Karen Carpenter and Princess Diana they share one thing in common. They all adhere to a linear, temporal understanding of 'emancipation' viewed in terms of development from a state of false consciousness ('virgin princess') to a new state of critical consciousness ('outspoken divorcee') (see Frank, 1995 on this 'redemption' narrative in medicine). Interestingly enough, Crystal's account does not follow this storyline. Rather than learning to overcome particular personality features, Crystal associates her recovery from bulimia and depression with learning to accept the different sides of her personality (the active and the extroverted, the passive and depressed, the masculine and feminine). This narrative approach presents an interesting alternative way of making sense and trying to overcome eating disorders (e.g. Hermans & Kempen, 1993; Maisel, Epston & Borden, 2004). The therapy encouraged Crystal not only to reflect on different sides of characters of her personality but also to reflect on their positive and negative aspects. The experience of, and therapies seeking to treat, eating disorders are often predicated on an absolutist notion of a healthy or right way of being in contrast with the sick and wrong way of being. In comparison, the narrative approach invites us to reflect on the empowering and disempowering aspects of all discourses that invite us to be certain way. This also comes back to Foucault's (1982) suggestion to be aware of the double-sided nature of discourses, which always both enable and constrain us. Such an approach allows us to critically reflect on how the ideal flexible self validates some valuable and suppressed feminine ways of being (emotional, caring, directed towards others) while also fuelling an individualist, politically and psychologically problematic idea that changing your life and the world is 'down to you'.

Conclusion

The two sets of stories contribute three points to critical feminist discussions on eating disorders.

First, the stories highlight that discourses on eating disorders are in no simple sense better, more emancipatory or healthier than discourses that arguably fuel eating disorders, such as beauty ideals. As my analysis indicates, public and media discourses on eating disorders, and the way they get articulated in personal stories, are much more complicated than that. Jeanne's personal story and media coverage of Karen Carpenter's anorexia reveal how the notion of the anorexic as falling victim of popular ideologies of beauty and success can be personally both healing and humiliating, and articulate both progressive cultural criticism and blatant sexism. Crystal's story and media narratives on Princess Diana highlight both the empowering and oppressing nature of the emerging association between eating disorders and rigidity, which suggests self-transformation and openness to the world as an alternative.

Second, the stories emphasise the old feminist observation that the personal is political. Both of the interviews and the media stories of the celebrities make it clear that the ideals accompanying discourses around eating disorders are deeply political and historical, articulating the political, economic and psychological sensibilities of their times. The differences between the narratives in terms of their emphasis on autonomy and adaptability also bring the historical contingency of these narratives into sharp relief, as the notion of independence resonates with the Cold War culture of masculine impermeability whereas the ideal of adaptability articulates a more recent enthusiasm with feminine fluidity and flexibility that is being espoused in contemporary politics, management and psychology (Martin, 1994).

Third, and coming back to the theoretical premise of this chapter, the analysis hopes to illustrate the fruitfulness of analysing experiences and representations related to eating disorders not as simple domination but as contestations. Interpreted from Volosinov's (1973) perspective the stories of the two women and the public representations of the two celebrities illustrate how contradictory social struggles, such as the post-war debates on mass culture or contemporary neoliberal or New Labour idealisation of flexibility translate into personal contestations. The experience, treatment and explanations of anorexia are frequently founded on normative absolutes about the right and wrong kind of self and body. By unpacking the complexities and contradictions embedded in personal and public understandings of eating disorders I have sought to foster a less simplistically judgemental and more nuanced and reflective approach to making sense of the relationships between the self, body, eating and politics.

References

Althusser, L. (1971). *Lenin and philosophy and other essays*. New York: New Left Books.
Blackman, L. (1999). An extraordinary life: The legacy of an ambivalence. *New Formations*, 36, 111–24.

Bordo, S. (1993). *The unbearable weight: Feminism, western culture, and the body.* Berkeley: University of California Press.
Bordo, S. (1997). *Twilight zones: The hidden life of cultural images from Plato to O.J.* Berkeley: University of California Press.
Braidotti, R. (1997). In the sign of the feminine: Reading Diana. *Theory & Event*, 1: 4. Available at: http://muse.jhu.edu/journals/theory_and_event/v001/1.4braidotti.html
Bruch, H. (1978). *The golden cage: The enigma of anorexia nervosa.* Cambridge, MA: Harvard University Press.
Day, K. & Keys, T. (this volume). Starving in cyberspace: The construction of identity on 'pro-eating disorder' websites. In S. Riley, M. Burns, H. Frith, S. Wiggins & P. Markula (Eds), *Critical bodies: Representations, identities and practices.* Basingstoke: Palgrave Macmillan.
Dennis, S. (1995). A shoulder to cry on; Di's new strength due to therapist. *Mirror*, 27 December 1995. Accessed through LexisNexis Database on 10 November 2006.
Denzin, N. (2002). The cinematic society and the reflexive interview. In J. Gubrium & J. Holstein (Eds), *Handbook of interview research.* (pp. 833–48). London: Sage.
Drury, P. & Nairn, J. (1997, 31 August). Goodbye my love; Together to the end ... the tragic lovers; Princess Diana and her lover Dodi Fayed died after horror car crash in Paris early this morning. *Sunday Mail.* Retrieved 1 December 2005, from Lexis Nexis Executive database.
Foucault, M. (1982). Afterword: The subject and power. In H. Dreyfus & P. Rabinow (Eds) *Michel Foucault: Beyond structuralism and hermeneutics.* (pp. 208–26). Chicago, IL: University of Chicago Press.
Fox, N., Ward, K. & O'Rourke, A. (2005). Pro-anorexia, weight-loss drugs and the internet: an 'anti-recovery' explanatory model of anorexia. *Sociology of Health and Illness*, 27(7), 944–71.
Frank, A. (1995). *The wounded story-teller: Body, illness and ethics.* Chicago, IL: University of Chicago Press.
Goodman, W. (1995, November 24). TV Weekend: In the opposite corner: The Princess of Wales, *The New York Times*, Accessed via LexisNexis database 1 November 2006.
Gremillion, H. (2003). *Feeding anorexia: Gender and power at a treatment centre.* Durham, NC: Duke University Press.
Grey, S. H. (2006). Exposing the backlash against Ally McBeal: Eating disorder allegory and feminism in public culture. *Communication and Critical/Cultural Studies*, 3, 288–306.
Harrison, K (2000). The body electric: Thin-ideal media and eating disorders in adolescents. *Journal of Communication*, 50, 119–43.
Hepworth, J. (1999). *The social construction of anorexia nervosa.* London: Sage.
The Herald (9 October 1996). Profuse apology offered by Sun; spy video of princess is a hoax, *The Herald* (Glasgow). Retrieved 1 December 2006, from LexisNexis Executive database.
Hermans, H. & Kempen, H. (1993). *The dialogic self: Meaning as movement.* New York: Academic Press.
Huyssen, A. (1986). Mass culture as woman: Modernism's other. In T. Modleski (Ed.), *Studies in entertainment: Critical approaches to mass culture.* (pp. 188–208). London: Routledge.

Kempley, R. (1989, 26 January). Drama of the dolls; 'Superstar's' riveting Carpenter metaphor. *The Washington Post*. Retrieved 1 December 2005, from LexisNexis Executive database.

Kitman, M. (1988). Two things on TV make me sick today, *Newsday*, 30 December 1988. Accessed via Lexis Nexis database on 1 December 2005.

Maisel, R., Epston, D. & Bordon, A. (2004). *Biting the hand that starves you: Inspiring resistance to eating disorders.* New York: W.W. Norton.

Malson, H. (1998). *The thin woman: Feminism, post-structuralism and the social psychology of anorexia nervosa.* London: Routledge.

Malson, H. (this volume). Deconstructing un/healthy body-weight and weight management. In S. Riley, M. Burns, H. Frith, S. Wiggins & P. Markula (Eds), *Critical bodies: Representations, identities and practices.* Basingstoke: Palgrave Macmillan.

Malson, H., Finn, D. M., Treasure, J., Clarke, S. & Anderson, G. (2004). Constructing the 'eating disordered patient': A discourse analysis of accounts of treatment experiences, *Journal of Community and Applied Psychology, 14*, 473–89.

Martin, E. (1994). *Flexible bodies: The role of immunity in American culture from the days of polio to the age of AIDS.* Boston: Beacon Press.

Moulding, N. (2003). Constructing the self in mental health practice: Identity, individualism and the feminization of deficiency. *Feminist Review, 75*, 57–74.

Pollack, D. (2003). Pro-eating disorder websites: What should be the feminist response? *Feminism and Psychology, 13*, 246–51.

Probyn, E. (1987). The anorexic body. In A. Kroker & M. Kroker (Eds), *Body invaders: Panic sex in America.* (pp. 201–11). New York: St Martin's Press.

Rich, E. (2006). The anorexic (dis)connection: Managing anorexia as an 'illness' and an 'identity'. *Sociology of Health and Illness, 28*, 284–305.

Ronai, C. R. (1998). Sketching with Derrida: An ethnography of a researcher/erotic dancer. *Qualitative Inquiry, 4(3)*, 405–20.

Rovner, S. (1983). Weight obsession & death; anorexia victims alarmed, *Washington Post*, 9 February1983. Accessed via LexisNexis database on 13 November 2006.

Saukko, P. (2000). Between voice and discourse: Quilting interviews on anorexia. *Qualitative Inquiry, 6(3)*, 299–317.

Saukko, P. (2006). Rereading media and eating disorders: Karen Carpenter, Princess Diana and the healthy female self. *Critical studies in media communication, 23(2)*, 152–69.

Saukko, P. (in press). *The anorexic self: A personal, political analysis of a diagnostic discourse.* Albany: State University of New York Press.

Volosinov, V. (1973). *Marxism and the philosophy of language.* New York: Seminar Press.

Walkerdine, V. (1999). The crowd in the age of Diana: ordinary inventiveness and the popular imagination. In A. Kear & D. L. Steinberg (Eds), *Mourning Diana: Nation, culture and the performance of grief.* (pp. 98–107). London: Routledge.

Wykes, M. & Gunther, B. (2005). *The media & body image: If looks could kill.* London: Sage.

3
Learning to Be Healthy, Dying to Be Thin: The Representation of Weight via Body Perfection Codes in Schools

Emma Rich and John Evans

Introduction

This chapter draws on data from a four-year research project within a leading clinic in the UK for the treatment of eating disorders, examining the role that schools play in the production of eating disorders (Evans et al. 2004; Rich and Evans, 2005). We draw attention to the way in which recent policies focusing on obesity encourage schools to engage with health issues rather simplistically in terms of weight management, rather than encouraging a more complex holistic outlook on and attitude towards health. With reference to the voices of the young women in our study, we reveal how schools now use what we refer to as 'body perfection codes' (Evans and Davies, 2004) to construct particular representations of weight, health and the body, and discuss how these codes can have negative implications for the relationships young people develop both with their own and others' bodies, weight and diet. Body perfection codes and their associated pedagogical modalities tend to carry particularly strong moral overtones in the notions of 'the body' they prescribe and define. An individual's character, value and their sense of embodied self comes to be judged essentially in terms of 'weight', size or shape. Moreover, because perfection codes define whose and what bodies have status and value, they also constitute acts of inclusion and exclusion; they help define relationships between individuals within and outside schools.

Our interest in exploring the relationship between schools and disordered eating are twofold. First, many previous studies have tended to explain eating disorders via accounts that either lean over-heavily on 'traits' of the individual, or, at the other extreme, focus blame on cultural factors such as the media and the 'cult of slenderness'. In our view, the tendency to reduce eating disorders to a 'pathological' individual condition diverts attention away from the role that social institutions (such as schools) may play in the development of disordered eating. Likewise, while acknowledging that body imagery, generated in particular by the media, may have a bearing on young people's relationships with their bodies and food, we do not believe that media imagery on its own can sufficiently account for the rise in disordered eating witnessed in recent years (see Grogan, 1999). In our research, we sought to address this lacuna by exploring how media imagery, school culture and peer pressure together intersect to create conditions that make problematic an individual's relationship with food, physical activity and their bodies. The second reason for a focus on schools was that, in the UK (as elsewhere), schools have been subject to a barrage of recent initiatives associated with tackling an 'obesity epidemic', invariably geared towards helping children and young people lose weight, become more active and change their eating patterns in and outside of school.

The context in which schools are charged with addressing obesity is one in which Government, public health agencies and the media continue to assert that the prevention of obesity 'should be amongst the highest priorities in public health' (Seidell, 2000, p. 28; see also Riley & Burns, this volume, for a discussion on obesity as a 'global epidemic'). Since concerns for tackling obesity are grounded in early intervention, a proliferation of agencies and organisations has been concerned with the focus on children's health, most notably schools. Increasingly, the UK Government now sees health as a 'whole school issue' (DoH, 2005) and the responsibility of all concerned with the education and wellbeing of young people, across a variety of sites. Central Government has sought joint action from its agencies, the Department of Health (DoH) and the Department for Education and Skills (DfES), to address health matters through policy, affecting the whole environment of schools. Many current initiatives in schools are being implemented as part of a Public Services Agreement Target: to halt, by 2010, the year-on-year increase in obesity among children under 11 in the context of a broader strategy to tackle obesity in the population as a whole.

Given that sociocultural factors have such a significant part to play in the development of eating disorders, it is somewhat surprising that schools – quintessentially agencies of social and cultural transmission – have received so little attention from social science research. Notwithstanding the volume of interest and a good deal of research on eating disorders, surprisingly scant-detailed attention has been given to the part that formal education may play, either alone or in conjunction with social practices outside school in the development of eating disorders, severe dieting, over-exercising or other negative relationships with food, the body and physical activity. For example, previous datasets exploring these issues have tended not to go beyond quantitative studies of body dissatisfaction and body esteem (e.g. Forbes et al., 2004).

Over a period of four years, our research has investigated the lives of forty girls and young women, all of whom have suffered from differing forms of clinically defined eating disorders, such as anorexia nervosa, bulimia or versions of disordered eating (e.g. orthorexia) and/or depression, over-exercising and other conditions of ill-health. All of these girls were full-time residents at a leading eating disorders centre in England, having been referred there either by a general practitioner, a child psychiatrist or paediatrician; their costs met either by the National Health Service (NHS) or private means (usually the family themselves). While relatively few people are impelled to take the dramatic actions of these girls, they nonetheless vividly reveal features of weight representations in schools to which many young people are subjected, and which may underlie the increasing levels of 'body disaffection' and 'dissatisfaction' now reported in Western societies (Grogan, 1999).

We located our research in a centre for the treatment of eating disorders rather than schools for a number of reasons. Our primary aim was to explore the links between obesity discourse, formal education and eating disorders through the voices of young people. As such, our first task was to identify a suitable number of young people with 'eating disorders' for inclusion in the study. We quickly discovered, however, that it is very difficult to identify young people so categorised through schools, as few 'surface' or present themselves as such to the system and the teachers within it. By contrast, the centre provided easy access to a sizeable number of young people of school age, the majority of whom had experienced mainstream education prior to their (usually two-week) stay at the centre, and would re-enter it on leaving. Research at the centre proved hugely valuable in providing opportunities for focus-group interviews, sustained periods of contact with the girls and young women, generating a depth of data that would not have been achieved had we pursued such girls/young women individually across many schools.

Our participants were asked to record and reflect on their experiences of mainstream schooling. A variety of data collection methods were used to gain access to participants' stories of the roles of formal mainstream education in the development of their disordered behaviours and relationships with their own and others' bodies. The methods used included interviews, diary keeping, focus groups, field notes, email correspondence, artwork and mapping techniques. We also interviewed teachers who work at the centre. In this chapter, we report on the young women's interview data unless stated otherwise. The young women were aged between 11 and 18 years, were white, of UK origin and able-bodied. Reflecting a wider demography of eating disorders (see Doyle & Bryant-Waugh, 2000) they, like most others attending the centre, come from 'middle-class' families and had attended what might be described as high-status comprehensive, grammar or private schools from across the UK. The centre also catered for males but received very few, and at the time of study no boys were available for inclusion in the research. Operating rather like a boarding school, the centre provided compulsory full-time education for the residents while liaising with the young person's school of origin to ensure continuity of work and to reduce the anxieties of re-entry to mainstream education.

Theorising representations of weight in school: The emergence of body pedagogies and body perfection codes

One of our research interests was to investigate how weight and health were being represented within schools and the impact these representations had upon the young women we interviewed. Given the recent barrage of initiatives aimed to combat obesity in schools, we were particularly interested in how the young women were learning about weight via the representation, practices and activities that were occurring in schools. In this sense, we were interested in how schools might play a role in constructing what we and others refer to as Body Pedagogies (Evans & Davies, 2004, 2006; Evans et al., 2008). Stated simply, pedagogy constitutes 'any conscious activity by one person designed to enhance learning in another' (Watkins & Mortimore, 1999, p. 3) and by 'body pedagogies' we refer to 'any conscious activity taken by one person, organisation, or a State, designed to enhance an individual's understandings of their own and/or others' corporeality' (Evans et al., 2008). We argue that body pedagogies define the significance, value and potential of the body in time, place and space and that these can combine with discourses available in wider society to damaging effect.

As argued throughout this book, discourses of neoliberal subjectivity, which produce an understanding of the body as a project that can be worked on, can combine with cultural ideals that idealise slimness and associate slimness with health and morality. These understandings are brought into schools to produce what we call 'body perfection codes'.[1] Body perfection codes are a form of educational code (Bernstein, 2000, 2001), an analytic that provides a way of understanding how wider social forces and trends relating to 'body perfection' are embedded in the cultures and structures of schools, and ultimately internalised as distinctive forms of embodied consciousness. The social bases of perfection codes have their origins in trends outside of formal education but are re-contextualised in school contexts (Evans and Davies, 2004). These social bases include the health and media industries and developments in medical research; for example, a shift to understanding common ailments such as heart disease in terms of unhealthy lifestyles. Such diseases are thus deemed to be potentially preventable by switching diet and reducing exposure to risk factors, and so individual accountability is at stake in such understandings of illness (Evans et al., 2004; Le Fanu, 1999).

In this chapter we argue that perfection codes ascribe value and meaning to particular body types and behaviours, and are embedded in educational practices that are specifically focused on body matters, for example, physical education (PE) (see, Evans et al., 2004). However, we also note that perfection codes are endemic in practices that extend way beyond the formal curriculum. They infuse the subcultures and informal structures of schools (such as playground structures and lunch breaks) so that within these contexts the body emerges as a project to be managed, regulated and measured in much the same way as academic work in school classrooms. Body perfection codes combine with body pedagogies so that the young women in our study learnt to focus on their bodies and associate health, morality and personal value with thinness in a context in which the body was represented as unfinished and never quite 'good enough'.

Learning 'weight' management

The young women in our research reported that weight management was a central feature of their experiences of school, in which they were taught to understand their bodies as a project that needed work, and to associate thinness with health and morality. For example, many of the participants reported that during PE, teachers often focused on the need to achieve 'fitness' and maintain a 'good weight'. In these classes the body was equated to machines with a focus on burning calories, losing weight or achieving a health status so that PE took on an inherently instrumental form:

> We learnt in PE that like exercise like ... burns calories and keeps you like ... at a good weight.
>
> (Jane[2])

Participants described critical moments when teachers made issues of weight and body management salient, which led these young women to change their behaviours, for example, to engage in extreme dieting.

> She [teacher] picked out this girl who was literally like this thick [pointing to a pole in the room] and she said 'now this looks like a girl who is the right weight'. That really upset me because I just thought I have to get [my weight] down quick, so yeah that probably had a big effect on me.
>
> (Lydia)

> I think it made me a bit worse ... there was the teacher ... she was saying like stuff like to all the pupils like 'oh you're all so lucky at the moment, you can eat like horses but you'll all be really fat when you're older if you carry on eating like this.
>
> (Jane)

Our data shows how perfection codes are incorporated into body pedagogies to produce particular understandings and representations of one's body. The young women's narratives reveal that as they experience instruction around health and exercise, they were also learning to regulate their own bodies and weight. As Burrows and Wright (2006) suggest, children and young people are being offered a number of ways to understand and change themselves, and take action to change others and their environments. The voices of those in our study suggest that perfection codes are not always transmitted straightforwardly, but are mediated by teachers, pupils and their peers in subtle and incidental ways. They become embedded in the cultures and structures of schools, defining what the body (in size, shape, predisposition and demeanour) is and ought to be; and how, for those who do not meet these ideals, there is treatment, repair and restoration (Evans & Davies, 2004; Evans et al., forthcoming).

These practices resonated with those noted by Kassirer and Angell (1998) who found that sometimes the focus in treatment of obesity has clearly been more on normalising the obese person's body, that is making the obese person thin rather than improving health (see also Aphramor & Gingras, this volume). In our study the perfection code represents a shift from a concern with repairing the 'physical body' through specific pedagogical action (for example, through PE and fitness regimes) to protecting/preserving the body through intervention and prevention. Thus, as Jane's extract above demonstrates, and Riley & Burns (this volume) have argued, everyone, regardless of size, becomes implicated in the need to be vigilant against weight gain.

Although criteria for being ' successfully healthy' are many and varied, health was reduced essentially to that which can be measured, so that weight, exercise and diet become 'gold standards' by which 'successful health' is defined. As Burns (2003) has pointed out, public anti-obesity messages are often oversimplified when re-contextualised as a focus on weight loss. In other words, the tendency is to reduce complex health issues to simple 'weight problems' and their solution, 'weight loss' and eating 'proper' food. This is because, as Campos (2004) suggests, much of the obesity discourse rests on the assertion that there is a correlation between being overweight and ill health and that losing weight will cure associated 'disease'. In a culture where everyone is assumed to be 'at risk', young people are pressed to make particular lifestyle choices to address these risks and avoid them. Thus health becomes primarily an obligation and individual responsibility (see Lupton, 1999; Nettleton & Bunton, 1995). The message these young women hear is that they are to take control of their health by making 'healthy choices', particularly in relation to diet:

> You just learn that some things are good for you and some things are bad and should be avoided. That's why I find it so hard here when they put a pasty in front of you because I just think 'fat'. You don't learn that there are other things in 'bad' foods that are also good for you, like protein and carbohydrates.
>
> (Lauren)

Perfection codes and the morality of weight

Perfection codes are not simply about working towards a particular representation of an ideal body by managing weight or eating 'good' foods, but are also connected to morality and virtue. In this sense, the regulation of the body is intimately bound up with moral imperatives around weight. By defining whose and what bodies have status and value, 'body pedagogies' also constitute acts of inclusion and exclusion. They carry particularly strong moral overtones in the notions of the body they prescribe and define, as Riley & Burns (this volume) also argue, an individual's character and value, their sense of self, can be judged essentially in terms of 'weight', size or shape. The 'overweight' body then represents an individual's moral failure to fulfil the requirements of neoliberal subjectivity since fatness comes to represent a self that is lazy, self-indulgent and lacking control. This representation produces hierarchies of the body relating to size, shape and weight, stigmatising the 'over weight' and evoking in them feelings of guilt and shame. The responsibilities placed on the individual to accept that correct diet and involvement in physical activity therefore become a moral as well as a physical obligation, what we refer to as 'new health imperatives'. In this sense, the processes through which bodies are being shaped are difficult to resist because of their pervasiveness and subtlety in exercising of power: health education is constructed here as 'in one's best interest', and about making 'informed choice'. As Brink (1994) notes, fat people are doubly stigmatised both for their physical appearance and their assumed moral weakness. Accounts used by our participants also allude to the ways weight loss was not simply about achieving a healthy slim body, but about how an individuals' character comes to be judged by others:

> Because I had hassle when I was fat. You know, I wouldn't get asked out by boys ... you know, every time I walked past a mirror I would hide myself.
>
> (Lydia)

> In a way I felt like I started losing weight first 'cos there was this girl that I really didn't like and she was really fat and me and my best friends used to pick on her 'cos she was fat and we were really horrible to her ... I really feel bad about it now ... but we were really horrible to her and we used to call her 'fat' and everything and she started losing weight and the very ... I remember thinking 'God she's gonna get thinner than me ... and I have to be thinner than her so I can keep the power of being horrible to somebody.
>
> (Lara)

The coupling of morality with body size thus enabled a form of bullying, as in the extract above, but also meant that for many of our participants 'guilt' was a routine feature of their relationships with food and exercise.

> If I see someone having something healthier than me I immediately feel guilty as I feel I am eating so much fat and it disgusts me.
>
> (Ruth)

For these young women, escaping the normalising effects associated with representations of weight was incredibly difficult. As we've elsewhere illustrated (Evans et al., forthcoming; Evans & Davies, 2006; Rich & Evans 2005), the pressures to evaluate and judge their own and others' bodies against unattainable social ideals and of routinely being evaluated, judged and displayed were ever present across all features of schooling. Indeed, what makes perfection codes different to previous forms of 'health promotion' in schools is that they were not confined to PE or Personal, Social and Health lessons, but were found across all features and structures of schooling, even within playgrounds and corridors. Lunchtimes, for example, were described as virulent environments in which the girls routinely surveyed not only their own, but also others' behaviour:

> Not many people were eating like a proper lunch so there was no way I was going to.
>
> (Viki)

> Everyone at school's got like food issues ... all the girls are always looking for like what's got the least fat and that ... and people will comment on each other like if someone has two chocolate bars someone will say like 'oh haven't you had one already' and stuff.
>
> (Tracey)

Collectively, our data points towards the way in which wider health imperatives seeping into school culture press young people to engage in a constant process of self-monitoring. Furthermore, the processes of self-regulation and monitoring of oneself provided a route for these young women to construct themselves as a 'good' subject:

> When I started dieting if I found out something was healthy, I had to have it. I felt that I was being different to most people eating chips and I suppose in a way that I would get recognised for being healthy.

I don't know why this felt good, it's as if people would think I was doing good and in the early stages I did get praised for taking care of myself. If I'd go to the canteen and there was something healthy I'd have to have it, anything to help me feel better.

(Ruth)

For many of our participants, weight loss, dieting and participating in physical activity constituted techniques through which they could be recognised as demonstrating autonomy, self-control and achievement. Thus, since health and 'weight' were strongly associated with morality, making 'good' and 'bad' choices or reducing one's body size became a way for these young women to demonstrate (and earn recognition) as a good person.

I always used to look at my friends and think that I wanted to be as good, or as pretty, or as clever as them. So I decided that not eating was a way that I could maybe achieve that.

(Hayley)

Mmm, but in some respects I did want it because it made me feel special, it made me feel that I was more important than everybody else, and I think in some ways that was why I couldn't get rid of it at school ... Because you have 'the dominants', 'the leaders', 'the thinkers', I was just 'the anorexic', that was who I was. And when this other girl at the school became anorexic, I felt that I had been pushed out of my place and I was furious ... It [anorexia] shows that you have a strength that others don't, because let's face it, not many people have the ability to starve themselves to death.

(Lauren)

Adhering to health becomes a way to stand out and achieve recognition within school cultures where 'authentic relationships are being replaced by judgemental relationships wherein persons are valued for their productivity or performances alone' (Ball, 2004, p. 146). As Lucey and Reay (2002) suggest, the constant striving for and achievement of high attainment that is particularly felt by middle-class girls can produce a sense of never being good enough. It is a culture that lends itself to alienation of the self as persons are constantly required to make themselves distinctive through 'practices of representation', judgement and comparison via what they eat, how they exercise or what they weigh. Unsurprisingly, as a consequence, some young people feel that they are not valued or recognised for who they really are. Mia, for example, commented:

> I've found that the teachers in this school, they're very cold and they never talk to you personally, like you're a person, they'll talk to you like you're a number to them and that's all it is basically.

Additionally, Ellie considered that her headmaster 'didn't really seem to care about his students', while Carrie commented that she felt students weren't 'treated as individuals' within school but just stereotyped or categorised in relation to abilities. For these young women, perfection code principles of 'slenderness' and 'weight loss' become 'the' credential for recognition and belonging, and diet becomes 'a rite of passage', a means of achieving and displaying high status by having the 'right' body and the 'right' commitment and attitude. Again, class seems relevant, since the 'qualities ascribed to femininity are understood as the central carriers of the new "middle-class" individuality, building upon the long-established incitement to women to become producers of themselves as objects of the gaze' (Walkerdine, 2003, p. 242).

Performative culture and the imperfect body

Achieving high status through body management, however, is a dangerous strategy. Part of the body perfection codes is that the body is understood as problematic, imperfect, unfinished, and so in constant need of work. Body perfection codes mean that you are never 'good enough', as in Anne's extract below, where she recalled how despite beginning to feel weak from her extreme dieting, teachers continued to emphasise the need for her to 'push herself' in terms of physical activity:

> Emmm ... they just sort of said 'push yourselves to the limit'... and I thought ... you know ... I sort of didn't kind of think I was fit enough sometimes ... near the end ... you know ... I was quite weak ... and they ... and they sort of made you push yourselves to the limit and I was like 'help I can't do this!'
>
> (Anne)

Anne's account is, we argue, an example of the way young women's subjectivities may be constructed within a performative culture, in which pressures to achieve 'excellence' (in terms of 'fitness' and diet regimes) become not only unbearable but impossible to achieve. The practices which she described as pushing her beyond boundaries with which she was comfortable were justified (by the teacher) with reference to the need to detect and address any deviation from 'normal' development in order to prevent obesity and associated diseases.

Although there are tensions between the variety of health discourses and modalities now found in schools, all, in one way or another, focus on the body as imperfect, unfinished or threatened (by the risks of modernity/lifestyles of food, over eating, inactivity) and to be ameliorated through physical therapy (e.g. circuit training, fitness through sport and a better diet). These accounts all represent the body as in need of care and change (Evans & Davies, 2004). Reflecting this, many of our participants reported being publicly weighed in schools. A further reflection of perfection code mentality, this act of weighing constructed bodies as either threatened by future excess fat or in need of changing if considered 'over-weight'. These experiences had a profound impact on our participants' relationships with their bodies; it was considered negative and demeaning, a humiliating and stigmatised encounter for those involved, as evidenced in extracts from Vicky's talk below.

> I used to be overweight, and I remember one time at school when the whole class got weighed. The teacher said, 'Oh, it's the big one' and I was the heaviest in the year.
> and my house mistress kept ... sort of coming into the common room and saying 'you've gotta be weighed now' and kind of saying it in front of everyone ... It was horrible.

We do not suggest that the schools explicitly supported problematic or harmful actions, rather that humiliation, among other techniques, is a process of normalisation in which young people's embodiment is regulated. In this way, body perfection codes operate to legitimise the public display and monitoring of young people's bodies. Such experiences can be particularly traumatic and problematic for young women. Harjunen (2002) suggests that during weighing the body is made public property and it is thus placed under the scrutiny, criticism and judgement of others. Despite increasing evidence of the damaging effects of weighing, the UK Government has plans under the Public Services Agreement Target to take body mass index (BMI) readings of primary school children in the UK (aged 4 to 10 years). Other research has reported further forms of surveillance, including lunchtime inspections being undertaken by teachers. In Australia, Leahy and Harrison (2003) report on the phenomenon known as 'fat laps' in primary schools, where children identified as exceeding recommended body weight norms were required to run around the school field in their lunchtimes.

Unattainable goals and shifting goalposts

The tendency to slip towards 'unhealthy' relationships with physical activity and the body was made worse by the variance in guidelines on healthy eating and exercise which are found within and across various institutions. For instance, recommendations for daily physical activity regimes continually change both in terms of intensity and duration. As such, 'health' emerges as an unattainable 'product' and a neverending project in which the body is to be continually worked upon and compared against others. One can always exercise more, eat less or lose more weight than someone else.

Our participants described engaging in behaviours that included collectively avoiding lunches, missing lunches because of sport and comparing weight loss with one another. Furthermore, body perfection codes produced conditions of possibility that led to the institutions being understood as sanctioning these behaviours.

> They [teachers] let them over-exercise and at times they even encourage them to over-exercise and I think that's a key thing. I mean, from our own experience ... over-exercise was a key element of it ... you know, swam a mile and before breakfast and would also go and do something else after the, the match ... and, emmm thought nothing wrong, saw nothing wrong with that ... and of course part of the problem then with over exercising is it then becomes a cycle, in the context of, of physical fitness is deemed to be ... an integral element of being well, in their minds ... and when you're trying to get them well, which involves attacking the physical fitness that's, that's a really difficult barrier to then break down.
>
> (Parent)

According to Foucault (1979), schools as disciplinary institutions can create disciplined subjects who conform to standards of normality concerning, for example, health, care for the body and docility. The imperative to adopt particular behaviours and achieve a particular weight for many of the girls, in our research, was therefore not about maintaining a healthy balanced lifestyle or enjoying physical activity as a lifelong pursuit, but an instrumental activity to gain recognition within the cultures of schooling, where the normality of thinness renders it not simply an issue of size, but a representation of qualities such as control, discipline and health.

Conclusions

Despite a growing body of research suggesting that the current 'facts' relating to obesity ought to be treated with a good deal more caution and far less certainty than their proponents would have us believe, the drive to tackle an obesity epidemic has become a rationale for the development of a range of school-based initiatives and policies.

Schools are a place where young people's bodies literally became a focus of continuous and close monitoring and control through the realisation of body perfection codes. All of the young women in our research reported that a narrow definition of health associated with weight loss had emerged from, and been reinforced, in both the formal and informal cultures of schools they attended. Health was not treated holistically, that is to say, as a state of becoming, subject to social, political, physical and emotional contingencies (and to visceral pleasures). Rather, it was represented reductively, as strongly associated with body size and appearance, such that the thin or slender body was taken to represent not only a state of good health but also an outward sign of self-control, virtue and of being a good responsible citizen. Health was configured as a personal attribute, as if young people were free of social, cultural, economic and physical constraints that may prevent them from making particular choices, or achieving a particular body size or health status. Thus, young people's moral decisions associated with physical activity and diet were ascribed to some flaw, or virtue, in their lifestyle. Such imperatives reify neoliberalism, a discourse that has remained central to performance cultures that are heavily regulated by the 'kind of meritocratic principles that explain any failure to "achieve" and to "have" as personal failure' (Lucey et al., 2003, p. 285). The consequence of all this is that the anxiety they feel within these performative cultures becomes a suppressed discourse. Their anorexia is constructed as part of the 'obligation to be free' within the biographical project, 'as if it were an outcome of individual choices' (Rose, 1999, p. ix).

Our research can only allude to the sort of experiences and sense of corporeality that our participants experienced within schools, as reported through their narratives. More research is needed to explore further how these processes are mediated through the pedagogical and power relationships that prevail between teachers and pupils, and among peers in schools and other spaces. In all of these young women's lives there are many other factors that have contributed to their decisions to embark on, learn and persist with the use of self-starvation as a means of bringing some meaning and control to their lives. The conditions of schooling cannot be ignored; they are represented as contributory factors in the development of 'disordered behaviour' when they should be involved in their prevention. The social injustice of placing such moral obligation and blame on individuals for their health/problems, and in ways, which depoliticise the roles that schools and other social influences play in people's lives must remain a pressing concern.

Notes

1. A code is a regulative principle, tacitly acquired, which selects and integrates: meanings, realizations contexts' (Bernstein, 1990, p. 14) later redefined as orientations to meanings; textual productions; and specialised interactional practices. Perfection codes determine 'what bodily acts are permitted and forbidden, the positive and the negative values of different possible behaviours of and on the body'. They determine and define simultaneously 'what 'the body' is and ideally ought to be' (Evans and Davies, 2004b: 215).
2. Pseudonyms have been used throughout the chapter.

References

Aphramor, L. & Gingras, J. (this volume). Sustaining imbalance: Evidence of neglect in the pursuit of nutritional health. In S. Riley, M. Burns, H. Frith, S. Wiggins & P. Markula (Eds), *Critical bodies: Representations, identities and practices of weight and body management*. Basingstoke: Palgrave Macmillan.
Ball, B. (2004). Performtivities and fabrication in the education economy: Toward the performative society. In S. J. Ball (Ed.), *The Routledge Falmer Reader in Sociology of Education*. London: Routledge Falmer.
Bernstein, B. (1990). *The structuring of pedagogic discourse: Volume IV, class codes and control*. London: Routledge.
Bernstein, B. (2000). *Pedagogy, symbolic control and identity*. Boston: Rowman & Littlefield.
Bernstein, B. (2001). From pedagogies to knowledges. In A. Morias, I. Neves, B. Davies & H. Daniels (Eds), *Towards a sociology of pedagogy: The contribution of Basil Bernstein to research*. New York: Peter Lang.
Brink, P. J. (1994). Stigma and obesity. *Clinical Nursing Research*, 3(4), 291–3.
Burns, M. (2003). Interviewing: Embodied communication. *Feminism and Psychology*, 13(2), 229–36.
Burrows, L. & Wright, J. (2006). Prescribing practices: Shaping healthy children in schools. Paper presented at Children and young people as social actors symposium, University of Otago.
Campos, P. (2004). *The obesity myth*. New York: Gotham Books.

Department of Health. (2005). *National healthy school status*. London: DH Publications.
Doyle, J. & Bryant Waugh, R. A. (2000). Epidemiology. In B. Lask & R. Bryant Waugh (Eds), *Anorexia nervosa and related eating disorders in childhood and adolescence*. Hove: Psychology Press, Taylor and Francis.
Evans, J. & Davies, B. (2004). The embodiment of consciousness: Bernstein, health and schooling. In J. Evans, B. Davies & J. Wright (Eds), *Body knowledge and control*. London: Routledge.
Evans, J. & Davies, B. (2006). The poverty of theory: Class configurations in the discourse of physical education and health (PEH*)*. Keynote paper *BERA PESIG*, Warwick University, September 2007.
Evans, J., Davies, B. & Wright, J. (2004) (Eds), *Body, knowledge and control*. London: Routledge.
Evans, J., Rich, E. & Allwood, R. (forthcoming). *Fat fabrications*. London: Routledge.
Evans, J., Rich. E., Allwood, R. & Davies B. (in press, 2008). Body pedagogies, policy, health and gender. *British Educational Research Journal*.
Forbes, G. B., Doroszewicz, K., Card, K. & Adams-Curtis, L. (2004). Association of the thin body ideal, ambivalent sexism and self-esteem with body acceptance and the preferred body size of college women in Poland and the United States. *Sex Roles*, 50, 331–45.
Foucault, M. (1979). *Discipline and punish*. Harmondsworth: Penguin.
Grogan, S. (1999). *Body image: Understanding body dissatisfaction in men, women and children*. London: Routledge.
Harjunen, H. (2002). The construction of the acceptable female body in Finnish school. In S. Vappu, J. Kangasvuo & M. Heikkinen (Eds), *Gendered and sexualized violence in educational environments*. Femina Borealis publication series no. 5: Oulu University.
Kassirer, J. P. & Angell, M. (1998). Losing weight – An ill-fated new year's resolution. *NEJM* 338, 52–4.
Leahy, D. & Harrison, L. (2003). Fat laps and fruit straps: Childhood obesity, body image, surveillance and education. *Educational research, risks and dilemmas: NZARE AARE conference handbook*, p. 335, NZARE, New Zealand.
Le Fanu, J. (1999). *The rise and fall of modern medicine*. London: Abacus.
Lucey, H., Melody, J. & Walkerdine, V. (2003). Uneasy hybrids: Psychosocial aspects of becoming educationally successful working-class young women. *Gender and Education*, 15(3), 285–99.
Lucey, H. & Reay, D. (2002). Carrying the beacon of excellence: Social class differentiation and anxiety at a time of transition. *Journal of Educational Policy*, 17(3), 321–36.
Lupton, D. (1999). (Ed.), *Risk and sociocultural theory: New directions and perspectives*. Cambridge: Cambridge University Press.
Markula, P., Burns, M. & Riley, S. (this volume). Introducing critical bodies: - Representations, identities and practices of weight and body management. In S. Riley, M. Burns, H. Frith, S. Wiggins & P. Markula (Eds), *Critical bodies: Representations, identities and practices of weight and body management*. Basingstoke: Palgrave Macmillan.
Nettleton, S. & Bunton, R. (1995). Sociological critique of health promotion. In S. Nettleton, R. Bunton & R. Burrows (Eds), *The sociology of health promotion*. (pp. 41–60). Hampden: Routledge.

Rich, E. & Evans, J. (2005). 'Fat ethics': The obesity discourse and body politics. *Social Theory and Health*, 3(4), 341–58.
Rose, N. (1999). *Governing the soul: The shaping of the private self.* Second edition. London: Free Associations Books.
Seidell, J. C. (2000). The current epidemic of obesity. In C. Bouchard (Ed.), *Physical activity and health* (pp. 21–30). Champaign, IL: Human Kinetics.
Walkerdine, V. (2003). Reclassifying upward mobility: Femininity and the neo-liberal subject. *Gender and Education*, 15(3), 237–48.
Watkins, C. & Mortimore, P. (1999). Pedagogy: What do we know? In P. Mortimore (Ed.), *Understanding pedagogy and its impact on learning.* London: Sage.

Section II Constructing Embodied Identities

Hannah Frith

The contributions in this section explore how representations and discourses of body and weight management inform the ways we think about ourselves and the kind of person it is possible to be. Critical approaches to understanding personhood and subjectivity share a suspicion of traditional approaches to the self in which the person is understood as unitary, internally consistent, stable and separate from social context and processes. Instead, as described in the Introduction, critical and constructionist approaches employ models of the self that conceptualise identity as a fluid process, as a kaleidoscope of understandings that are made sense of through interaction, and which may be fractured, contradictory or only partially formed. In this section we offer three different forms of analysis that are informed by critical and constructionist conceptualising of subjectivity in relation to weight and body management. Each chapter also deals with a different type of body-management practice by drawing on diverse research sites. Day and Keys conduct a discursive analysis of textual material from 'pro-eating disorder' websites that explores how the construction of alternate anorexic and bulimic selves takes place. Gill presents an analysis of interview and focus-group data in which boys and men discuss their responses to media images of male bodies and their own appearance management behaviours. Finally, Heenan explores the usefulness of feminist object relations psychoanalytic theory for understanding the connections between discourses of consumerism and women's gendered developmental processes. These chapters take up a number of themes which are key to critical, social constructionist and post-structural/modern conceptualisations of self and identity.

Critical psychology asserts that all knowledge is historically and socially specific and therefore work drawing from this approach often challenges the notion of knowledge (including psychological knowledge) as self-evident, 'fact' or 'truth'. This includes a scepticism about how psychologists typically understand 'the person' as a self-contained individual, unique unit with an integrated and coherent inner world of emotions, awareness, judgements, personalities and ways of reasoning. Using this model of 'the person' traditional approaches in psychology tend to examine phenomena in terms of the properties and characteristics of individuals and are concerned to categorise, measure and describe individuals and their characteristics (such as the anorexic, the over-eater, the obese). These characteristics are assumed to be stable, internally coherent and consistent over time. In contrast, as noted in the Introduction, critical and constructionist psychologists have questioned the idea that individuals are the owners of relatively stable, distinct and coherent personalities by demonstrating the flexibility and variability in the ways in which individuals account for themselves in different social contexts for different interactional purposes. In this volume, for example, Gill notes the diverse range of responses to changing media representations of male bodies both between different men and within individual men's accounts, and the competing tensions between being interested in and concerned about their bodies but not being vain, narcissistic or obsessional.

One consequence of the mainstream approach to 'the person' as unique, bounded and the centre of awareness and action is that 'the problem' (which for our purposes might be defined as over- or under-eating or being over- or under-weight) becomes located within the individual who is deemed deficient and who is given responsibility for 'curing' themselves. Critical psychologists deconstruct these taken-for-granted categories of people typically described and deployed by mainstream psychology and medical establishments to demonstrate how these can be a feature of social conditions and power relations rather than 'naturally' occurring phenomena. Social constructionists are concerned with identifying how particular categories of person ('the anorexic', 'the bulimic', 'the obese' etc.) come into being and come to have particular meanings. Importantly, they are concerned with how these meanings or discourses come to define what kind of person it is possible to be. Critical psychologists often draw on the notion of 'positioning' (Davies & Harré, 1990) to emphasise that it is through language and interaction that identities and subjectivities are accomplished, produced and displayed. Discourses make available particular subject positions from which individuals can speak (e.g. a medical discourses makes the subject positions of doctor and patient available) and enable and constrain how people can speak, think, be or act when they are so positioned. For example, the chapters by Day and Keys, and Heenan describe how psychiatric and medical discourses of normality and abnormality serve to separate out some women (those who are 'over' eaters, 'excessive' dieters or 'overvalue' their appearance) from others, locate the source of pathology within the individual, and focus attention on symptom reduction for individuals. Rather than assuming that disordered eating is a problem located within individuals the meaning of which is already knowable and established by psychological knowledge, both of these chapters are concerned with examining the process of meaning-making and how meaning is made of particular behaviours, actions and identities. Day and Keys explore how alternative meanings of anorexia and bulimia are created on 'pro-eating-disorder' websites, which give rise to alternative subject positions. Instead of being positioned as sick, mentally ill or overly affected by media messages, on these sites those with anorexia are positioned as virtuous, strong-minded girls and women who actively choose to control their food intake. Similarly, Gill explores how young men make meaning of their own embodiment while simultaneously making meaning of media representations of the bodies of other men. In this way, they are engaged in the task of understanding how they are positioned as men by these images, and the kinds of masculinities available to them. This focus on meaning-making is important for understanding the intersection of practices and identities from the perspective of social actors themselves, and for generating alternative knowledges which may be of practical benefit. For example, by explicating the ways in which those contributing to websites make sense of what it means to be anorexic or bulimic, Day and Keys highlight what girls and women may be giving up if they move away from these behaviours and identities. Similarly, Heenan argues that by re-conceptualising eating disorders as the expression of social tensions, the function of the therapist may be to work with and facilitate the individuals' sense of self and agency in order to explore the unconscious meaning and functions of an eating disorder. By stepping outside of discourses of 'madness' (e.g. anorexia as a mental illness) or 'badness' (e.g. obesity as a moral failing) and working with individuals' own meanings new insight and alternative ways of working can be identified. This section thus showcases three analyses that seek to avoid problematising individuals (e.g. as sick or ill) by examining how identities and behaviours which may be deemed pathological can be meaningful, reasonable and even rational when explored in context.

Traditional psychology's tendency to prioritise the individual, and to see society and the individual as separate has been challenged by critical psychologists who argue that the world we experience (and our experience of ourselves) is a product of social processes. In attempting to subvert the gap between the individual and society, common in mainstream psychology, and to explore the self as inherently embedded within and inseparable from social context, social constructionists are often accused of social or cultural determinism. Social constructionism, as both Day and Keys, and Gill acknowledge, must recognise the importance and centrality of cultural representations for the construction of subjectivity, while avoiding positioning of individuals as 'passive victims' of social cultural forces such as media representations. Both these chapters emphasise the active construction of selves through the manipulation, take-up, resistance to, and reframing of a multitude of competing and often contradictory subject positions which are socially available. For example, Day and Keys demonstrate how pro-anorexia websites operate as discursive spaces for the active construction of 'anorexic selves' which challenge the medical model of an 'ill self' by constructing anorexia as a positive lifestyle choice adopted by elite, disciplined, virtuous individuals. Similarly, Gill criticises conceptualisations of 'media effects' which give rise to the simplistic message that 'thin models cause anorexia' and challenges researchers to find a way to retain a notion of social and cultural influence of the media, while remaining sensitive to the ways in which these images/messages are consumed by their audience and are internalised to the extent that they are seen to be unique individual choices rather than socially imposed ideas (also see Malson, Section I of this volume). This challenge is taken up by Heenan who provides an overview of feminist object relations theory which explores how eating problems are linked to the psychodynamics of consumerism which is built on the tension between desire and constraint, and how bodily scrutiny and eating behaviours could be seen as a means of enacting unconscious conflicts about women's place in society. Although, as Heenan points out, psychoanalytic theories of eating disorders have been contentious among feminists and social constructionists because of their a-historical and a-cultural concerns with the 'inner world', a focus on the unconscious does provide a means for understanding the socially constituted nature of subjectivity which does not rely on individuals being able (or willing) to articulate these processes of construction for themselves. A feminist-informed psychodynamic approach is one way, then, for theorists to understand women's participation in their own oppression as apparently natural, desirable and freely chosen. Collectively these chapters explore how representations of the body and bodily practices (like those identified in Section I) can be taken up, negotiated, resisted and re-worked in the dynamic construction of embodied subjectivities.

References

Davies, B. and Harré, R. (1990). Positioning: The discursive production of selves. *Journal for the Theory of Social Behaviour,* 20, 43–63.

4
Starving in Cyberspace: The Construction of Identity on 'Pro-eating-disorder' Websites

Katy Day and Tammy Keys

Introduction

'The self' has often been central to analyses of 'eating disorders' and problems with food and 'body image'. However, in mainstream psychology notions of the self have often been situated within a false dichotomy between the subject and the social world, a dichotomy that has been deconstructed by critical theorists, particularly those writing from a social constructionist perspective (e.g. Burkitt, 1991). This chapter explores these debates and trends in theorising of the self, and reports on a study that analysed the discourse on pro-eating-disorder websites from a feminist social constructionist perspective. The analysis highlights the active discursive construction of feminine identities within these spaces and how this is closely bound with punitive regimes on the female body such as self-starvation. Through our analysis, the chapter challenges notions that the self can be understood as a separate, 'pre-existent' or static entity in understandings of self-starvation. Rather, 'anorexic selves' are constructed, worked on, multi-faceted and shifting, and an understanding of the discursive locatedness of these is important for fuller understandings of body modification and the self.

The self and 'eating disorders'

Within mainstream psychology, theorising around the self has generally characterised the self as an entity that is unitary and internally consistent, relatively stable (that is, does not, as a matter of course, change or fluctuate) and separate (or at least separable) from the surrounding social context and social processes (Burr, 1995). This has had a number of consequences for theorising around disordered eating as well as clinical and therapeutic practices, as these have largely drawn upon psychological knowledge.

One result has been a widespread belief within psychology that it is possible to measure aspects of the self and categorise individuals. There is a common acceptance that 'anorexia' and 'bulimia' are recognisable, definable categories or conditions, which has the effect of immediately separating some girls and women from others (Hepworth, 1999). There is also an implication that when we refer to 'anorexia' or 'bulimia', we are not just referring to practices or behaviours, but also to certain traits or tendencies that the individual possesses, which are usually internally consistent or 'hang together' in some way. For example, the research literature around anorexia reports that 'anorexics' tend to be 'control freaks', perfectionists and value asceticism (see Lupton, 1996; Smith, 2002). In addition, attributes such as negative affect, low self-esteem and body dissatisfaction have been linked to disordered eating (see Bettle et al., 2001; Burns & Gavey, this volume; Cervera et al., 2003; Willcox & Sattler, 1996). Mainstream psychological understandings of the self have therefore informed individualistic deficiency models that conceive of disordered eating as a problem that emanates essentially from within the individual. These form the basis of mainstream scientific and clinical conceptions of 'eating disorders' (Hepworth & Griffin, 1995) in which the wider context is obscured or under-theorised and where resulting interventions (for example, cognitive-behavioural therapy) have focused upon changing the problematic individual.

Some analyses of 'eating disorders' have attempted to move away from this focus on the individual to pay greater attention to the wider sociocultural context of disrupted eating and the role of factors such as the media (Bemis, 1978; Cumella, 2002; Field, 2000; Stice et al., 1994). Feminist analyses have made a notable contribution here. For example, feminist writers have pointed to the strongly entrenched Western cultural requirement that women must be thin in order to be considered worthwhile and attractive to men (Bartky, 1988; Bordo, 1993; Orbach, 1978, 1986; Wolf, 1990). This has resulted in attempts on the part of women and girls to modify their bodies through weight loss (see Lee, 1998). In addition, feminists have argued that a failure to eat on the part of women often results from and is a form of resistance towards feminine roles characterised by a lack of power, obedience, restraint, self-denial and self-sacrifice (Eichenbaum & Orbach, 1983; Lawrence, 1979; Orbach, 1978, 1986), and so is about more than just the pursuit of physical beauty.

However, despite the contributions of such work in placing gender and society as central, many feminist analyses have been accused of reproducing or inadvertently supporting models of the self that are characteristic of mainstream psychology (for examples of this critique see Hepworth and Griffin, 1995; MacSween, 1993; and Saukko, this volume). Criticisms of feminist analyses that have been accused of reproducing mainstream models of the self are threefold. First, these studies may maintain problematic distinctions and typologies; second, these analyses have located problems (and hence solutions) within the individual; and third, these texts have tended to have a white and Eurocentric perspective.

Addressing these criticisms in turn we note, for example, that the problems associated with the categories 'anorexic' and 'bulimic' have been variably acknowledged in light of continuities between those diagnosed with an eating disorder and those not (Chernin, 1986; Lawrence, 1984; MacLeod, 1981), yet these categories have largely been retained, thus reproducing the notion that those experiencing problems with food can be categorised into 'types'. Instead, Hepworth and Griffin (1995) argue for an analysis of self-starvation and binge-purging behaviours as extreme variations of women's 'normal' reactions to social and cultural forces, as opposed to medical and psychological disorders. They argue that in order to achieve this, it is necessary to deconstruct such pathologising categories (hence, a preference for terms such as 'body distress', 'self-starvation' and 'body modification' among such critics). Their position is supported by Bordo (1993) who notes that a preoccupation with slenderness in women has become normative, and so to locate such problems within a sub-group of types is problematic.

In addition, although Heenan (this volume) makes a case for a feminist-informed psychodynamic analysis, MacSween (1993) points out that this approach produces analyses in which sociocultural factors (for example, social pressures to be thin) are often conceived of as 'going to work' on a fundamental self. A self described by Orbach (1986) as organised around a core of bodily needs and desires, and by Chernin (1986) as comprised of innate female qualities. This self is then distorted, fragmented or prevented from fully developing as a result (MacLeod, 1981; Orbach, 1986). The implication here is that although the self may be affected by social processes, it is conceptualised as existing separately to them. Following from this, the realisation of a more well-integrated ego (Orbach, 1986) or authentic self (MacLeod, 1981), and getting in touch with one's bodily needs and desires (Orbach, 1986) is often presented as the way forward. Thus, the individual rather than the wider social context is located as the source of transformation, which, according to Robertson (1992), underplays the need for social change via collective political action. MacSween (1993) also points out that the assumption that women can realise a self-contained and autonomous 'true self' underestimates the power of gender ideologies and is based upon a masculine model of the self which is not achievable for many women in patriarchal societies (who, in contrast, are often encouraged to be dependent and connected to others). In sum, such critics argue that adding a feminist perspective to existing psychological and psychiatric orthodoxies that draw upon concepts such as the 'authentic self' is insufficient and that critical theorists need to deconstruct and critique these.

Finally, mainstream models of the self have been critiqued for being Eurocentric because it can be argued that the understandings of the self produced in these models (for example, as separable from social processes) are reflective of the sociocultural contexts in which observations of 'anorexics' and 'bulimics'. This work, most notably in the UK and the US, tends to be reflective of Western ideologies of individualism (Parker, 1989; Sampson, 1993). This argument is given weight if we consider cross-cultural variations in understandings of the self, most notably, within those cultures that are often described as 'collectivist', such as those in Asia, Africa and Latin America. Smith and Bond (1993) argue that within such cultures, the notion of a self-contained individual that can be separated from or exist independently of social relations does not figure prominently. Rather, the self is often defined in terms of relationships with others, such as family members, work colleagues and friends. From this perspective, understandings of the self within mainstream psychology, and detectable in the literature on 'eating disorders', can be understood as socially and culturally located constructions, rather than forms of knowledge that reflect 'truth'. The next section of the chapter turns to social constructionism as a theoretical approach which can and has been usefully applied to the study of disordered eating and addresses the problems outlined above.

Constructing the self: Knowledge production and power

Critical theorists writing from a social constructionist or post-structuralist perspective have rejected the individual/society dichotomy in favour of a view of the self as always embedded in and inseparable from the surrounding social context. Notions of an authentic or true self that is independent from this are problematised, as is the notion that any experience of the body outside of social categorisations is possible. For example, MacSween (1993) argues that the body is not a simple biological given, but a social construction, and that any experience or understanding that we have of our bodies is necessarily mediated by social discourse and the social context. As such, embodied identities are constructed or forged from the systems of meanings operating within the contexts in which the person is situated (see Curt, 1994; Stenner & Eccleston, 1994). In addition, our subjectivities are fragmented and multifaceted because the discourses surrounding our activities, the groups that we belong to and our bodies are often multiple and contradictory. For example, drawing upon the work of French philosopher Foucault, and conceiving of identities as discursively produced, Eckermann (1997) argues that the contradictory discourses surrounding self-starvation serve to constitute the subjectivities of women and girls practising this as both 'super-compliant' (for example, complying to the demands of the thin ideal) and as defiant rebels (for example, defying the needs of the body). This challenges unitary understandings of the self, pointing instead to the self as occupying different and conflicting subject positions. (See also Saukko, this volume, for a discussion on the contradictory nature of discourses).

However, this is not to say that we simply absorb cultural messages in a deterministic, straightforward manner – rather, the construction of identity is viewed as a process that is active and dynamic (Griffin, 1989). One problem with much theorising around 'eating disorders' is that girls and women who experience problems with food and the body have been positioned as 'passive victims' of sociocultural forces and expectations. Such analyses arguably obscure notions of agency and suffer from an oversimplification of processes of power (Saukko, in this volume). Clearly, ideologies of gender and the female body are powerful and pervasive and often have real and damaging consequences. However, Weedon (1987) argues that the subject is able to reflect upon the discourses and discursive relations that constitute her and has some leeway in choosing from the options available. Further than this, according to those such as Eckermann (1997), women and girls actually have the potential to 'rewrite' gender ideologies, their actions and identities in beneficial ways. Here, Eckermann is drawing upon a Foucauldian analysis of power that conceives of power as operating in a circular as opposed to a 'top-down' manner, whereby local processes of knowledge production have the potential to subvert and overthrow more widespread and institutionalised discourses. This offers up the possibly of change without relegating it either to the level of the individual on the one hand (for example, realising a more 'authentic' self) or to a radical transformation in social structures on the other (for example, dismantling the patriarchal order). (Also see Gill, this volume, for a discussion on how we might analyse the subtle and complex ways that men may engage with ideologies of gender and the embodied identity.)

Recently, writers such as Harris (2001), Lyons (2000) and Giroux (1998) have identified the Internet as one place where a rewriting of gendered ideologies may be occurring. For example, Harris (2001) and Giroux (1998) have argued that young people have identified virtual spaces on the Internet as new spaces for expression in which they attempt to construct 'choice biographies' (Harris, 2001, p. 130), or in other words, rewrite their actions and identities in ways that resist or challenge dominant images and representations. These often take the form of sub-cultural sites such as 'gurl' web pages. It also appears that struggles over meaning may be occurring on the recently emerged 'pro-eating-disorder' websites, a characteristic of which is the promotion of 'eating disorders' as a 'lifestyle choice' rather than as 'disease' (Paquette, 2002), and which are believed to be accessed mainly by girls and young women aged between 13 and 25 (Fraser, 2003). Angerer (2004) proposes that one reason why the Internet may appeal to those who experience issues with their bodies is because in cyberspace, bodies become invisible or inconsequential, thus allowing for 'disembodied' identities. The content of the pro-eating-disorder websites often contains images of ultra-thin bodies and endless discussions of body weight and size, so within these spaces, the physical body is far from inconsequential. However, as Angerer (2004) also points out, people in cyberspace are permitted to 'set themselves in scene ... uninhibited by an objective reality' (p. 24), so this allows for constructions of one's body that may not be a reflection of its actual physicality.

The emergence of these websites is generally regarded as a worrying development. Women and girls posting on the sites often swap tips on how to achieve and maintain a low body weight via practices such as self-starvation and self-induced vomiting, and it has been argued by Fraser (2003) that the sites often attract teenage girls seeking advice on how to get thinner, and may even be stumbled upon accidentally. Therefore the sites may act as a form of 'initiation' into such practices (although the extent to which this is the case is unknown). We certainly do not wish to dispute the notion that these sites are highly problematic. However, Robertson (1992) argues that a problem with much literature on 'eating disorders' is that girls and women have become the silent objects of discourse around this as opposed to its originators. We regarded the websites as offering the opportunity to explore the 'sense-making' and active construction of identity that occurs within these spaces, outside of a therapeutic or 'face-to-face' research context.

The study

The aims of the study were to identify discourses around femininity, the female body, food and its (non-) consumption, as well as 'anorexia' and 'bulimia', on the websites and examine how these were taken on board, reworked and resisted by the contributors. We were interested in this discursive activity in light of the 'sense-making' occurring; how these meanings and the use of them informed the construction of identity and the 'pro-eating-disorder' phenomenon.

Data collection involved searching for 'pro-eating-disorder' websites using popular search engines (for example, 'Google' and 'Yahoo!'). Some search engines proved more useful than others, as some service providers have attempted to remove all links to the sites. This has only been partially successful. For example, it was found on subsequent searches that sites visited previously had disappeared, only to be replaced by new ones. A more recent, follow-up search indicated that none of the websites accessed for the study are now in existence, although new ones continue to surface.

Regular searches were conducted between September 2002 and April 2003 by one of the authors (TK), and material was downloaded for analysis, which gave a total of 13 sites. Following the ethical guidelines produced by the Association of Internet Researchers (AOIR), we decided to use public web pages and chat exchanges in publicly accessible forums only, avoiding 'lock and key' sites where greater privacy is assumed. In addition, steps were taken to ensure that nobody would be identifiable from the analysis, such as the removal of all names (even obvious pseudonyms) and any other information that may lead to personal identification. Further, no attempts were made to deceive those visiting the sites by, for example, TK 'posing' as a self-starver or someone seeking advice on weight loss. Rather, a method of 'lurking' was adopted (reading the messages without taking part).

The websites were formatted in various ways, but most commonly contained links to such subsections as 'Tips': including how to maintain and hide an 'eating disorder'; 'Ana Commandments': the rules that a 'true anorexic' should live by; and 'My Journal': the site creator's account of her daily life. Some websites contained discussion boards where girls and women discussed their lifestyles with others in a similar situation. Practically all of the websites had links to images of emaciated women, but we decided to focus on the written text as this appeared to be the richest source of discourse in relation to the construction of identities. All of the material found at each of the websites was included in the analysis to ensure a good variety. On virtually all of the websites, 'anorexia' was referred to as 'Ana' and 'bulimia' as 'Mia'[1].

The data were analysed using a post-structuralist form of discourse analysis informed by a feminist perspective, following guidelines provided by Willott and Griffin (1997). The material from the websites was read repeatedly until we were familiar with it. It was then broken into 'chunks', with each chunk representing a block of text or series of interactions centring on a theme or issue. The 'chunks' were then coded using in-vivo themes including, for example, 'resistance', 'theology' and 'thinspiration'. Eventually 25 themes were identified. In this chapter we examine themes that focused on identity concerns, which included 'the Other', 'control and discipline' and 'religion'. All 'chunks' coded using the same in-vivo theme were selected and the ways in which this theme was represented or constructed were documented, noting similarities, differences and contradictions. This process was repeated until the major discursive patterns had been identified for each in-vivo theme. The final stage was to develop a theoretical account of these discursive patterns. We present the analysis below.

'Saints' and 'sinners': Discourse around femininity, food and eating

Members of the 'pro-eating-disorder' community constructed their practices around food and body weight as central to their identity and self-worth. For example, the 'good anorectic' who successfully restricts their food intake is characterised on the sites as a type of 'secular saint':

Extract 1:
Thou shall not eat without feeling guilty.
Strict is my diet. I must not want. It maketh me to lie down at night hungry.
It leadeth me past the confectioners. It trieth my willpower
I believe in calorie counters as the aspired word of God ...
I believe in bathroom scales as an indicator of my daily successes and failures.

(Site 11)

Extract 2:
When you feel empty, it means you are empty of your sins.

(Site 1)

Theological discourse and imagery pervaded the material from the sites, and many of the regimes described and promoted are reminiscent of the practices of inflicting pain and punishment on the body, including self-starvation, among latter-day female saints in expiation of sin (Vandereycken & van Deth, 1990). Some writers have drawn parallels between these practices and more contemporary instances of 'anorexia', for example, as both being characterised by asceticism (Bell, 1985; Walker Bynum, 1991). Similarly, Griffin and Berry (2003), in their discussion of 'holy anorexia' (Bell, 1985), describe how throughout the ages 'fasting', and the demonstration of independence from bodily needs, has often been regarded as a route to salvation for women. This is perhaps associated with constructions of femininity that closely bind femaleness with nature, bodily desire and the 'primitive', things that have come to be devalued (in preference of rationality and restraint) and which must be kept under control. However others such as MacSween (1993) and Malson (1998) have cautioned against drawing such parallels because of the very different meanings that food and self-starvation carried in medieval and twentieth-century Europe. For example, fasting as an instrument of spirituality.

One way to explain these themes of religion and morality, and the construction of those who self-starve as secular saints in contemporary times is to draw from Griffin and Berry (2003) whose analysis of messages portrayed in Western advertisements for food showed that food consumption (particularly high-fat foods) is culturally associated with debauchery, sin and weakness. This operates alongside recent health promotion campaigns and a Western media concerned with promoting 'healthy eating/living' that are often pervaded by moral discourse (see Madden & Chamberlain, 2004 and other chapters in this volume including Burns & Gavey; Rich & Evans; and Aphramor & Gingras). Here, eating certain types of food and occupying an overweight body becomes not just a sign of being 'unhealthy', but also a marker of moral weakness and inferiority (Markula, Burns & Riley, this volume; Lupton, 1996). Madden and Chamberlain (2004) argue that such discourse has implications for subjectivities that become closely bound with eating practices (and body size). For example, a failure to discipline one's desires, and to eat 'bad' food is to take up the negative position of 'sinner' (Wetherell, 1988). Thus while religious discourses were employed on these sites to make sense of restricted eating, maintaining a discursive relationship between religion, morality and food since mediaeval times, we can theorise that there have been shifts in these meanings (see Curt, 1994) for a discussion of texuality and tectonics).

On the sites analysed, the notion of the uncontrolled 'sinner' was detectable:

Extract 3:
[The voice of Mia] Your fingers will be inserted down your throat and not without a great deal of pain, your food binge will come up. ... You fat cow you deserve to be in pain!

(Site 8)

As in Extract 3, overindulgence and 'fatness' (however measured) is construed on these sites as unacceptable and as warranting physical (self) punishment. It could be argued that this discourse is enabled by the contemporary obsession with healthy eating and the 'obesity epidemic' (see Markula, Burns & Riley, this volume). For example, Eckermann (1997) argued that ironically health promotion campaigns may create obsessive concerns about weight, shape and eating (a point raised more recently by Burns & Gavey, 2004 and Rich & Evans, this volume). However, we argue that the role of gender and femininity requires further examination. Sied (1994) argues that women are often regarded as the guardians of 'moral virtue' and numerous authors have pointed out that the denial of bodily needs and the denouncement of pleasure have and continue to be closely bound with images of, and discourses around, normative/desirable femininity (e.g. Orbach, 1978, 1986; Eichenbaum & Orbach, 1983). This indicates then that the impact of moral and theological discourse around food and eating on feminine subjectivities in particular is likely to be more pronounced, creating the conditions of possibility (Foucault, 1972; see also Malson, this volume) for identities that associate denial of food with 'good' femininity. Thus the girls and women contributing to the sites we analysed appeared to be attempting to construct a valued identity for themselves through reduced food intake, one that clearly set them apart from the 'weak' and 'inferior':

Extract 4:
It's not our fault [that] others have no control over their own bodies and live in a fast-food, fat-soaked existence.

(Site 5)

Extract 5:
Hot open-face roast beef sandwich, lobster roll, sloppy Joes, roast chicken dinner, beef stew & biscuits, chicken pot pie ... all of my

co-workers eat this shit every day. It's gross! This morning, they ordered breakfast. When it arrived, I didn't know it was here yet and I could smell something gross. I said 'Do you guys smell poop?' someone said 'No, but I smell our breakfast' and then they started eating all this greasy gross stuff. I'm so glad I don't eat that crap. It's friggin gross. I haven't eaten anything yet today. Just gum and a cup of coffee!

(Site 7)

Extract 6:
If you're anti-Ana or anti-Mia why do you even bother posting here? I don't understand, what would you think if I got on your Fat and Obese website and posted against you? Is there such a thing as anti-fat? Cuz I think that I am!

(Site 9)

The extracts above (4–6) serve as examples of a collectively constructed identity that is strong and virtuous and in opposition to the 'fat', 'gluttonous', 'uncontrolled' Other: an opposition that provides the pro-ana community with an 'elite' or special status (see also Rich & Evans, this volume, for a discussion on the relationships between representations of morality, subjectivity and thinness). Indeed, the discursive activity occurring on the sites appears to be as much about the collective construction of a positive identity as sharing advice and swapping 'tips' on how to maintain a low body weight. For example, those posting on the sites often referred to themselves and to each other as 'Ana' (anorexic) or 'Mia' (bulimic) which in these contexts were presented as positive and valued forms of identity, as opposed to, for example, illnesses or practices.

Cohn (1986) argues that women are engaged in a constant struggle to assert a (satisfactory) female identity in a world where female identities are often denied independence or value or remain hidden (see also Heenan, this volume). Research has shown that a characteristic of identity construction is that it often occurs in relation to other groups who are perceived as holding less social power because of, for example, their gender or class status, thus allowing for a powerful and positive group identity (e.g. Day, 2003; Gough & Edwards, 1998). Our analysis suggests that the relational construction of identity occurring on the sites was enabled and informed by a wider cultural denigration of 'fat' bodies and 'gluttonous' practices which are linked to discourses of morality in terms of being a certain type of unrestrained, immoral personhood.

In Extract 6, the poster poses the question 'Is there such a thing as antifat? Cuz I think that I am!', reproducing the current wider sociocultural discourse that is critical of obesity (such as the 'war on obesity', see Markula, Burns & Riley, and Malson, this volume). Her posting appears to function more as a statement of difference as opposed to an exploration of a serious question. The widespread promotion of the thin ideal (e.g. Bartky, 1988; Bordo, 1993; Markula, Burns & Riley this volume; Orbach, 1978, 1986; Wolf, 1990) and discourses around normative/ desirable femininity which emphasise restraint and denial of bodily needs (e.g. Eichenbaum & Orbach, 1983; Heenan, this volume; Orbach, 1978, 1986) thus open up the pursuit of a thin body and moral virtue as ways in which women can achieve a positive identity (see also Rich & Evans, this volume).

The active self: The language of struggle, self-determination and choice

A second theme identified did not draw on discourses of traditional femininity, but what may be considered to be 'new', more marginalised or subversive forms of knowledge, what Harris has described as 'choice biographies' (2001, p. 130). For example, a pattern of discursive activity that occurred on the sites was one that positioned girls and women who severely restrict their food intake and/or who binge and purge as a determined group of people who were actively in control of their bodies and lives with language that was at times suggestive of political struggle. For example, 'mission statements' such as the ones below were typical on the sites:

Extract 7:
Our authority is our control over our own bodies.

(Site 5)

Extract 8:
I believe in perfection and strive to attain it.

(Site 11)

Extract 9:
This site is for those of us who will fight to be the best we can be and the best we can be is the thinnest we can be. We will not allow those around us to detour our missions. We will do whatever it takes to reach our goals. This is a place for the elite who, through personal

determination in their ongoing quest for perfection, demonstrate daily that the Ana way is the only way to live.

(Site 5)

Such posts could be read as an active attempt to resist and subvert medicalised and psychiatric constructions of self-starvation which position girls and women who practice this as passive victims of a disease that they have no or little control over. Research has demonstrated how widespread such ideas are (Benveniste, LeCouteur and Hepworth, 1999; Saukko, this volume). Rather, on the pro-ana sites we analysed, extreme forms of body modification are constructed in terms of choice and personal determination, and as a cause of pride and celebration. This construction has been noted by others as a prominent characteristic of pro-eating-disorder websites (e.g. Paquette, 2002). Girls and women who self-starve can thus either 'take up' the subject positions that 'pathology' discourse offers (for example, the 'sick self') or they can rework and resist such discursive positioning, which is what appears to be occurring on the sites. There is much at stake for these girls and women, especially if we consider arguments presented by those such as Laing (in Liversidge, 1988) that pathologising categories and labels are often used to strip people of their civil liberties. Indeed, the material from the sites we analysed indicated that some of the girls and women contributing had been in forced treatment at one time or another as accounts of this, as well tips on resistance, were offered.

The positioning of those who self-starve as active and agentic subverts socially deterministic discourses of the self-starving girl/woman as a victim of social forces. For example, Wooley (1994) argues that the objectification of women's bodies disenables them from experiencing the self as active and agentic, a contention that was challenged on the sites. This is a position that is also problematic in light of Western bourgeoisie, patriarchal ideologies that value independence and autonomy, and which devalue social conformity. On the sites, severe restriction of food intake was often articulated in terms of nonconformity:

Extract 10:
This isn't a place for the weak. This site isn't looking to rescue you. This is a place for those who don't conform to the gluttonous world we live in.

(Site 5)

Extract 10 incorporates a note of social criticism in relation to overconsumption in the contemporary Western world. Drawing upon a discourse of 'anti-consumerism' this posting serves to position members of the movement as 'non-conformist' in this context and helps to establish the 'differentness' of those who 'are Ana'. In addition to an anti-consumerist standpoint, dominant Western ideologies that value independence and autonomy were also in evidence. Wetherell (1988), and Burns and Gavey (2004) have identified a need for women who are pursing thinness to negotiate a cultural context in which independence (from social pressures) is valued (see Gill, this volume, for an analysis of this cultural context in relation to men's embodied identities). Such repertoires included drawing upon a range of discourses and interpretative repertoires that, for example, portrayed their failure to eat as the result of 'natural' appetite as opposed to pursuit of the thin ideal (Wetherell, 1988) and by tapping into a health discourse which constructs thinness as healthy (Burns & Gavey, 2004 and this volume; Wetherell, 1988). In the study reported here, self-starvation was constructed in terms of an attempt to regain control over the female body, as acts of non-conformity in a fat, gluttonous world and as the pursuit of physical perfection. A key difference between this study and the aforementioned studies appears to be the extremity of the practices described on the sites we analysed, which renders accounting practices drawing explicitly on notions of health or natural appetite problematic. However, a similarity is that ideologies of individualism and choice appear to be central in that identity construction occurs in a way that attempts to incorporate these ideals in addition to the pursuit of thinness.

MacSween's (1993) analysis of feminine identities in bourgeois patriarchal cultures may be instructive here. She argues that within such cultural contexts, women are encouraged to be conformist and passive (for example, conform to cultural ideals such as the thin ideal, self-sacrifice and restraint), but that this requirement also has to be negotiated in light of the (male) values of independence and autonomy that are promoted and valued. One of the ways in which this is dealt with (albeit a precarious one) is for girls and women to combine a culturally validated thin body (thus conforming to cultural ideals) with extreme control over food intake (thus demonstrating independence from physical needs and self-determination) (see Heenan, this volume for a similar discussion in relation to fashion models). It appears that those posting on the sites may be faced with the task of negotiating a satisfactory collective feminine identity in the face of potential accusations that they are conforming to cultural ideals and yielding to social pressures, such 'social conformity' being out of line and incompatible with ideologies of individualism and the autonomous self in Western cultures. They counter this by constructing themselves as self-determined agents and protestors.

The discourses of subjectivity explored in this study produce both 'hyper feminine' and 'resistance to femininity' accounts. This illustrates Foucault's notion of the 'active self' (1981), capable of using discourses to variably create the self. However, Foucault (1979, 1980) also argued that the surveillance of bodies has created the conditions for self-surveillance and self-discipline, and that these processes are all the more powerful when people see themselves as acting out of 'choice' (also see Malson, this volume). The aim of the analysis presented here is to explore the reasons why those contributing to the sites constructed themselves as active agents in light of wider meanings surrounding their subjectivities and practices, but this is not treated here as an unproblematic reflection of 'truth', and indeed, the power of ideologies surrounding femininity, food and the female body, and their relationship with the 'pro-eating-disorder phenomenon' has been explored here. Further, our analysis identifies an additional paradox, in 'choosing' a pro-ana lifestyle its proponents who argue that 'the Ana way is the only way to live' (extract 9) simultaneously undermine notions of choice.

In conclusion

To date, discussions of 'pro-eating-disorder' websites and communities have concentrated largely on the 'dangerous content' of these and the functions of them in promoting unrealistic body ideals (e.g. Fraser, 2003; S.C.a.R.E.D., 2003). However, these sites and communities are also important because these provide discursive contexts in which sense is made of food and its consumption, femininity and the female body, and in which the active construction of 'anorexic selves' occurs. Our analysis has shown that those who contributed to the sites that we examined were active discourse users forging identities that were multifaceted and contradictory and enabled by a wider discursive context that produced particular understandings of femininity, denial, consumption, autonomy and choice. For example, identities were identified that were both 'hyper feminine' (e.g. being virtuous through denial) and also resistant to traditional notions of femininity (e.g. as passive).

Understanding the construction of identities in these virtual spaces is important for understanding the maintenance and promotion of punitive regimes on the female body among those who contributed material, as this is closely bound up with their subjectivities. There will also have undoubtedly been interactions with other social structures such as class. This seems possible given the location of practices such as self-starvation within middle- and upper-class groups of girls and women in particular (see Logue, 1991; Vandereycken & van Deth, 1990; Colman, 1987), and representations of working class femininity as obese and uncontrolled (see Skeggs, 1997). Although in the sites we analysed class markers did not seem obviously apparent, a focus on this may be beneficial in future research. Similarly, a psychoanalytic analysis (see Hollway, 1983, 1989, 1995; Malson, 1998; Walkerdine, 1987) may yield useful insights into the emotional content of these sites, as there was often an angry and even vengeful tone to many of the posts. This emotive aspect of the data is not analysed in depth here because of the theoretical approach of the study which was concerned with the use of discourse and social construction of identity.

At this stage we'd like to conclude by summarising the advantages of research that takes a social constructionist approach, in which the self is discursively constituted, active and dynamic. 'Anorexic selves' are not a pre-existing entity which then 'cause' certain behaviours and 'attitudes' with regard to food and the body, rather they are created and 'worked on'. Nor is the 'anorexic self' a unitary, one-dimensional entity that is separable from the social context. As illustrated in the chapter, a matrix of (often contradictory) discourses and meanings can be taken up, reworked and resisted in variable ways by girls and women who modify their bodies in order to forge identities that are multifaceted and shifting (for example, 'the saint' versus 'the sinner', 'the conformist' versus 'the rebel'). We argue for the importance of analyses of 'eating disorders' that acknowledge the locatedness of such meanings and discursive work in order to move away from static and unitary conceptions of the self and embodied identities.

Note

1. It is important to note that the terms 'Ana' and 'Mia' do not always have equal status on the sites, with 'Mia' often being depicted as the lesser 'sidekick' of or accompaniment to Ana.

References

Angerer, M. L. (2004). Cyber@rexia: Anorexia and cyberspace. In C. Reiche & V. Kuni (Eds), *Cyberfeminism: Next protocols* (pp. 19–31). New York: Autonomedia.

Aphramor, L. & Gingras, J. (this volume). Sustaining imbalance – Evidence of neglect in the pursuit of nutritional health. In S. Riley, M. Burns, H. Frith,

S. Wiggins, & P. Markula (Eds), *Critical bodies: Representations, identities, and practices of weight and body management*. Basingstoke: Palgrave Macmillan.

Association of Internet Researchers (2002). *Ethical decision-making and internet research: Recommendations from the AOIR working committee*. Retrieved 25 January 2003 from http://www.aoir.org/reports/ethics.pdf

Bartky, S. L. (1988). Foucault, femininity and the modernisation of patriarchal culture. In I. Diamond & L. Quinby (Eds), *Feminism and Foucault: Reflections on resistance* (pp. 61–85). Boston, MA: Northeastern University Press.

Bell, R. (1985). *Holy anorexia*. Chicago: University of Chicago.

Bemis, K. M. (1978). Current approaches to the aetiology and treatment of anorexia nervosa. *Psychological Bulletin*, 85, 593–617.

Benveniste, J., LeCouteur, A. & Hepworth, J. (1999). Lay theories of anorexia nervosa: A discourse analytic study. *Journal of Health Psychology*, 4, 59–69.

Bettle, N., Bettle, O., Neumarker, U. & Neumarker, K. (2001). Body image and self-esteem in adolescent ballet dancers. *Perceptual & motor skills*, 93 (1), 297–310.

Bordo, S. (1993). *Unbearable weight: Feminism, western culture and the body*. Berkeley: University of California Press.

Burkitt, I. (1991). *Social selves: Theories of the social formation of personality*. London: Sage.

Burns, M. & Gavey, N. (2004). 'Healthy weight' at what cost? 'Bulimia' and a discourse of weight control. *Journal of Health Psychology*, 9 (4), 549–65.

Burns, M. & Gavey, N. (this volume). Dis/Orders of weight control: Bulimic and/or 'healthy weight' practices. In S. Riley, M. Burns, H. Frith, S. Wiggins, & P. Markula (Eds), *Critical bodies: Representations, identities, and practices of weight and body management*. Basingstoke: Palgrave Macmillan.

Burr, V. (1995). *An introduction to social constructionism*. London: Routledge.

Cervera, S., Lahortiga, F., Martinez-Gonzalez, M. A., Gual, P., de Irala-Estevez, J. & Alonso, Y. (2003). Neuroticism and low self-esteem as risk factors for incident eating disorders in a prospective cohort study. *International Journal of Eating Disorders*, 33 (3), 271–81.

Chernin, K. (1986). *The hungry self: Daughters and mothers, eating and identity*. London: Virago Press.

Cohn, N. (1986, January). By love possessed. *The New York Review*, 3–4.

Colman, A. (1987). *Facts, fallacies and frauds in psychology*. London: Hutchinson.

Cumella, E. J. (2002). Recognising the unique treatment needs of eating disorders. *Behavioural Health Management*, 22 (6), 10–15.

Curt, B. (1994). *Textuality and tectonics: Troubling social and psychological science*. Buckingham: Open University Press.

Day, K. (2003). *Women and alcohol: Contemporary discourses around femininity and leisure in the UK*. Unpublished doctoral thesis, Sheffield Hallam University.

Eckermann, E. (1997). Foucault, embodiment and gendered subjectivities: The case of voluntary self-starvation. In A. Peterson & R. Bunton (Eds), *Foucault, health and medicine* (pp. 151–69). London: Routledge.

Eichenbaum, K. & Orbach, S. (1983). *Understanding women: A feminist psychoanalytic approach*. New York: Basic Books.

Field, A. E. (2000). Media influence on self-image: The real fashion emergency. *Healthy Weight Journal*, 14 (6), 88–90.

Foucault, M. (1979). *Discipline and punish*. New York: Random House.

Foucault, M. (1980). *Power and knowledge: Selected interviews and other writings, 1972–1977*. New York: Pantheon Books.
Foucault, M. (1981). *The history of sexuality 1: An introduction*. Harmondsworth: Penguin.
Fraser, M. (2003). Anorexia on the web. Retrieved April 28, 2003 from http://www.capitalnews9.com/content/health_team_9/?ArID=6973&SecID=17
Giroux, H. (1998). Teenage sexuality, body politics and the pedagogy of display. In J. Epstein (Ed.), *Youth culture: Identity in a postmodern world* (pp. 24–55). Malden: Blackwell.
Gough, B. & Edwards, G. (1998). The beer talking: Four lads, a carry out and the reproduction of masculinities. *Sociological Review*, 46 (3), 419–35.
Griffin, C. (1989). 'I'm not a women's libber, but ...': Feminism, consciousness and identity. In S. Skevington & D. Barker (Eds), *The social identity of women* (pp. 173–93). London: Sage.
Griffin, J. & Berry, E. M. (2003). A modern day holy anorexia? Religious language in advertising and anorexia nervosa in the west. *European Journal of Clinical Nutrition*, 57, 43–51.
Harris, A. (2001). Revisiting bedroom culture: New spaces for young women's politics. *Hecate*, 27 (1), 128–38.
Heenan, C. (this volume). Feminist object relations theory and eating 'disorders'. In S. Riley, M. Burns, H. Frith, S. Wiggins, & P. Markula (Eds), *Critical bodies: Representations, identities, and practices of weight and body management*. Basingstoke: Palgrave Macmillan.
Hepworth, J. (1999). *The social construction of anorexia nervosa*. London: Sage.
Hepworth, J. & Griffin, C. (1995). Conflicting opinions? 'Anorexia nervosa', medicine and feminism. In S. Wilkinson & C. Kitzinger (Eds), *Feminism and discourse: Psychological perspectives* (pp. 68–85). London: Sage.
Hollway, W. (1983). Heterosexual sex: Power and desire for the Other. In S. Cartledge & J. Ryan (Eds), *Sex and love: New thoughts and old contradictions*. London: Women's Press.
Hollway, W. (1989). *Subjectivity and method in psychology*. London: Sage.
Hollway, W. (1995). Feminist discourses and women's heterosexual desire. In S. Wilkinson & C. Kitzinger (Eds), *Feminism and discourse: Psychological perspectives* (86–105). London: Sage.
Lawrence, M. (1979). Anorexia nervosa: The control paradox. *Women's Studies International Quarterly*, 2, 93–101.
Lawrence, M. (1984). *The anorexic experience*. London: The Women's Press.
Lee, C. (1998). *Women's health: Psychological and social perspectives*. London: Sage.
Liversidge, A. (1988, April). Interview with R. D. Laing. *OMNI Magazine*, 56–63.
Logue, A. W. (1991). *The psychology of eating and drinking: An introduction*, 2nd edn. New York: W.H. Freeman.
Lupton, D. (1996). *Food, the body and the self*. London: Sage.
Lyons, A. (2000). Examining media representations: Benefits for health psychology. *Journal of Health Psychology*, 5 (3), 349–59.
MacLeod, S. (1981). *The art of starvation*. London: Virago Press.
MacSween, M. (1993). *Anorexic bodies: A feminist and sociological perspective on anorexia nervosa*. London: Routledge.
Madden, H. & Chamberlain, K. (2004). Nutritional messages in women's magazines: A conflicted space for women readers. *Journal of Health Psychology*, 9 (4), 583–97.

Malson, H. (1998). *The thin woman: Feminism, post-structuralism and the social psychology of anorexia nervosa*. London: Routledge.

Malson, H. (this volume). Deconstructing un/healthy body-weight and weight management. In S. Riley, M. Burns, H. Frith, S. Wiggins, & P. Markula (Eds), *Critical bodies: Representations, identities, and practices of weight and body management*. Basingstoke: Palgrave Macmillan.

Markula, P., Burns, M. & Riley, S. (this volume). Introducing critical bodies: Representations, practices and identities of weight and body management. In S. Riley, M. Burns, H. Frith, S. Wiggins & P. Markula (Eds), *Critical bodies: Representations, practices and identities of weight and body management*. Basingstoke: Palgrave Macmillan.

Orbach, S. (1978). *Fat is a feminist issue*. London: Hamlyn.

Orbach, S. (1986). *Hunger strike: The anorectic's struggle as a metaphor of our age*. London: Faber & Faber.

Paquette, M. (2002). Bad company: Internet sites with dangerous information. *Perspectives in Psychiatric Care*, 38, 39–40.

Parker, I. (1989). *The crisis in modern social psychology and how to end it*. London: Routledge.

Rich, E. and Evans, J. (this volume). Learning to be healthy, dying to be thin: The representation of weight via body perfection codes in schools. In S. Riley, M. Burns, H. Frith, S. Wiggins, & P. Markula (Eds), *Critical bodies: Representations, identities, and practices of weight and body management*. Basingstoke: Palgrave Macmillan.

Robertson, M. (1992). *Starving in the silences: An exploration of anorexia nervosa*. Sydney, Australia: Allen & Unwin.

Sampson, E. E. (1993). *Celebrating the other: A dialogic account of human nature*. New York: Harvester Wheatsheaf.

Saukko, P. (this volume). 'I feel ridiculous about having had it' Critical readings of lived and mediated stories on eating disorders. In S. Riley, M. Burns, H. Frith, S. Wiggins, & P. Markula (Eds), *Critical bodies: Representations, identities, and practices of weight and body management*. Basingstoke: Palgrave Macmillan.

S.C.a.R.E.D. *Support, concern and resources for eating disorders*. Retrieved 17 January 2003 from http://www.eating-disorder.org/prosites.html

Sied, R. P. (1994). Too 'close to the bone': The historical context for women's obsession with slenderness. In P. Fallon, M. A. Katzman & S. C. Wooley (Eds), *Feminist perspective on eating disorders* (pp. 3–16). London: Guilford Press.

Skeggs, B. (1997). *Formations of class and gender*. London: Sage.

Smith, J. L. (2002). *The psychology of food and eating*. Basingstoke: Palgrave.

Smith, P. B. & Bond, M. H. (1993). *Social psychology across cultures: Analysis and perspectives*. Hemel Hempstead: Harvester Wheatsheaf.

Stenner, P. & Eccleston, C. (1994). On the textuality of being: Towards an invigorated social constructionism. *Theory and Psychology*, 4 (1), 85–103.

Stice, E., Schupak-Neuburg, E., Shaw, H. E. & Stein, R. I. (1994). Relation of media exposure to eating disorder symptomatology: An examination of mediating mechanisms. *Journal of Abnormal Psychology*, 103 (4), 836–40.

Vandereycken, W. & Deth, R. van (1990). *From fasting saints to anorexic girls: The history self-starvation*. London: Athlone Press.

Walker Bynum, C. (1991). *Fragmentation and redemption: Essays on gender and the human body in medieval religion*. New York: Urzone Inc. Zone Books.

Walkerdine, V. (1987). No laughing matter: Girls' comics and the preparation for adolescent sexuality. In J. M. Broughton (Ed.), *Critical theories of psychological development* (pp. 87–125). New York: Plenum Press.

Weedon, C. (1987). *Feminist practice and poststructuralist theory*. Oxford: Basil Blackwell.

Wetherell, M. (1988). Fear of fat: Interpretative repertoires and ideological dilemmas. In J. Maybin & N. Mercer (Eds), *Using English: From conversation to cannon* (pp. 36–41). London: Routledge.

Willcox, M. & Sattler, D. N. (1996). The relationship between eating disorders and depression. *Journal of Social Psychology*, 136 (2), 269–71.

Willott, S. & Griffin, C. (1997). 'Wham bam, am I a man?': Unemployed men talk about masculinities. *Feminism and Psychology*, 7, 107–28.

Wolf, N. (1990). *The beauty myth*. London: Chatto & Windus.

Wooley, O. W. (1994). And man created 'woman': Representations of women's bodies in western culture. In P. Fallon, M. A. Katzman & S. C. Wooley (Eds), *Feminist perspectives on eating disorders* (pp. 17–52). London: Guilford Press.

5
Body Talk: Negotiating Body Image and Masculinity

Rosalind Gill

Introduction

'Why do you run?' asks an advert for Puma running shoes. 'Because my friends keep setting me up with fat guys' comes the answer from the advert's lithe, young female subject. A smiling, overweight man – his facial features constructing him as a figure of fun – is pictured holding a bouquet of flowers.

Adverts like this derive their force from the powerful symbolic links established between weight or fat, sexual unattractiveness and lack of social power. While these connections are well documented in relation to images of women, these representations are part of a growing trend in contemporary visual culture to pathologise overweight *male* bodies, and to cast doubt upon the 'masculinity' of men who are deemed to be fat. Men's fleshy bodies are increasingly presented as objects of shame, ridicule or moral failure, and a myriad of reality-based makeover television programmes focus on overweight men and boys (examples in the UK include *Fat Camp* and *Ian Wright's Unfit Kids*). The accompanying iconography – plates of greasy chips, large beer bellies and stomachs that are bursting out of ill-fitting and cheap shirts – points to the profoundly classed and racialised nature of this phenomenon (see also Aphramore & Gingras, this volume). But above all, this representational practice is gendered in significant and complicated ways. While the hostility meted out to women who fail to live up to normative standards of bodily size and shape (informed as it is by long histories of misogyny, cultural assumptions about the body and highly sexualised attributions about weight) seems to have few parallels for men, it is interesting to note the choice of the middle-aged, working class, white male as the emblematic icon of obesity in contemporary media discourse. How men negotiate media representations of men and their bodies is an underresearched area and one that is addressed in this chapter.

This chapter draws on two linked studies of British and Australian men to examine the impact of changes in media representations of men. The research was not carried out with a particular focus on food, eating or weight issues, though all these topics featured in the interviews, but rather its focus was on young men's sense of self at a moment when masculinity was said to be both 'in crisis' and increasingly defined 'through their bodies' (Gill, 2006). The research involved interviews and focus groups with 140 men and showed the complex psychosocial negotiations that men make in relation to practices around weight, including shopping, cooking, dieting and various forms of exercise. This chapter describes the multiple discourses that men can draw on when responding to media images of men's bodies and then explores one discourse, that of 'pressure' which appeared particularly salient within the data. The chapter then examines how other discourses of masculinity can interact with accounts of 'pressure', arguing that issues of weight and body image need to be re-contextualised within a larger framework concerned with masculine identity and embodiment.

Masculinity, representation and body image

Since the mid-1980s there has been a profound shift in the ways that men's bodies are depicted in the media, with the growing visibility of an eroticised, young, toned ideal (Edwards, 1997; Mort, 1988; Nixon, 1996). Where once images of young, scantily clad women dominated public space, increasingly, muscular males took up positions on billboards, magazine covers and in advertising (Gill, 2006). As I have explored elsewhere (Gill, 2003; Gill, Henwood & McLean, 2000) this was significant not only for the new and relatively sudden 'hypervisibility' of a particular kind of male body in visual culture, but also because it represented a departure in terms of representational practice. It broke what John Berger (1972) describes as the 'unwritten law' that 'men act and women appear' (p. 47). Men's bodies were put on display (as women's long had been) in ways that constructed them as (sexual) objects, highlighting their 'to-be-looked-at-ness', men they became objects as well as subjects of the gaze.

The reasons for this shift are multiple and complex, and have been explored in detail in a number of studies (Chapman & Rutherford, 1988; Edwards, 1997; Gill, 2003; Mort, 1988; Nixon, 1996). They include the impact of the growing visibility of gay culture and the economic significance of the pink pound/euro/dollar; the ongoing impact of feminist critiques of masculinity, with the corresponding hunger for a 'new man'; the significance of changes within the fashion industry and attempts to attract men as consumers of style; and the political economy of the magazine industry, seeking (in the mid-1980s) to produce mainstream men's magazines that would satisfy advertisers eager to sell expensive cars, hi-fis and watches to a powerful high-spending demographic. More significant than the causes of this shift, for the purposes of this chapter, are its consequences in terms of men's self-esteem and bodily practices.

New pressures are said to be contributing to the 'crisis' in masculinity, as men's bodies are becoming the centre around which the identity is built (Drummond, 2002). Even as rates of eating disorders have increased among the male population, and popular anxieties about a range of 'body-image-related disorders' have extended to men, there has been little research exploring this. Research which has explored men's 'body image' (a person's thoughts, perceptions and feelings about his or her body) suggests that men are increasingly dissatisfied with their bodies and feel under increasing pressure to conform to a new cultural ideal of masculinity that is lean, well toned and muscular (Grogan 1999; Mishkind et al., 1986). However, estimates of body image dissatisfaction are largely based on quantitative, questionnaire-based research which, as Grogan & Richards (2002) have argued, tells us little about 'why men are dissatisfied and how this dissatisfaction affects their behaviour in relation to exercise and diet' (p. 21). Much research in this field is also compromised by inadequate conceptualisations of 'media effects' (Wykes & Gunter, 2005), in which the media are seen to operate through single, unitary stereotypes, exerting determining effects on attitudes and behaviour. This position has been extensively critiqued (Barker & Petley, 1997; Carter & Weaver, 2003), not least for its hypodermic conceptions of meaning, its assumption of audiences as passive and its lack of insight about the processes through which influence works. Within research on anorexia, this position has sometimes been stretched to such an extent that eating disorders appear to be, fundamentally, *reading disorders*, that is, based on faulty relationships to the media (see Brain, 2006 for a fuller discussion and Saukko, this volume, for an examination of the literature regarding the role of the media in the production of 'eating disorders').

In a field that is highly medicalised and further dominated by the power of psychiatry, it is pertinent and politically important to resituate eating disorders within a context that includes dominant cultural representations and may, in this sense, shift the site of assumed pathology.

Yet most conceptualisations of media effects remain problematic. The Body Image Summit hosted by the UK government in 2000 has come to exemplify a certain strand of thinking about this topic. On the one hand it offered a long overdue recognition that 'representations matter' and they occupy a profoundly moral or ethical space (Silverstone, 2006). Yet the glib, facile way in which subtle and complex ideas were reduced to sound bites during and after the Summit offered little in the way of hope to people who have engaged and struggled with conceptualising these issues. It has left public discourse seesawing between a view of media power as total, overbearing domination versus a view of consumers as active, free and entirely autonomous, unaffected by cultural representations of bodily desirability.

The overemphasis on 'media effects' is further troubled by today's focus upon obesity: no one could make a serious argument that being fat is promoted by the media (although, of course, many products that contribute to body fat are advertised heavily), yet it appears that weight is increasing among the population, and is constructed as a major health problem facing Western societies (however true or not this may be, see Monaghan, 2005 and Aphramor and Gingras, this volume). What role, then, can be accorded to the media here? And is it really sustainable to argue that the media promote anorexia, yet have no impact whatsoever on obesity? Equally, the notion of free 'choice' invoked to reject the view of media power as pervasive and all-encompassing simply sidesteps and avoids all the difficult, but crucially important, questions about how socially constructed ideals are internalised and made our own – that is, *really, truly our own*, not experienced as impositions or as socially constructed, but felt to flow from individual convictions, from uniquely personal choices. Media power clearly needs to be re-thought. To argue that the media effects paradigm is flawed, then, is not to call for some neoliberal view of choice, but to recognise the complexity of subjectivities as the spaces in which these processes take place (see Gill, 2007). A major challenge for contemporary researchers is to hold on to a notion of social/cultural influence, yet remain sensitive to the different ways in which the public habitat of images impact on individuals (the opportunities for negotiation, resistance, rejection and so on) and to the ways in which our engagement with cultural representations is a complex product of individual and social biographies. It suggests that an understanding of body image can only really come from an appreciation of embodied identity, that is, the ways in which bodies live, feel and experience the world. Such a perspective is very different from the simplistic claim that 'thin models cause anorexia'.

The approach to the research

The research reported in this chapter is based on semi-structured interviews with 140 boys and men aged between 15 and 35 in 4 British regional locations in the UK (London, Bangor, Manchester & Newcastle) and interviews with 30 men in Australia. Most of the interviews were carried out between 1998 and 1999, with the remainder conducted in 2000–2001. A third phase of research, based in the western suburbs of Sydney, took place in 2003. The participants were recruited from a variety of sites, deliberately chosen to vary the extent to which, and ways in which, the men might be expected to be 'body conscious'. Sites included gyms, nightclubs, shopping centres, schools, universities, youth clubs and gay organisations. The sample was socially diverse in terms of class, 'race', ethnicity and sexuality, but did not contain any men who were visibly disabled or who identified as such, and this is certainly an important omission.

The participants took part in one of the two types of interview, namely, individual-life-history interviews or focus-group interviews, in which they were in discussion with two or three other men, as well as the (usually male) interviewer. The two types of interview were designed to be complementary. In the individual life history interviews topics were more personal and intimate: the young men were asked to reflect upon significant moments in their own biographies (e.g. moving from primary to secondary school, their first sexual relationship, leaving home), as well as more obviously body-focused topics related to bodily changes and body care. In the focus groups the emphasis was less upon individuals' biographical accounts than upon discussion of issues and concerns (e.g. body modification, pressures on men today, health and fitness). The individual interviews and focus-group interviews did not only differ in terms of substantive content, but also differed markedly in tone (cf. Frosh et al., 2001). There was generally (as expected) greater personal disclosure in the life-history interviews while the focus groups were characterised by an ongoing banter and repartee that can be variously understood as humorous, defensive or competitive, and which we have analysed as part of the performance of gender and *'doing masculinity'* in the interviews (see Gill et al., 2005).

The topic of body image was approached in the interviews in a variety of ways. Men were shown a series of 'prompt' images from contemporary publications (e.g. advertisements, magazine covers from *Men's Health*) and were asked about their responses to them. Men were also asked about their own practices in relation to their appearance, touching on topics that included exercise, 'grooming', clothing the body and cosmetic surgery. Additionally they were asked to talk about other men's bodies in a variety of ways. For example, men participating in individual interviews were asked for reflections on how their own body, body image and sense of identity differed from that of their father or other significant men in their life. Finally, there were a number of general questions about body image and body modification practices. As we have discussed elsewhere, contrary to the dire warnings we received from friends and colleagues about how unlikely it was that men would be prepared to be interviewed about their bodies, we found our respondents were willing and able to discourse articulately on a whole range of topics related to masculine embodiment (Gill et al., 2005).

Contradictory subjectivities: Multiplicity and fluidity in men's responses

When asked what they thought of the shift in the portrayal of men's bodies, the majority of the men in our study responded using words like 'stressed' or 'under pressure'. In this respect the findings seem to confirm fears among academic researchers that the increase in the circulation of unrealistic and idealised images of men has lead to a corresponding increase in men suffering from various body image disorders. However, our research found something that other studies have not yet highlighted: namely, that the men also had a whole range of other ways of talking about the impact of this representational shift upon their lives. Coded thematically, we identified no fewer than eight different sorts of reactions, as set out below:

1. *Aspirational.* Though most of the men accepted that contemporary representations of the male body were designed to be aspirational, surprisingly few claimed to aspire to the kind of look or body depicted in aftershave advertisements or on magazine covers. Those who saw the images as aspirational also saw them as *achievable.* Thus, interestingly, men did not aspire to that which they did not feel they could achieve.
2. *Pressurising.* From this perspective, idealised representations of the male body put men under pressure and gave them impossible new templates to try to live up to.
3. *Generating resentment.* Some men felt anger or hostility towards the new representational practice or the men represented. Often this was

accompanied by a strong orientation to justice, against which 'perfect' male bodies were seen to offend.
4. *Body culture as shallow.* This critical response highlighted the superficiality of body culture and of being judged by one's looks. A significant number of gay men in the sample articulated this perspective.
5. *Narcissistic.* This reaction was correlated with a discomfort with male concerns about appearance, as distinct from the more moral or politicised rejection evidenced by the description of body culture as shallow. Those who saw the representations as uncomfortably narcissistic were more likely to be younger, to be working class and to reject the images as unduly feminine or homoerotic.
6. *Uniform.* Men adopting this perspective highlighted the tedious uniformity of representations of male attractiveness, sometimes joking that there was 'just one man' in all the photo shoots for all the different products and magazines. It was connected to a discomfort with the increasingly narrow notion of beauty being promoted and the lack of diversity in the images.
7. *Irrelevant.* A number of men claimed that the representations have no significance for them at all, and were a complete irrelevance to their lives and sense of self. These men neither aspired to the look nor felt pressured, resentful or critical of the images; they simply imbued them with little significance. All these men were heterosexual and two kinds of arguments were put forward: first, that they were 'insulated' from this imagery by being in a long-term relationship and secondly, that the look presented was not appealing to women and therefore of little significance to them.
8. *Desirable/inaccessible.* A significant number of gay men articulated feelings of desire in relation to the representations. Some heterosexual men also communicated this idea (in complex ways, see Gill et al., 2000). However, some gay men felt disappointed about the *failure* of these representations to produce feelings of desire in them. In these rare cases men talked about the inaccessibility of the models, their flat, intimidating, off putting nature, and the absence of any sense of vulnerability of frailty or openness that might allow space for desire.

I will return to the most prevalent type of response that highlighted the stress or pressure created by these new images below. But initially, two points are crucial to note. First is the sheer variety of different reactions to this imagery suggesting that it is not just experienced in terms of pressure. Secondly, there were profound ambivalences both between different men and, significantly, within individual men's accounts.

We can highlight this by analysing one passage from an interview with a London-based gay man we have called Rich.

> Interviewer: I mean, just from a personal perspective, what do you, what do they say to you? What's your initial reaction to these? [Showing him images from advertising campaigns]
> Rich: Oh God! You'll think this is really weird, but it pisses me off, they've all got the same body type.
> Interviewer: What pisses you off about that?
> Rich: Well, it's not my body type! [Laughs]. Plus of course, you know I don't look like this. And I suppose I do feel as though I should. I don't feel as though I, you know, morally as though I should. Obviously I know that, but it does make me feel a bit more ugly, I suppose. And, and there's a real thing about youth and no hair on the body. And you know, I've got quite a hairy chest, and, you know, for years I've been covering it up and trying to make sure that people don't see it. Specifically because I know so many people are grossed out by it. I think these sorts of things are. They really add to that. I mean, they are sexy, I will say, I think. But they're starting to get boring. I think in a few years, maybe people will get bored of this type of, you know, like stomach. [Sighs] No, I suppose they never will.

In this single extract, Rich employs a variety of different ways of talking about the representations from criticising the uniformity of the bodies displayed ('they are all the same body type'); to explaining how this makes him, a person with a different body type, feel 'a bit more ugly'; to finding these representations sexy; before finally concluding that perhaps they were sexy, but now they are just boring. Rich deploys several different types of discourse about representations and also depicts several different emotional states, including anger, shame, insecurity, desire and boredom, all in the space of a few moments (lines). These responses are not mutually exclusive alternatives: it is possible to have multiple and contradictory responses to these representations (see Burns & Gavey, this volume, for a discussion on multiplicity). Like Rich, most of the men interviewed did not have a single, fixed viewpoint, but moved between a variety of reactions, emotions and subject positions. How could a questionnaire-survey hope to capture the subtlety and fluidity of this? Any research looking for a singular account of the impact of these representational shifts would do violence to the complexity of Rich's subjectivity.

The pressures on men to live up to new masculine ideals

I want to turn now, to what was by far the most common way of talking about idealised representations of the male body, which was the way media images produced pressure or stress. A typical response came from a 24-year-old student from Newcastle. Talking generally about representations of men he argued:

> I think blokes are starting to get paranoid, you know, about how they look and stuff.
> When shown the advert for Calvin Klein fragrance 'Escape for Men', he went on I think that a bloke would look at that and, well I would look at that and I think I'm a bloke and I'm supposed to look like that am I?

A similar response was given by a London-based gay man who worked in the media. He talked about his desire to 'block out' all the images of male toned bodies because of the pressure they put on him:

> Josh: I tend to screen a lot of those out because I think it's too stressful to think I'm pudgy and and they're not really. Um, I, to be perfectly honest, this is a very. That Escape advert for example, I'd probably pay far more attention to it if he was dressed.
> Int: Why do you think that would be?
> Josh: Because that's quite stressful, as someone who hasn't got a body like that, um, and has stopped working out and all that marlarkey. I tend to [...] lots of filters in your head. I tend to go 'oh, go away! Stop it!'

One of the questions that academics and policymakers ask repeatedly is about the effects of these new pressures. Will they translate into low self-esteem and depression or into the adoption of positive health behaviours? Policymakers might take heart from the following interview with Gavin, a young, heterosexual-identified man from Bangor when he said, 'I mean, you definitely see more adverts like this than you maybe used to in the past. Well it makes you want to go out and do 100 sit-ups as well' and the later added 'Yeah, looking at that now makes me want to get back in the gym', which directly attributes the imagery of the toned body to the impetus to work out. However, what was striking was how rare such accounts are, and how reluctant the men were to admit that their behaviour had been influenced by either media images or other people's judgements.

In the remainder of this chapter, I look briefly at some of the discursive 'trouble' occasioned by expressions of 'feeling pressurised'. I argue that such a position was difficult for many men to occupy because of three competing injunctions that operate to structure much of the talk about masculinity. These are the injunctions that men should be different/be independent, that men should not be narcissistic or vain and that they should not be obsessional. Finally, I examine a fourth injunction: that men should not 'let themselves go'.

Discursive trouble

'Being different'

One of the most widely shared and taken-for-granted themes in the interviews concerned individualism and the value attached to 'being your own man' and 'being different'. It is somewhat paradoxical that the thing that most united these 140 men was their conviction that they were different from other men. Few men attempted to account for their sense of difference, either in terms of their personal biography or social location/identity; for the vast majority it was asserted as a self-evident truth. The men in our sample used three means to accomplish themselves as individuals who are 'different', in addition to outright assertion. First, there was a widely shared attack on uniformity and conformity, and the self-construction as a 'rebel'. As I have discussed elsewhere (Gill et al., 2005) this generational cohort of men aged between 15 and 35 might be known as 'rebels without a cause', with little substantive evidence of revolutionary attitudes, yet a strong attachment to the notion of rebellion, as expressed through the desire to 'be different'. Second, men asserted their individualist, rebellious identity by claiming complete independence and autonomy in relation to all bodily choices. Connell (1987, 1995) has argued that the value of 'independence' is a central feature of hegemonic masculinity (see also Day & Keys, this volume). We found that many men attached significantly greater authority to choices that had (apparently) been made independently of any outside influence. It is this injunction that produced men's considerable discomfort and ambivalence about conceding that their perceptions of physical attractiveness might be in any way influenced by marketing or advertising. Significantly, only those who were critical of these processes admitted that they might play a part in structuring desires and subjectivity (Gill et al., 2000). Perhaps as a consequence of the necessary reflexivity occasioned by being homosexual in a heterosexist society, gay men were most likely to take up this position. But generally, most men, gay or straight, were keen to characterise any decision, particularly those about their bodies, as unaffected by influence from parents, teachers, friends, lovers or the media. Finally, individual men were also able to claim being 'different' by constructing a number of implicit and explicit contrasts with other men. For example, one man argued that men's magazines are bought by people who need someone to 'tell them how to live their lives', but that he did not need this. Men frequently compared their own autonomous choices with those of other men depicted as 'sheep-like', 'fakes' or 'clones', as in the focus group extract below.

> Owen: Well I hate. Everyone buys the same. You see all the lads on a Friday, Saturday night, and they're all wearing the same shirts.
> [words ommitted]
> Gareth: There's no individualism, you know.

The contradictory themes of 'feeling under pressure' from idealised images of the masculine body, yet not wanting to acknowledge that one's desires or bodily practices were generated anything other than entirely autonomously and independently produces an ideological dilemma (Billig et al., 1988) for many men. Only those men who had reflected extensively upon the impact of the media and body culture, and positioned themselves as critical of it, were able to talk about the ways in which their own ideals and behaviours had been impacted. The 'trouble' produced by this tension, is underscored by the other powerful injunctions operating in relation to masculinity.

Rejecting vanity

Vanity was repeatedly discussed as something to be condemned and guarded against at all costs. Being thought vain or narcissistic was profoundly feared by the vast majority of men we interviewed, who employed frequent disclaimers about any aspect of their behaviour that might conceivably attract the label. Although several men in our sample used skin care products, including cleansers and moisturizers, their use was universally justified in instrumental terms (i.e. to maintain healthy skin) rather than in relation to appearance. For example, one working class man from Newcastle offered a detailed justification of his use of hand cream by reference to the damage engendered by his work as a welder. Working out at the gym was also frequently characterised in terms of health rather than appearance, even by men who had previously told us they felt pressurised by contemporary idealised images of the toned male body. Others suggested alternative instrumental justifications including the need to train to get acceptance to the fire service, or build muscle for self-defence. Gay men were more likely than straight men to admit that they were concerned about their appearance, but they too were sensitive to potential criticisms of themselves as narcissistic (cf. Levine & Kimmel, 1998).

It appears overall that the desire to achieve a particular look must be presented in a way that does not transgress the taboo about appearing vain. This came out especially clearly in men's talk about cosmetic surgery. On the one hand, a strongly libertarian discourse organised around the claim that 'it's your body so you should do what you like with it' was salient. Yet on the other, this libertarianism was undercut at precisely the point where vanity could be invoked. The particular place where men drew the line between a legitimate reason for surgery and vanity is less significant than the fact that they all believe that a line *can and should be drawn* and that a division between appropriate concern about one's appearance, and vanity or narcissism was deemed a meaningful one. Their vocabularies (both verbal and psychological) for making sense of embodiment are profoundly individualistic and there was little space for even thinking about what might lead someone to regard cosmetic surgery as the least-worst option for them. This represents a stark contrast with research about women (cf. Davis, 1997). It seems that the notion of vanity or narcissism has become a kind of catch-all category for explaining all of the things that are impossible to think of in purely individualistic terms. Vanity and narcissism here, then, are crucial constructs used by men to understand their own and others' experiences of embodiment, if only negatively, and to construct a meaningful psychological and moral universe.

Against obsession

Further discursive trouble was produced by the requirement of normative masculinity that one should not be obsessional, and indeed should not take anything too seriously. In the interviews there was a consistent rejection of obsession. Several men said that what they disliked about the gym was the obsessiveness of the people who used it. This kind of talk also spilled over into discussions of surgical body modification, with phrases like 'perfectionism' or 'hyper-perfectionism' standing in for obsession. An implicit norm about obsession was deployed. The term was used almost exclusively to characterise others' behaviour, occasionally being applied to one's own behaviour only when it was safely in the past. So, for example, those who went to the gym three times a week would be seen by non-gym users as obsessional, and they in turn would regard their own behaviour as reasonable and well balanced, with men who trained six or seven days a week earning the 'obsessive' tag. Thus while being an entirely flexible category, being obsessional was agreed by most men to be a 'Bad Thing'.

In contrast, not taking yourself too seriously was widely championed. Several men praised the young men's magazines *FHM* and *Loaded* for having this quality, and the ability to laugh at themselves. Perhaps not surprisingly this was most highly valued by the younger heterosexual men who came closest to contemporary definitions of the 'lad'. The elevation of 'having a laugh' and 'not taking yourself too seriously' fits in with contemporary ideas about postmodernism in popular culture, in which an ironic distance is said to characterise representations. There was a powerful sense in some of the interviews with young heterosexual men that being seen to take yourself seriously contravened some unwritten rule. Men were keen to distance themselves from being seen as too serious, too committed, too earnest – things that were likely to attract a comment about obsession.

Respect, or, 'not letting yourself go'

Finally, there was considerable talk around the notion that you should take care of yourself. This was (again) a highly individualistic discourse in which men were constructed as the individual 'managers' of their own bodies. Men had to negotiate a delicate path between an appropriate level of care and attention to one's body, and the twin pitfalls of vanity or obsession. If they appeared too concerned about their body or their looks they laid themselves open to accusations of vanity or obsession; if they seemed unconcerned they were at risk of being accused of 'letting themselves go'. Men tended to handle this 'ideological dilemma' through the notion of 'self-respect', as Sean said, 'well, you still make the same effort don't you, every morning? It's self respect'.

As well as being an individualistic discourse, 'respect' was a highly moralistic repertoire. Drawing on neoliberal subjectivity (see, for example, Markula et al., this volume), this discourse sets up the individual to discipline their own body and then finds them morally culpable if they fail. Interestingly, this was seen most clearly in relation to being overweight, which attracted great disapproval. As writers in a Foucaultian tradition have argued, such accounts draw on an understanding that the body can be read as an indicator of self-control and self-discipline. In this way, fat represents not simply excessive flesh, but an inability to control oneself (Bordo, 1993; also see Rich & Evans, this volume, for another example of morality discourses around weight and body management).

The men in this study bore witness to this coupling of morality with body size. They explained how they would be teased about their appearance and that the beginnings of a paunch would attract playful, but nevertheless critical, comments from friends. They argued for the need to 'take care' of their bodies. These accounts can be read in the extract below in which not taking care of one's body is elided with fat, lack of interest in life and a conformist lifestyle, with fat symbolising a variety of negative characteristics that have no direct relevance to body weight.

> Dominic: I just don't want to, I would like to look after myself and I, I mean, the really important thing is still to be fit and healthy as you get older, and take care of your body and your mind, and. I don't want to end up like some people I know. Some people in my, even in my family and people I see around, you know. They just sort of let them go. Themselves go, get fat and lose interest in everything, don't they. Do their 9 to 5 job, sit in front of the TV, and that's their life. That's not for me.

Conclusion

This chapter in part confirms the growing concern among academics and policymakers that men are feeling under increasing pressure to live up to idealised, muscular and youthful depictions of the male body. But it also highlights a range of other ways that the men in our study talked about the impact of such representations in advertising and magazines many of which are critical of and resistant to these representations. Crucially, it shows that men move between and combine different orientations to body image in a way that a simple, singular notion of 'men under pressure' does not capture. The emphasis among the vast majority of men on being different and independent, and their reluctance to acknowledge any social or cultural influence on their (bodily) decisions means that there is no simple correspondence between subjective experiences of 'pressure' and particular behaviours. Things are further complicated by the powerful injunctions which structure men's talk about their own bodies – namely, the requirements not to be vain, not to be obsessional and not to let oneself go. Such elements of hegemonic masculinity produce their own pressures for men, who have to discursively negotiate these complex and contradictory requirements about being a man.

This chapter points to the value of research locating concerns about weight and body image within a broader understanding of gendered, embodied identities and practices. Feelings about shape, size and appearance, and practices that have a bearing on health matters cannot be split off from the rest of men's lives. This is true in terms of 'structural' variables such as age, class or sexuality, and here we have highlighted some of the differences in ways that heterosexual and gay men orientated to such issues, but it's also true in terms of men's intimate relationships to themselves and others. Understandings of 'weighty issues' will be strengthened by this psychosocial focus on subjectivity, and policy interventions in this field will be flawed unless they attend to the complex web of socio-emotional meanings that embodied subjects give to their bodies.

References

Aphramor, L. & Gingras, J. (this volume). Sustaining imbalance – Evidence of neglect in the pursuit of nutritional health. In S. Riley, M. Burns, H. Frith, S. Wiggins, & P. Markula (Eds), *Critical bodies: Representations, identities and practices of weight and body management*. Basingstoke: Palgrave Macmillan.

Barker, M. & Petley, J. (1997). *Ill effects: The media/violence debate*. London: Routledge.

Berger, J. (1972). *Ways of seeing*. London: Penguin Books.

Billig, M., Condor, S., Edwards, D., Gane, M., Middleton, D. & Radley, A. R. (1988). *Ideological dilemmas: A social psychology of everyday thinking*. London: Sage.

Bordo, S. (1993). *Unbearable weight: Feminism, western culture, and the body*. Berkeley: University of California Press.

Brain, J. (2006). Hungry for meaning: Discourses of the anorexic body unpublished Ph.D. thesis, LSE, University of London.

Burns, M. & Gavey, N. (this volume). Dis/Orders of weight control: Bulimic and/or 'healthy weight' practices. In S. Riley, M. Burns, H. Frith, S. Wiggins & P. Markula (Eds), *Critical bodies: Representations, identities, and practices of weight and body management*. Basingstoke: Palgrave Macmillan.

Carter, C. & Weaver, K. (2003). *Violence and the media*. Buckingham: Open University Press.

Chapman, R. & Rutherford, J. (eds). (1988). *Male order – Unwrapping masculinity*. London: Lawrence & Wishart.

Connell, R. W. (1987). *Gender and power: Society, the person and sexual politics*. Sydney: Allen & Unwin.

Connell, R. W. (1995). *Masculinities*. Sydney: Allen & Unwin.

Davis, K. (1997). 'My body is my art': Cosmetic surgery as feminist utopia? *The European Journal of Women's Studies*, 4 (1), 23–38.

Day, K. & Keys, T. (this volume). Starving in cyberspace: The construction of identity on 'pro-eating-disorder' websites. In S. Riley, M. Burns, H. Frith, S. Wiggins, & P. Markula (Eds), *Critical bodies: Representations, identities, and practices of weight and body management*. Basingstoke: Palgrave Macmillan.

Drummond, M. (2002). Men, body image and eating disorders. *International Journal of Men's Health*, 1 (1), 79–93.

Edwards, T. (1997). *Men in the mirror: Men's fashion, masculinity and consumer society*. London: Cassell.
Frosh, S., Phoenix, A. & Pattman, R. (2001). *Young masculinities: Understanding boys in contemporary society*. Basingstoke: Palgrave Macmillan.
Gill, R. (2003). Power and the production of subjects: A genealogy of the new man and the new lad. In B. Benwell (ed.), *Masculinity and men's lifestyle magazines*. Oxford: Blackwell.
Gill, R. (2006). *Gender and the media*. Cambridge: Polity.
Gill, R. (2007). Critical respect: The difficulties and dilemmas of agency and 'choice' for feminism: A reply to Duits and van Zoonen. *European Journal of Women's Studies*, 14 (1), 65–76.
Gill, R., Henwood, K. & McLean, C. (2000). The tyranny of the sixpack: Understanding men's responses to idealised male body images in popular culture.' In C. Squire (ed.), *Culture in Psychology*. London: Routledge.
Gill, R., Henwood, K. & McLean, C. (2005). Body projects and the regulation of normative masculinity, *Body & Society*, 11, 37–62.
Grogan, S. (1999). *Body image: Understanding body dissatisfaction in men, women, and children*. London: Routledge.
Grogan, S. & Richards, H. (2002). Body image: Focus groups with boys and men. *Men and Masculinities*, 4 (3), 219–32.
Levine, M. P. and Kimmel, M. S. (1998). *Gay Macho*. New York: New York University Press.
Markula, P., Burns, M. & Riley, S. (this volume). Introducing critical bodies: Representations, identities and practices of weight and body management. In S. Riley, M. Burns, H. Frith, S. Wiggins & P. Markula (eds), *Critical bodies: Representations, identities and practices of weight and body management*. Basingstoke: Palgrave Macmillan.
Mishkind, M. E., Rodin, J., Silberstein, L. R. & Striegel-Moore, R. H. (1986). The embodiment of masculinity: Cultural, psychological and behavioral dimensions. *American Behavioral Scientist*, 29, 545–62.
Monaghan, L. F. (2005). Big handsome men, bears and others: Virtual constructions of fat male embodiment. *Body and Society*, 11 (2), 81–111.
Mort, F. (1988). Boy's own? Masculinity, style and popular culture. In R. Chapman & J. Rutherford (eds), *Male order: Unwrapping masculinity* (pp. 193–224). London: Lawrence and Wishhart.
Nixon, S. (1996). *Hard looks: Masculinities, spectatorship and contemporary consumption*. London: UCL Press.
Rich, E. and Evans, J. (this volume). Learning to be healthy, dying to be thin: The representation of weight via body perfection codes in schools. In S. Riley, M. Burns, H. Frith, S. Wiggins, & P. Markula (Eds), *Critical bodies: Representations, identities, and practices of weight and body management*. Basingstoke: Palgrave Macmillan.
Saukko, P. (this volume). "I feel ridiculous about having had it" Critical readings of lived and mediated stories on eating disorders. In S. Riley, M. Burns, H. Frith, S. Wiggins, & P. Markula (Eds), Critical bodies: Representations, Identities, and Practices of Weight and Body Management. Basingstoke: Palgrave Macmillan.
Silverstone, R. (2006). *Media and morality: On the rise of the mediapolis*. Cambridge: Polity Press.
Wykes, M. & Gunter, B. (2005). *The media and the body: Looks could kill*. London: Sage.

6
Feminist Object Relations Theory and Eating 'Disorders'[1]

Colleen Heenan

Most psychoanalytic theory draws upon modernist notions of the self and has been criticised for promoting a masculinist view of the world in which women are conceptualised as lacking (Appignanesi & Forrester, 1992; Buhle, 1998). While it might appear that psychoanalysis is incompatible with feminist and/or post-structuralist analysis, it is psychoanalysis's differing theories of unconscious processes that have appealed to a number of contemporary feminist and/or post-structuralist writers (see, for instance, Chodorow, 1999a; Frosh, 1987; Grosz, 1990; Hollway, 1989). Although this remains a controversial move, feminist and post-structuralist writers have drawn on psychoanalytic theory to mount challenges to psychiatric discourses of women's embodiment that maintain a dichotomy between normal and abnormal behaviours, and which marry discourses of weight with discourses of morality.[2]

In this chapter I plot some of the historic and theoretical shifts in feminist psychoanalytic thinking that have challenged traditional psychiatric discourses on women's eating, particularly relating to clinical populations. I outline a psychoanalytic understanding of the centrality and complexity of the processes of need and desire, separation and attachment, and agency and control in human development, and the role of food and eating within these processes. I demonstrate how these developmental processes have particular significance for women because the function of hunger, food and feeding takes on particular gendered meanings. I also argue that consumer culture is particularly toxic for women because the psychodynamics of consumer culture not only resonate with these processes but also because women's identities are so firmly embedded with their corporeality. First, though, I examine in more detail the feminist psychoanalytic critique of psychiatric discourses around women, food and 'eating disorders'.[3]

Fat is a Feminist Issue

The publication of Susie Orbach's (1978) *Fat is a Feminist Issue* marked a turning point in many contemporary Western women's unhappiness with and desire to 'manage' their bodies. First, Orbach unusually positioned 'compulsive eating' and 'excess' body weight as gendered and embodied manifestations of women's contradictory social and sexual status. Orbach was part of the second-wave North American and European feminist movement, which included the development of 'consciousness-raising' (CR) groups that aimed to help women 'take control' of their lives by deconstructing the micro-politics of gender (Enns, 1993). Not surprisingly, the appropriation and surveillance of women's bodies as enacted through domestic violence or reproductive rights were subjects to the fore. However, a further focus was that of the gendered mandates surrounding women's physical appearance. Rather than continuing to attempt to 'fit in' and 'adapt' to dictates about body size, Orbach's anti-diet *Fat is a Feminist Issue* aimed to raise participants' awareness in two ways. Firstly, weight-reduction dieting was reinterpreted as another gendered form of body regulation which could be refused. Secondly, participating in bodily scrutiny was reframed as a gendered means for enacting the cultural constraints of women's gendered subjectivities (never having the 'right' body; how to *manage* an appetite) while also de-politicising that struggle by individualising it as a personal struggle (to 'get' the right body) (Orbach, 1978). Embedding an individual analysis of bodily scrutiny within a social constructionist framework offered a means for the political articulation and expression of many women's unhappiness.

Second, Orbach drew on psychoanalysis to theorise eating behaviour and 'excess' body size as unconscious expressions of women's unhappiness in the face of these contradictions. Her use of psychoanalytic thinking (see also *Hunger Strike*, 1986) mirrored that of a growing number of feminist authors (Benjamin, 1988; Chodorow, 1978, 1999a; Dinnerstein, 1976; Mitchell, 1974) who regarded it as a means for elaborating aspects of gendered subjectivities. *Fat is a Feminist Issue* introduced the controversial idea that psychoanalytic theory might be a useful *feminist* tool for understanding bodily scrutiny as an unconscious means for women to enact rather than articulate themselves. For instance, women's concerns about physical appetite might be regarded as expressing unconscious (and conscious) conflicts about having needs – particularly when these were not likely to get met. Similarly, feeling 'out of control' around food could be a displacement for articulating feelings of helplessness about living in a patriarchal society; and focusing on weight loss might be a woman's only means of exerting power – through transforming body shape and size. Indeed, Orbach argued that eating more and becoming bigger than is socially sanctioned may be a covert expression of anger about women's social limitations. By embedding a psychoanalytic approach within a feminist social constructionist framework, Orbach was emphasising that women may not put their thoughts and feelings into words – perhaps because they may feel they will not be taken seriously. Instead, thoughts and feelings may be enacted through socially sanctioned forms of gendered displacement onto and into the body. For instance, she suggested that the thinness of the anorexic is a gendered protest offering an over-exaggerated parody of women's culturally specified body size. In turn, the bulimic woman has found a private solution to the paradox of living in a society in which the pressure to consume and constrain live side by side (Bloom et al., 1994; Cooper, 1987); this conformity masks a hidden rebellion, in which 'unladylike' bingeing is controlled through purging or starving.

Orbach (1978) further challenged traditional psychiatric discourses of eating disorders by arguing that some women may actually unconsciously prefer being fat and fear being thin. Being fat is one way of taking up more space in a patriarchal society, whereas being thin could feel like being invisible. Thus, being fat could be understood as an overt refusal to conform to prescribed body images for women. Indeed, the physical strength required of women in order to attend to others' domestic needs may necessitate having a body size which reflects the demands made of it. A further outgrowth of CR groups was the development of 'self-help' therapies which provided a springboard for the development of feminist therapists; that is, a variety of psychotherapeutic models (in North America this was mainly humanistic and cognitive while in the United Kingdom it was psychoanalytic) were adapted for use within feminist frameworks (Enns, 1993; Heenan and Seu, 1998; Worell and Remer, 1992).

As I noted at the beginning of this chapter, the turn to psychotherapeutic theory and practice, particularly psychoanalysis, is a move that divides many feminists today (Heenan, 1995; Kitzinger and Perkins, 1993). Psychoanalytic theories of eating disorders have been particularly repugnant to feminists because of their a-historical and a-cultural concerns with the internal world (Orbach, 1986, 1994). This has resulted in positioning eating disorders as signs of women's immaturity (Crisp, 1980; Dally, 1969) or their inability to adapt to their environment (Hsu, 1989). However, it was the inability of feminist theory and political action to offer the means to both understand women's participation in their oppression, as well as to bring about change in these conditions, which prompted authors like Orbach (1978, 1986), Lawrence (1987), and later Bloom et al. (1994), to adopt British[4] Object Relations theory as a tool for explicating both the onset and maintenance of eating disorders.

For many feminists the attraction of British object relation theory is its attention to the intersubjective process of development in the creation of self or subjectivity. This provides a means to understand the socially situated nature of unconscious processes – the subject of the following sections.

Development is a Feminist Issue

Within psychoanalysis there are a variety of schools of thought in relation to the nature of the self and subjectivity. British object relations theorists subscribe to a modernist notion of a 'unitary self of substance' as belied by Winnicott's notion of 'true and false' selves (see Greenberg & Mitchell, 1983). More contemporary and feminist readings of British object relations theory (Benjamin, 1995, 1998; Chodorow, 1999b; Flax, 1990, 1993) focus not on the 'self' but on 'subjectivity', *'the point of contact* between identity and society' (Parker, 1992, p. 117 [original emphasis]). However, Flax (1990) argues that feminists and post-structuralists need to retain some way of thinking about those 'core' or 'organising' selves which enable us to theorise these very issues of subjectivity, without sliding into notions of 'unitariness'. Further, contemporary readings of clinical practice emphasise the *intersubjective* function of therapy as 'co-constructing' narratives rather than 'discovering' truths (Hamilton 1992; Ogden 1994). In summary, feminist object relations theory could best be described as a 'feminist standpoint theory' (Ramazanoglu and Holland, 2002) clearly steeped in clinical practice. This results in some epistemological disparities with postmodern thinking. One of these is the feminist object relations' focus on the role of unconscious processes in the interaction of food, the body and gender in women's psychosocial development and the development of eating problems.

Given the physical vulnerability and dependency of the human infant, it is perhaps no surprise that food and feeding have such key functions in psychosocial development (Bloom et al., 1994). Within British object relations' theory (Greenberg and Mitchell, 1983), the feeding process is understood as the somatic and unconscious introjection of the caretaking relationship between infant and caretaker. Thus, psychophysical experience of hunger is 'one of the most basic and discrete avenues by which need is learned about altogether' (Bloom and Kogel, 1994, p. 41). The repetitive need to express hunger and others' response provides ongoing opportunities for the infant to develop a sense of psychophysical agency, 'object' constancy (if I cry, I know someone will come) and psychophysical boundaries (this is me, that is you). The infant's sense of agency is thus inextricably bound up with another's response, confirming its intersubjective and interdependent basis. The role of food and feeding in this process is that both are emotionally imbued with complex and often unconscious emotions relating to fundamental states of vulnerability and dependency. Thus, they have a key role in the development of a sense of agency and control, issues which are inherent aspects of eating disorders. From a psychoanalytic perspective, if hunger is continually met inappropriately and inconsistently, particularly at early stages of life, this can result in not just confusion about the cue, but fear because of the infant's inability to discriminate between parts of self, as well as its inability to feel it can effectively engage others in meeting its needs. This means that hunger no longer becomes primarily a signal for eating, but a signal which comes to disturb.

Bloom et al. (1994) suggest that food's material and symbolic connection with the infant's primary caretaker makes it a key 'transitional' object (Winnicott, 1971) in development that continues to have significance throughout life. In this way, food is imbued with complex and unconscious emotions which relate to states of vulnerability, dependency, comfort and security, and agency and control, which are all implicated in the development of subjectivity. Winnicott suggested that a key part of the developmental process of psychological separation and individuation involves the infant projecting feelings about the self and other onto 'transitional objects' (teddies, blankets and items of food, for instance). The infant's capacity to creatively imbue these objects with emotional and symbolic meaning allows them to be used to manage feelings, impulses and desires. For example, particular foods may be a source of comfort that can be used to manage anxiety about separation from the caregiver by maintaining a fantasised bond to the mother. In turn, with increased physical separation from the caretaker, objects can be kept near such that the infant's lessening sense of omnipotent control is compensated for by an increasing sense of achievement over the environment. For instance, the infants growing realisation that food (and therefore comfort and security) is provided by someone who is separate and 'not me' is compensated for by the infant's ability to both get an accurate response from its caretaker to its demands for feeding. In addition, its increasing ability to feed itself marks points of accomplishment within psychophysical and emotional maturation. The infant can experience the emotional pleasure of sensing that a separate other takes part in assuaging needs by, for example, providing food. Furthermore, by expressing both of a wish for, or a rejection of, specific foods the infant can attempt to establish autonomy and a sense of self distinct from others, as well as develop a more finely tuned expression of desire.

While this highlights how particular foods and the process of consumption may have individual significance, feminists are also interested in how the function of hunger, food and feeding takes on particular gendered meanings, as does the sense of an embodied self. The acquisition of gender identity and the process of separation and individuation occurs differently for female and male children within culturally, historically and sexually specific circumstances. For women in contemporary Western society, separation, individuation and the expression of desire are contentious issues; food and eating offer culturally and gender-syntonic means for the manifestation of these tensions. Eichenbaum and Orbach (1982) suggested that female babies in contemporary Western society may be more prone to disturbances in feeding because the social context of their upbringing means that women experience a 'cycle of emotional deprivation' because of their 'second-class' status (p. 38). These tensions may be conveyed to daughters through curbing their hunger and censoring their demands for food; that is, raising them to not expect their needs to be met. Eichenbaum and Orbach (1982) argued that this could result in the defensive splitting off of unmet needs leading to the development of an external 'false' but compliant and pleasing self, again something which is gender-syntonic for women.

In addition, consolidating gender identity involves an early stage in which children seem to want to have their corporeal self not just confirmed but admired. However, Bloom and Kogel argue that 'a little girl's mandate to appear (rather than to act or be) and to focus on her appearance is confirmed as intrinsic to her being and equal to being an adequate female' (1994, p. 49). The authors remind us of the 'female culture mother' (p. 49) in which mothering occurs and to which daughters both identify and attach. In contemporary Western culture, acting *on the body* through the available practices of femininity (Bartky, 1988; Bordo, 2003) enables women to perform their subjectivities, predicated on corporeal malleability. As Orbach puts it, '[a]s though they were hemlines that could be shortened or lengthened seasonally, the current aesthetic of women's bodies has been changing almost yearly' (1986, p. 71). This simultaneously reinforces a sense that the female body is not good enough to be accepted as it is. Indeed, Orbach suggests that the ongoing social construction and reconstruction of 'choices' about body size and shape within consumer societies means some women may develop a 'false body' as 'a malleable vehicle for survival through attempted compliance' (1994, p. 169; see also Rich & Evans, this volume, for a discussion of the female body as imperfect). Orbach argues that this feeds into and exacerbates women's underlying sense of body insecurity that derives from this gendered mandate to 'transform the self'.

Consumerism and transformation

Bloom et al.'s (1994) feminist psychoanalytic thesis of psychosocial development is embedded within a postmodern framework which posits life in contemporary Western society as a 'project of the self' in which the 'performing subject' cultivates an inner and outer self (Giddens, 1991; see Markula, Burns and Riley, this volume, for a discussion on neoliberal subjectivity and weight). The private concerns of the inner body, expressed as both physical and mental health, become a vehicle for not only appearing but also for participating in public life (also see Rich and Evans, this volume). Featherstone (1991) describes consumer culture as 'latch[ing] onto the prevalent self-preservationist conception of the body, which encourages the individual to adopt instrumental strategies to combat deterioration and decay (applauded too by state bureaucracies who seek to reduce health costs by educating the public against bodily neglect) and combines it with the notion that the body is a vehicle of pleasure and self-expression' (1991, p. 170). At the same time, appearance and participation are prescribed.

Bloom et al. argue that in contemporary Western society consumerism forms part of the '"maternal" matrix to which individuals consciously and unconsciously attach' (p. xiii); active participation in consumer culture resonates with individuals' developing psychological structures and provides a means for bridging the gap between the public and private. It also provides a means for individuals to feel 'interpersonally connected' (Gutwill, 1994a, p. 18), thus assuaging feelings of vulnerability, dependency, autonomy and agency. Consumer culture functions as a cultural parent by promising to satisfy wants and needs through the culturally specific and gender-specific meanings embodied in these consumer/transitional objects (such as food) which actively encourage attachment through possession. Indeed, the emotional and economic power of consumerism is that its cultural symbols seem to 'know' (like parents) not just what the consumer *wants* but what she *needs*. The paradox of consumerism is its ability to position the consumer as someone who is free and informed enough to make 'choices' about consumption and thus encourages active participation and sense of autonomy. However, for consumerism to reproduce itself, it requires its products to have an inbuilt lack of durability, or failure to satisfy, in order for more goods to be required, while the appearance of newer and better goods must be presented as if the goods were required by the consumer, in order to successfully appeal to customers' apparent needs. Fairbairn (1952) argues that blaming the self functions as a way of managing this disappointment. He argued that the internal object world consists only of 'bad' objects, those linked with unhappy feelings. Internalising only the 'bad' enables the infant to retain some kind of attachment to the real (m)other, in the face of disappointment. This is achieved by blaming the self and not the other on whom one depends (Fairbairn's 'moral defence'). Finally, one attempts to turn the self into whatever the internalised bad object (the persecutory superego) suggests (symbolically) is required. This defence mechanism thus allows for hope of future assuagement through transforming the self, while preserving the other (and self) from the disturbing feelings which have arisen (see Greenberg and Mitchell, 1983 for a fuller account of this).

Gutwill (1994b) suggests that it is the 'subject seeking' nature of consumer culture (the search for a 'better' or 'perfect' self) which makes it particularly toxic for women. Consumer culture provides the right parental combination of authority and nurturance through prescribing what is right and encouraging consumers to look after themselves by 'getting the best'. The culturally symbolic and gender-specific meanings attached to items or activities enables introjection of and attachment to mass culture. The diet industry represents one of the most gendered and toxic ways in which consumerism 'seeks out' women. It tantalises by tapping into beliefs that women's bodies *should* be worked on, indeed transformed ('wouldn't you like a *new* body?'). Diets seductively promise help – 'wouldn't you look great if you trimmed down your thighs – here's a diet which will tackle those troublesome areas' – while threatening rejection and exclusion should the consumer *not respond* ('want to wear those new fashions – get the right look'). Many different weight-reduction diets may appear to be actively chosen (and, indeed, cultural discourses of dieting thrive on notions of personal autonomy and control) and promise transformation. However, they are ultimately not sustainable and fail to satisfy – yet there is always the assurance that success is possible with the next diet. Although dieting is 'a business that thrives on failure' (Gutwill, 1994b, p. 32), failure is located within the woman with the promise of endless chances of redemption through other diets resulting in internal conversation like, 'If only I could stay on this diet, I could be acceptable and lovable. But the truth is that I am *not* good enough; I am selfish, fat, stupid for wanting and needing, ugly, and weak. I deserve all I get. It's my own fault' (ibid., p. 31).

Orbach (1978) suggested that, as women are discouraged from having either emotional or physical 'appetites', they may feel anxious and frightened when their emotional needs are stirred up, quickly 'translating' these feelings into feelings of hunger – a corporeal need. They then admonish themselves as being 'greedy', then feel fat, then ugly, and then in need of losing weight. Undertaking to eat less, they are put in touch very acutely with material physical hunger, on top of the emotional hunger they already experience from being positioned as the 'emotional nurturer' to others. By removing food, they may be removing one of the few things which they feel does offer them some comfort and satisfaction, something which makes no demands upon them, something which they can have *all for themselves*. Moreover, consumerism's capacity to make women's bodies an integral part of appeals to women's gender-specific sense of agency; that is, a belief in the importance of 'acting upon themselves' and 'making things right for others', adds to its toxicity.

Yet consumer culture also de-centres the viewer, *constructing* a sense of subjectivity through a false belief in agency. Through constantly 'viewing' their bodies, women may not feel they 'own' them. Orbach (1978) suggested that when they look into the mirror, women tend to focus on culturally syntonic hated aspects of the body, fantasising about how they would look *if* they lost weight, or exercised more. Given that there are many 'social' mirrors which offer negative, undermining, messages alongside seductive images of how things *could and ought to be*, this is not surprising. As noted by other contributors to this book, Bordo and Bartky appropriated Foucault's (1978) notion of 'panopticons'[5] as part of the modernist project of self-regulation. They suggested it offers a way of understanding the *gendered* regulation of the body in consumer culture; through the private and public practices of femininity, women are not only constantly observed but also learn to observe themselves and others without apparent coercion. As Bartky further elaborates: 'In contemporary patriarchal culture, a panoptical male connoisseur resides within the consciousness of most women: they stand perpetually before his gaze and under his judgment' (1988, p. 72). Consumer culture, then, is underpinned by the 'project of the self', the notion that the body is something to be regulated and worked on as well as a means for pleasure and self-expression. It promises to satisfy needs and wants while ultimately failing to do so. The psychodynamics of consumerism and of dieting, both revolve around issues of desire and constraint. As such, they resonate with and tap into the dynamics of women's gendered developmental process. Feminists' use of British object relations theory offers valuable insights into the gendered psychodynamics of contemporary corporeal subjectivities by exploring the points of contact between society and identity in the development of eating disorders.

Feminist therapy and eating disorders

From a psychoanalytic perspective, eating problems represent a withdrawal into an internal bodily world in an attempt to provide a replacement for and a means to assuage feelings about, a dissatisfying external world. They are not *conscious* acts of resistance but *unconscious* expressions of individual distress. Indeed, for some women, the symptoms and obsessions of an eating problem becomes a 'substitute for life' (Bloom and Kogel, 1994, p. 58), while for others 'it serves to modulate anxiety, need states, and esteem' (ibid.). It is the combination of an ambivalent focus on her own bodily state, along with her attunement to others' needs that culminates in a split between body/self, with the body attaining the status and function of an object. The body comes to be the regressive site for, a substitute for, and even the sole means of relating. This results in the body – and food – being used expressively and defensively. In turn, these individual psychodynamics are exacerbated by and mirrored within the ways in which women's bodies are made use of by consumer societies.

Feminist psychoanalytic psychotherapy explores the ways in which unconscious processes act as a gendered panopticons. It reminds us that there is an internal unconscious world and a set of internal (object) relations which not only mirror the toxic dynamics of consumerism but are structured by culture. Paradoxically, the 'symptoms' of eating disorders can provide the necessary sense of 'cohesion' at the very time when the 'eating disordered' woman feels she is falling apart (Hamburg, 1989, p. 134). Indeed, the insidiousness of eating disorders is that they can function 'agentically' by appearing to act as solutions. However, the solution 'robs' the woman of any sense of agency in that it acts 'on' her, offering an identity (see Day and Keys, this volume, for such examples).

One of the major differences between postmodern and psychoanalytic frameworks is that the aim of the therapist is to facilitate a *self* and facilitate a client's capacity to *act on* the self in more helpful ways (Flax, 1990), albeit within the particular pedagogic frameworks which discursively constitute any psychotherapy (Rose, 1990). The feminist therapist aims to facilitate a patient's subjectivity in order for the woman to develop an alternative *self*. For instance, a sense of agency is required to contemplate the notion that an eating disorder may have an unconscious function and meaning – as opposed to working within discourses of madness or badness. In turn, agency is required to engage and articulate other aspects of self more directly. It could be said that the experience of being subjectified (in the Foucauldian sense of being tied to an identity) is reframed by the feminist therapist as a defence mechanism which prevents the woman from having 'no self' – or one expressed solely through her body and its functions.

Bloom et al.'s work is extremely useful in interweaving ideas from postmodern thinking within a psychodynamic framework in order to understand how the gendered tensions within contemporary Western society get acted out through women's bodies. Crucially, they also shift emphasis away from the mother as 'at fault'. Fairbairn's thesis (of 'moral defence', see above) can be employed in theorising the cultural context in which women develop and maintain eating disorders. Culturally dystonic feelings, such as loneliness, futility or despair can be articulated through the culturally syntonic terrain of women's bodies. Further, the persecutory feelings which many women experience as a result of consumerism's misogyny can be managed through displacement onto appetite or the body, both of which are morally and culturally imbued with notions of excess and the need for regulation.

Finally, while theorising how unconscious processes are structured by culture, Bloom et al. (1994) also remind us that psychoanalytic practice is equally influenced by consumerism's 'cultural violation' (p. 201) – a full breach of the 'public/private' divide; that is, they remind readers of the intersubjective nature of psychotherapy in which the gendered panopticons of consumer culture are also at work on the *therapist*. Woolley (1991) described this as a 'counter-transference' to consumer culture[6] which can manifest itself in a number of worrying ways. For instance, they argue that practitioners may disregard women's expressions of unhappiness with their bodies or food as so 'gender-syntonic' for women as not warranting serious exploration, or as signs of immaturity – a failure to 'rise above' or separate off from culture. Further, the psychoanalytic emphasis on unconscious processes may precipitate the belief that these are defences against something more important (the 'real' underlying issue) or even that they need to be *controlled* – either through the therapist's regulatory action of hospitalising the patient or by telling the client to 'pull themselves together' – perhaps by *going on a diet*. Gutwill (1994c) argues that references to a wish to diet need to be understood as not simply another expression of 'feminine body dissatisfaction' but as an expression of underlying despair. In reminding the reader of how the individual is enculturated, she points out that female therapists and clients may in turn feel equally envious or repulsed by each others' bodies. Clients for instance, may believe that if the therapist's body is bigger than the norm, that she is inadequate as a therapist – her failure to regulate her body 'speaking' her failure as a woman. In turn, therapists may well feel that a client's failure to regulate weight undermines therapeutic success. Alternatively, feminist therapists may feel traumatised by the ways in which women are so culturally violated by consumerism that they re-enact this process over and over.

However, one of the difficulties of texts such as Bloom et al.'s (1994) 'Eating Problems' is that it does not recognise that it privileges gender as the salient issue for women in consumerism. The authors thus implicitly adopt a model of 'woman' as white, Eurocentric, heterosexual, middle class and able-bodied, and risk making universalistic claims about women and about women's bodies. Thompson (1994) argues that by privileging gender we exclude race, class and sexual orientation as equally important influences on eating. This may skew notions of prevalence and the epidemiological profile of eating disorders by presuming that 'other' women are less likely to be affected by the impact of the 'culture of thinness'. As such, large numbers of studies may simply reflect particular populations of women. Thompson further argues that '[t]here is no monolithic "American" culture: the messages girls receive about body sizes and eating are shaped by ethnicity, nationality, class, race, *and* individual family members' personalities' (1994, p. 371, emphasis in the original). This means that the ways in which culture is understood and introjected cannot be dominated by theories of gender as this is only one of the salient factors. *Intra*cultural variations in parenting suggest a need to rethink ideas about socialisation as a *singular* process (see, for instance, Nakano Glenn et al., 1994). It is not simply enough to think about particular clients' 'special' circumstances (for example, as black women, Asian women, or disabled women) as such an approach belies the ways in which white women continue to position 'other' women as 'different' in relation to the norm of whiteness or heterosexuality or other privileges.

Trepagnier (1994) suggests that privileging gender also means that white feminists do not have to think about the ways in which we benefit from upholding the order. So, for instance, although women in general may feel coerced and constrained by 'the beauty myth' (Wolf, cited in Trepagnier, 1994, p. 201), this myth is based on the norm of whiteness. Thus, she argues that white women may actually *benefit* by participating in the 'disciplines of femininity' (Bartky, 1988); that is, while white women may be both enticed and rejected by 'the beauty myth', they are at least being offered the chance to become 'real' women. In contrast, black women are simply being offered the chance to become 'more like white women' (Joseph and Lewis, 1981, cited in Trepagnier, 1994, p. 202).

Some of these objections can clearly be extended to postmodern feminists' universalising rather than definitive focus on *which* woman's bodies they are concerned with. In turn, there is a tendency to privilege the discursive function of gender over other forms of power. These issues certainly need to be addressed and the above critiques will help to inform the necessary shifts. The idea of attachment to consumer culture as monolithic rather than specific needs to be addressed although Nasser et al. (2001) suggest theorising the monolithic impact of consumerism on women's bodies on a global scale. In turn, the notion of 'cultural transference' could be augmented by incorporating issues of power and difference *between* women. 'Cultural transference' could also prove a useful deconstructive tool in understanding the power of other issues 'at work' in feminist postmodernist approaches to women's bodies. For instance, is the postmodern delight in *abstraction* an emotional defence against some of the corporeal horrors being enacted? Is this an intellectual displacement for eroticised feelings? Does the current feminist fascination with *thin* bodies belie a culturally syntonic disgust with *fat* or even provide a means to express *envy*? While there is certainly a desire to further explicate these issues, perhaps this also reflects the gendered mandate to continually 'work on' women's bodies, whichever ones they are.

This chapter has grounded feminist psychoanalytic thinking about women, food and bodies within a postmodern framework. It has shown ways in which aspects of British object relations theory can be drawn on, not to demonstrate women's 'lack', but instead, to theorise how consumerism elides the boundaries between the private and public (Bloom et al., 1994). While women's ongoing 'work on the self' offers a means for establishing and maintaining a coherent sense of identity, these practices occur within social structures which simultaneously tap into and exacerbate unconscious anxieties about inclusion and exclusion. Although this chapter has focused on the usefulness of these ideas for clinical practice,

I would argue that feminists' current 'transference' to the culture of postmodernity exacerbates a tendency to reify abstraction of what remains a highly emotive issue with numerous personal resonances.

Notes

1. Parts of this chapter have appeared in a previous publication: Heenan, M. C. (2005) 'Looking in the Fridge for Feelings': The Gendered Psychodynamics of Consumer Culture, in J. Davidson, L. Bondi & M. Smith (Eds) *Emotional Geographies* Burlington, VT & Aldershot: Ashgate, pp, 147–60.
2. See Markula, Burns & Riley (this volume) for further discussion and critique of the impact of dichotomising abnormal and normal body-related practices, the gendered nature of weight and body management and the association of morality with weight.
3. My use of the label 'eating disorder' to describe obesity and compulsive eating (as well as anorexia and bulimia nervosa) is clinically strategic. The label paves the way for accessing therapy (if wanted) to a group of women who are precluded from mainstream 'treatment' because they are not deemed to be 'mad' but 'bad'; that is women who are 'overweight', obese or 'compulsive/binge eaters'. As such, it can be a relief to obtain clinical 'status' and a thoughtful analysis of what is usually regarded by psychiatrists or doctors as greed or stupidity. Again, 'labelling' need not be constrained by particularities; for instance, some compulsive eaters do use 'compensatory behaviours'; some are obese, others are not. However, 'labelling' clearly works to construct identities and social practices, and I return to this point later in the text.
4. The term 'British' object relations theory denotes the difference between this group of theorists and the more biologically based 'object relations' work of Melanie Klein (see Greenberg and Mitchell 1983 for a fuller explanation).
5. The term 'panopticon' refers to the way in which, through the private and public practices of discipline such as femininity (Bartky, 1988), as much as the panopticons within prisons, people are not only constantly observed but they also learn to observe themselves and others without apparent coercion. Bartky (1988) and Bordo (1988) further elaborate how internal gendered mirrors function as if the observer were male.
6. The term 'counter-transference' derives from the theory of 'transference' – the belief that feelings about early caretakers may be re-invoked in the patient in the present – exploration of which forms an essential part of psychoanalytic psychotherapy. 'Counter'-transference describes the feelings generated in the therapist by the patient which also have an impact on therapy (Bateman & Holmes, 1995).

References

Appignanesi, L. & Forrester, J. (1992). *Freud's Women*. London: Virago.
Bartky, S. Lee (1988). Foucault, Femininity, and the Modernization of Patriarchal Power. In I. Diamond and L. Quinby (Eds), *Feminism and Foucault: Reflections on Resistance.* (pp. 61–86). Boston: Northeastern University Press.

Benjamin, J. (1988). *The Bonds of Love: Psychoanalysis, Feminism, and the Problem of Domination*. London: Virago Books.
Benjamin, J. (1995). *Like Subjects, Love Objects*. New Haven, CT: Yale University Press.
Benjamin, J. (1998). *Shadow of the Other: Intersubjectivity and Gender in Psychoanalysis*. London: Routledge.
Bloom, C., Gitter, A., Gutwill, S., Kogel, L., Zaphiropoulos, L. (1994). *Eating Problems: A Feminist Psychoanalytic Treatment Model*. New York: Basic Books.
Bloom, C. & Kogel, L. (1994). Tracing Development: The Feeding Experience and the Body. In C. Bloom, A. Gitter, S. Gutwill, L. Kogel & L. Zaphiropoulos (Eds) *Eating Problems: A Feminist Psychoanalytic Treatment Model* (pp. 40–56). New York: Basic Books.
Bordo, S. (2003). *Unbearable Weight: Feminism, Western Culture, and the Body* (10th Anniversary edn) Berkeley, California: University of California Press.
Buhle, M.J. (1998). *Feminism and Its Discontents: A Century of Struggle with Psychoanalysis*. Cambridge, MA: Harvard University Press.
Chodorow, N. (1978). *The Reproduction of Mothering: Psychoanalysis and the Sociology of Gender*. Berkeley, CA: University of California Press.
Chodorow, N. (1999a). *The Reproduction of Mothering: Psychoanalysis and the Sociology of Gender* (2nd edn) Berkeley, CA: University of California Press.
Chodorow, N. (1999b). *The Power of Feelings: Personal Meaning in Psychoanalysis, Gender and Culture*. New Haven, CT: Yale University Press.
Cooper, T. (1987). Anorexia and Bulimia: The Political and the Personal. In M. Lawrence (Ed.) *Fed Up and Hungry: Women, Oppression and Food*. London: Women's Press.
Crisp, A. H. (1980). *Anorexia Nervosa: Let Me Be*. London: Academic Press.
Dally, P. (1969). *Anorexia Nervosa*. London: William Heinemann Medical Books.
Dinnerstein, D. (1976). *The Rocking of the Cradle and the Ruling of the World*. London: Souvenir Press.
Eichenbaum, L. & Orbach, S. (1982). *Outside In, Inside Out: Women's Psychology, A Feminist Psychoanalytic Approach*. Harmondsworth, Middlesex: Pelican.
Enns, C. Zerbe (1993). Twenty Years of Feminist Counseling and Therapy: From Naming Biases to Implementing Multifaceted Practice. *The Counseling Psychologist*, 21 (1) 3–87.
Fairbairn, R. (1952). *An Object Relations Theory of Personality*. New York: Basic Books.
Featherstone, M. (1991). The Body in Consumer Culture. In M. Featherstone, M. Hepworth and Bryan S. Turner (Eds) *The Body: Social Process and Cultural Theory* (pp. 170–96). London: Sage.
Flax, J. (1990). *Thinking Fragments: Psychoanalysis, Feminism, and Postmodernism in the Contemporary West*. Berkeley, CA: University of California Press.
Flax, J. (1993). Mothers and Daughters Revisited. In J. van Mens-Verhulst, K. Schreurs & L. Woertman (Eds) *Daughtering & Mothering: Female Subjectivity Reanalysed*. London: Routledge.
Foucault, M. (1978). *Discipline and Punish: The Birth of the Prison*, trans. Alan Sheridan. New York: Vintage Books.
Frosh, S. (1987). *The Politics of Psychoanalysis: An Introduction to Freudian and Post-Freudian Theory*. Basingstoke: Macmillan.
Giddens, A. (1991). *Modernity and Self-Identity*. Cambridge: Polity.
Greenberg, J. R. and Mitchell, S. A. (1983). *Object Relations in Psychoanalytic Theory*. Cambridge, MA: Harvard University Press.

Grosz, E. (1990). *Jacques Lacan: A Feminist Introduction*. London: Routledge.
Gutwill, L. (1994a). Women's Eating Problems: Social Context and the Internalization of Culture. In C. Bloom, A. Gitter, S. Gutwill, L. Kogel & L. Zaphiropoulos (Eds) *Eating Problems: A Feminist Psychoanalytic Treatment Model* (pp. 1–27). New York: Basic Books.
Gutwill, L. (1994b) The Diet: Personal Experience, Social Condition, and Industrial Empire. In C. Bloom, A. Gitter, S. Gutwill, L. Kogel & L. Zaphiropoulos (Eds) *Eating Problems: A Feminist Psychoanalytic Treatment Model* (pp. 28–39). New York: Basic Books.
Gutwill, L. (1994c). Transference and Countertransference Issues: The Impact of Social Pressures on Body Image and Consciousness. In C. Bloom, A. Gitter, S. Gutwill, L. Kogel & L. Zaphiropoulos (Eds) *Eating Problems: A Feminist Psychoanalytic Treatment Model* (pp. 144–171). New York: Basic Books.
Hamburg, P. (1989). Bulimia: The Construction of a Symptom. *Journal of the American Academy of Psychoanalysis*, 17 (1), 131–40.
Hamilton, N. G. (Ed.) (1992). *From Inner Sources: New Directions in Object Relations Psychotherapy*. Northvale NJ: Jason Aronson Inc.
Heenan, M. C. (1995). Feminist Psychotherapy – A Contradiction in Terms? *Feminism and Psychology*, 5 (1), 112–17.
Heenan, M. C. & Seu, I. B. (1998). Introduction. In I. B. Seu & M. C. Heenan (Eds) *Feminism & Psychotherapy: Reflections on Contemporary Theories and Practices* (pp. 1–12). London:Sage.
Hollway, W. (1989). *Subjectivity and Method in Psychology*. London: Sage.
Hsu, L. K. George. (1989). The Gender Gap in Eating Disorders: Why are the Eating Disorders More Common among Women? *Clinical Psychology Review*, 9, 393–407.
Kitzinger, C. & Perkins, R. (1993). *Changing Our Minds*. London: Onlywomen's Press.
Lawrence, M. (Ed.) (1987). *Fed Up and Hungry – Women, Oppression and Food*. London: The Women's Press.
Markula, P., Burns, M. & Riley, S. (this volume). Introducing Critical Bodies: Representations, Identities and Practices of Weight and Body Management. In S. Riley, M. Burns, H. Frith, S. Wiggins, & P. Markula (Eds), *Critical Bodies: Representations, Identities and Practices of Weight and Body Management*. Basingstoke: Palgrave Macmillan.
Mitchell, J. (1974). *Psychoanalysis and Feminism*. Harmondsworth, Middlesex: Pelican Books.
Nakano Glenn, E., Chang, G. & Rennie Forcey, L. (Eds) (1994). *Mothering: Ideology, Experience, and Agency*. New York: Routledge.
Nasser, M. Katzman, M. A. & Gordon, R. A. (Eds) (2001). *Eating Disorders and Cultures in Transition*. London: Brunner-Routledge.
Ogden, T. (1994). *Subjects of Analysis*. London: Karnac Books.
Orbach, S. (1978). *Fat is a Feminist Issue*. London: Paddington Press.
Orbach, S. (1986). *Hungerstrike*. London: Faber and Faber.
Orbach, S. (1994). Working with the False Body. In A. Erskine & D. Judd (Eds), *The Imaginative Body: Psychodynamic Therapy in Health Care* (pp. 165–79) London: Whurr Publishers Ltd.
Parker, I. (1992). *Discourse Dynamics: Critical Analysis for Social and Individual Psychology*. London: Routledge.

Ramazanoglu, C. & Holland, J. (2002). *Feminist Methodology: Challenges and Choices*. London: Sage.

Rich, E. and Evans, J. (this volume). Learning to be healthy, dying to be thin: The representation of weight via body perfection codes in schools. In S. Riley, M. Burns, H. Frith, S. Wiggins, & P. Markula (Eds), *Critical bodies: Representations, identities, and practices of weight and body management*. Basingstoke: Palgrave Macmillan.

Rose, N. (1990). *Governing the Soul*. London: Routledge.

Thompson, B. (1994). Food, Bodies and Growing Up Female: Childhood Lessons about Culture, Race, and Class. In P. Fallon, M. Katzman & S. Wooley (Eds) *Feminist Perspectives on Eating Disorders*. (pp. 355–80). New York: Guilford Press.

Trepagnier, B. (1994). The Politics of Black and White Bodies. *Feminism and Psychology*, Special Issue on Shifting Identities, Shifting Racisms. 4 (1),199–205.

Winnicott, D. W. (1971). *Playing and Reality* Routledge: London.

Wooley, S. C. (1991). The Female Therapist as Outlaw. In P. Fallon, M. Katzman & S. Wooley (Eds) *Feminist Perspectives on Eating Disorders*. (pp. 318–38). New York: Guilford Press.

Worell, J. & Remer, P. (1992). *Feminist Perspectives in Therapy: An Empowerment Model for Women*. New York: John Wiley & Sons.

Section III Meanings of Body Management Practices: Women's Experiences

Pirkko Markula

The previous sections identified cultural connections between health, weight, body size and shape in the landscape of weight and body management. These chapters examined how representations of 'healthy weight' may be engaged within the production of subjectivity. They further demonstrated how we come to understand ourselves in the interaction with culturally available discourses. This interaction creates the terms through which we make sense of the actions, behaviours and material experiences around us. The same discursive milieu of health, weight and body size produces the representations, subjectivities and practices around the contemporary cultural understanding of the body. Therefore, social constructionist and critical approaches situate people's practices within the discursive logic that is part of their cultural and social context(s). This section focuses specifically on practices that individuals use to manage their body weight.

The chapters in this section examine three different weight related practices: practices associated with the eating disorder 'bulimia' (Burns & Gavey), dieticians' advice and working practices with 'over weight' clients (Aphramor & Gingras) and participation in commercial weight-loss programmes (Gimlin). They further highlight how women may make sense of their bodies within a larger discursive context of health, weight and (feminine, heterosexual) beauty, age and class.

From a post-structuralist perspective, our ideas about what constitutes a healthy body are socially constructed. The meanings attached to 'health' can be multiple, but certain meanings accumulate within a specific cultural and historical context. Health can be understood as a discursive formation that is based on theories, concepts and descriptions from several disciplines such as psychology, nutrition, physiology, epidemiology and medicine. Based on such knowledge certain health practices, such as dietetics, hospital care, doctor surgeries and media health campaigns, are formed. In addition, such individual health practices as hygiene, non-smoking, moderate drinking, dieting or exercising become meaningful based on what we know (that is, what we consider to be 'truths') about health. Therefore, knowledge and practice are inextricably linked in the discourse of health. In this section, for example, Aphramor and Gingras demonstrate how the scientific knowledge of 'energy balance equation' (that body weight is a function of the amount of calories consumed minus the amount of calories expended) underpins nutritional advice, powerfully shaping the dieting practices offered to clients. Through its discursive formation, knowledge also turns into a vehicle of power, in terms of what is considered to be true, who has the rights to speak and what may be spoken. For example, Aphramor and Gingras argue that nutritional advice based on the 'energy balance equation' positions 'fatness' as always unhealthy. Evidence that contradicts this logic is effectively silenced by excluding it from the education of dieticians and the scientific publications on nutrition. Indeed, all the chapters in this section identify the 'energy balance equation' underlining women's body management practices albeit in very different ways. Aphramor and Gingras challenge the 'energy balance equation' for its lack of scientific evidence; Gimlin examines its employment in commercial weight loss programmes that advocate weight loss through 'planned and reasoned eating'; and Burns and Gavey show how the 'energy balance equation' is drawn upon to justify such weight control behaviours as purging.

The authors in this section also point to the impact of psychological, medical and nutritional knowledge on individuals' understandings of their (healthy) bodies. All of the three chapters focus on women's body reduction practices, locating their work in the current cultural moment where thinness has come to signify health, making all of us 'weight watchers'. Thus, the authors in this section examine women's body management practices against the panic caused by the 'obesity epidemic'. Burns and Gavey show a shared discursive culture between women who engage in 'bulimic' practices and 'Weight Watchers' literature in which food consumption is understood as something to be 'earned'; Aphramor and Gingras critique the focus on weight over fitness in dieticians professional practices; and Gimlin explores how the need to lose weight becomes imbricated in discourses of health, age and beauty. The authors demonstrate that the social construction of the healthy body as a good looking, thin body translates into a variety of practices including purging and smoking (Burns & Gavey), non-evidence-based dietician advice

(Aphramor & Gingras) and older women's attendance at commercial weight-loss groups (Gimlin).

The chapters in this section further locate body management practices within what the authors identify as problematic and simplistic health promotion messages. As we stated in the introduction for this book, public representations of body size are tied to an understanding of 'neo-liberal subjectivity' in which the individual is understood to be responsible for his/her behaviour. The authors in this section demonstrate that medical discourse on obesity and commercial discourse on the ideal body blame women for a lack of willpower, the inability to exercise self-control around food and their consequently bulging bodies. Aphramor and Gingras critique health promotional material that engenders guilt and shame on large-bodied individuals. In their chapters, Gimlin, and Burns and Gavey point to the media's role in the current consumer culture for fostering women's personal responsibility for their bodily appearance. Similar to medical discourse on dieting, the popular media instructs women to take charge of becoming slender which, in these media messages, has become synonymous with health, beauty, success and self-control.

Social constructionism allows us to examine how knowledge is (re)produced through social practices. It also assumes that individuals play an active part in this process as they engage in multiple practices within similar discursive conditions. Saukko (Chapter 2, this volume) argues that discourses are multifaceted and contradictory and they can be simultaneously both empowering and disempowering. To examine the complexity of individuals' engagement with the discursive culture, Burns and Gavey, for example, explore how their participants validate their 'bulimic' behaviours by arguing that since a slim *looking* body is a sign of health, then as 'healthy' persons they are not a drain on health services. Gimlin examines how the same Weight Watchers' cooking and eating regime can be understood as empowering for older women who have previously not cooked with their own needs in mind, but disempowering for younger women who are not in control of their household food management and have to negotiate their mothers' associations between food, love and rejection.

While they share a concern with 'weight watching' the chapters in section three examine practices associated with differently sized bodies: women who maintain a slim body through 'bulimic' practices or larger (men and) women seeking professional or commercial help in reducing their body size. The chapters also employ three different forms of critical analysis to examine body management practices. Burns and Gavey are critical psychologists who take a post-structuralist perspective to perform discourse analyse on weight-loss literatures (e.g. magazines) and participant interviews; Aphramor and Gingras use their background as dieticians and poets to produce an evidence-based ideological and poetic analysis of scientific literature. Alternatively, Gimlin, a sociologist, combines a Grounded Theory-informed thematic analysis of participant interviews with ethnographic participatory observation to examine practices in commercial weight-loss programmes.

The chapters in this section showcase a range of theoretical and methodological approaches to the study of weight and body management practices. They do, however, share an understanding that discursive cultures provide the conditions of possibility for a variety of practices (such as purging, dieticians' professional practices and attendance at commercial weight-loss programmes). Individuals may take up these practices in creative ways within a shared discursive milieu. As Saukko reminds us, Foucault (1982) emphasised 'the always double-sided nature of discourses, which produce us both as active subjects, capable of acting on our own behalf (as gays, anorexics etc.) and as passive objects constrained by the legacy of the discourse (which has defined homosexuality and anorexia as pathologies)' (this volume). These chapters highlight the dominance of the socially constructed association between health and slenderness. In addition, they examine the different ways individuals make sense of this association to create different weight management practices. This section, therefore, aims to depart from the idea of body troubles as individual pathology to understand corporeality as socially constructed with the contemporary culture of body (reduction) practices.

7
Dis/Orders of Weight Control: Bulimic and/or 'Healthy Weight' Practices

Maree Burns and Nicola Gavey

As mentioned in the introduction to this volume, current concerns about the health risks of obesity (e.g., Aronne, 2001; Visscher & Seidell, 2001) are regularly translated into a more generalised anxiety about 'overweight' bodies, and the risks they pose for health. In response to this threat, public health strategies in Westernised countries have been encouraging their populations to maintain a 'healthy weight', and this impetus has been enthusiastically capitalised on by the food, fitness, fashion, weight loss and cosmetic industries and in popular media. Within this healthy weight discourse a healthy weight is medically defined in terms of body mass index (BMI [weight to height ratio]) and is portrayed as the effect of a well-calibrated balance between food intake and energy expenditure. To suggest a relationship between this ubiquitous promotion of healthy weight and the eating disorder 'bulimia' (bulimia nervosa) makes little sense at face value. In this chapter, however, we argue that 'bulimia' can be understood with reference to such broader cultural emphasis on, and particular representations of, health. In this context, we suggest bulimic practices have a logic that is continuous with the contemporary conflation of health with the slender, female body.

The current trend in medical research and in public health to construct obesity as a health problem of epidemic proportions has significant implications for the ways in which non-slender bodies are regarded. In Westernised cultures adiposity has become associated with being 'at risk' for the future development of health problems regardless of the actual health status of fat or 'weight-gaining' bodies (Ryan & Carryer, 2000). The medicalisation of high body weights also supports contentions about the universal desirability of weight loss, which relies on disputed assumptions that dieting is achievable, sustainable and improves health

(Austin, 2001; Berg, 1999; McFarlane, Polivy, & McCabe, 1999). Furthermore, public health strategies for obesity prevention and the wider promotion of healthy weight derived from these assumptions land in a cultural domain that is already highly charged with potent values that cohere around food, consumption and body size. These values are also profoundly gendered. A gendered aesthetic of slimness for women has long been strongly entrenched in the Western cultural requirements of femininity and heterosexual attractiveness (Bartky, 1988; Bordo, 1993). That is, regardless of its health status Western cultural ideals of women's bodies already idealise and reinforce sinewy slimness and marginalise overweight bodies.

The social production of bulimia

Considering the (Western) cultural milieu into which health messages are delivered, it is not unreasonable to speculate that intersections between directives specifically encouraging weight control for health and gendered constructions of fatness as embodied deviance have implications for women's embodiment and body management practices. Indeed, commentators (e.g., Austin, 1999a; Cogan, 1999; Germov & Williams, 1996) have suggested that such intersections operate to sanction the 'dieting epidemic' and to fuel related eating disturbances including 'anorexia' and 'bulimia' for women in Western cultures (Austin, 2001). Although a relatively small percentage of women are diagnosed with 'bulimia' (American Psychiatric Association, 1994), the feelings and behaviours associated with it, such as body dissatisfaction, 'obsessive' concerns with weight, dieting, bingeing and purging practices are reportedly so widespread that they have been described as normative (Rodin, Silberstein, & Streigal-Moore, 1985).

Taking the sociocultural context as central, postmodern theorists (e.g., Bordo, 1993; Burns, 2004, 2006; Hepworth, 1999; Malson, 1998; Malson & Burns, forthcoming) have challenged the traditional understanding of women's eating difficulties as individual pathology and have emphasised the constitutive nature for subjectivity and practice, of contemporary constructions of gender and the gender-specific values and practices of Western culture. From this perspective investigators have suggested continuities between contemporary 'healthy living' rhetoric and the body management practices that women engage in, noting that discourses of health and discourses of dieting both assume that the ideal female body is slender and this slender-looking female body is heterosexually attractive (Chapman, 1999; Davies, 1998; Lupton, 1996; Neumark-Sztainer & Story, 1998; Spitzack, 1990).

The study

In this chapter we take one step further the scholarship that posits a relationship between 'healthy living' rhetoric and women's problematic or 'distressed' body management. For this we examine the accounts of women who desire a slender body and who practise strict caloric regulation and compensation (consistent with diagnostic descriptions of 'bulimia') alongside cultural texts that contain messages about healthy weight control. First, we present cultural texts in order to illustrate the societal instantiations of a healthy weight discourse and to demonstrate a problematic continuity that exists between these normalised ideas and those traditionally pathologised descriptions of bulimic practices. This includes health promotion advice taken from magazines, adverts, websites, public health promotion and obesity prevention material. Our use of this material rests on the idea that bulimic bodies are crafted in conjunction with culturally contingent, gendered notions of consumption, dieting, fitness, health and body management, all of which are implicated to varying degrees in discourses of healthy weight. As our key focus implies, we consider that the societal manifestations of these discourses form (at least in part) the cultural conditions of possibility that contribute to disordered eating and problematic body-management practices. The second set of data is the interview accounts of 15 women who practise 'bulimia' (see Burns & Gavey, 2004 for details).

In the analyses that follow we have deployed a discursive approach informed by feminist post-structuralism (see Burns & Gavey, 2004) to explore the two main topics that emerged from women's talk around health: (1) a healthy body is slender and (2) meticulous regulation of the body's energy intake and expenditure, despite its bulimic rationality, constitutes healthy body management. For each of these ideas we briefly illustrate elements of the cultural context in which a discourse of healthy weight renders fat bodies problematic and promotes weight control as a healthy practice. We then examine women's talk about their desire for slenderness and their practices in relation to this discourse of healthy weight.

Health as toned and muscular slenderness

Cultural context

> Body weight is a very visible and easily understood marker of a person's physical status. An optimal range can be defined and the further outside this range the greater the health risks.
>
> Agencies for Nutrition Action, 2001, p. 1)

As suggested previously, concerns with food, weight, diet and fat are not the sole domain of women with eating/body difficulties or eating disorders, but rather reflect an inescapable Western cultural fixation with weight control. Women are inundated with images and messages that glorify slenderness and that urge dieting, exercising and body shaping. Increasingly, and in concert with the global 'panic' surrounding rising rates of obesity and its so-called associated health risks, these messages are infused with a healthy weight discourse. As the following examples illustrate, a discourse of healthy weight is articulated in a number of diverse cultural sites. Healthy weight rationale is obvious on 'healthy living' websites where individuals are invited to calculate their BMI, assess their risk for health problems and then utilise the various weight-loss techniques listed. Food advertising also often exploits the slim/healthy link. Weight Watchers suggest that their cereal bars 'keep your bottom line looking really healthy' (Weight Watchers, 2001b, p. 63). Lifestyle magazines announce the weight-loss efforts of celebrities and write about their healthier (thinner) physiques. *Who Weekly* writes of singer Sophie Monk, '"eating disorder? No way", says the pop star who's dropped two dress sizes [from size 12 to 8] through exercise and sensible eating: "I feel so much healthier now"' (Noonan, 2001, p. 1). More serious media coverage also deploys healthy weight rhetoric. News items and television documentaries warn of a global epidemic of obesity and state, 'we are eating ourselves to death and over the next 20 to 30 years it is our single biggest challenge in New Zealand' (Gillespie, 2000). As these examples illustrate, medical and public health discourses regarding the dangers of excess weight are reproduced in many popular sites where they are generalised in a way that constructs any weight gain as potentially unhealthy and to be avoided. The result is that everyone is implicated in a discourse of healthy weight in a way that implies a responsibility to at least practise weight control, and continuously be vigilant about potential weight gain.

Women's talk

Most of the participants in this study responded to questions about what slenderness means by describing the slender female body in what are now familiar ways, as heterosexually attractive and as a sign of success and/or control. In addition many of the women also suggested that the thin and toned female body was healthy and reflected fitness, well-being and vitality.

Slenderness looks/is healthy

> Alison: I know this girl Leeann from the running club. That would be my ideal. She's quite skinny – she's not that tall but she's really slender, very slim ... sort of ... very athletic ... yeah, not skinny, not Kate Moss type thing. More of an Elle McPherson type of build but not quite so statuesque.
> MB: and what is it about that figure that you like?
> Alison: Well, it looks healthy, yeah healthy, you know – athletic, fit, that kind of thing.

> MB: So is having a certain type of body important to you?
> Pam: Yeah.
> MB: Why?
> Pam: [long pause] I personally like the ... toned, athletic body. So ... fit in body, fit in mind. My motto.

In these excerpts the toned, slender physique is portrayed as an ideal body indicative of physical health, athleticism, mental well-being and fitness. However, Alison also links 'healthy' slenderness with two well-known models and simultaneously constructs such a figure as 'beautiful'. This ties in with the idea that appearing 'healthy' for women is inextricably linked with the requirements of traditional feminine physical attractiveness (Spitzack, 1990). For women a 'healthy' body is not only the socially constructed 'well' body but can also be a sexualised and objectified body, restoring connotations of traditional heterosexual beauty and passivity.

> Alison: But it [being slender] does have some health benefits because I think ... we're lesslikely to develop diabetes and heart disease and all these things [laughing]. It's gotta be good for the country and the health thing, doesn't it?

Here Alison deploys the discourse of healthy weight in which slenderness is associated with a reduced risk of disease. This construction of health paradoxically produces Alison's account of her attempts to be thin (which include running compulsively and vomiting several times a week) as worthwhile attempts at avoiding 'illness'. Being slender is not only good for her but also for 'the country and the health thing'. The irony of this is not lost on Alison whose laughter underscores the contradictory nature of her comments about purging for health.

Presumably her weight control is good for the country because as a slender person Alison is a 'responsible citizen' who will not be consuming more than her fair share of the national health budget by developing the expensive and 'preventable' diseases attributed to obesity (see Swinburn, Ashton, Gillespie, Cox, Menon, Simmons, & Birkbeck, 1997). Indeed, health promotion recommendations concerning weight control are often premised on warnings about the rising costs related to obesity and the 'potential for long term savings in health care costs through effective obesity prevention and management' (Agencies for Nutrition Action, 2001, p. 5). Within a discourse of healthy weight Alison's potentially unhealthful practices and her desire for slenderness have a certain logic that cannot simply be dismissed as an outcome of her eating 'pathology'. 'Good citizen Alison' and her slimming body management practices are legitimated and her motivations to be slender are set apart from other narcissistic, frivolous or pathological concerns.

Conflict between the 'look' of health and 'being' healthy

Although the desire for a slender physique was defended by many of the participants as a reflection or measure of a healthy and active lifestyle, at times it was the 'appearance of health', the thin, toned figure, that was overtly sought after rather than any experience of well-being. As well as careful attention to diet and getting lots of exercise, most of the women also described body management practices such as taking diet pills, being prepared to undergo liposuction, excluding certain foods from their diets (e.g., bread), fasting, using self-induced vomiting, exercising for up to 20 hours a week and misusing laxatives. These practices, while they may help to reduce weight and strip fat and therefore increase the chances of attaining the socially constructed 'healthy looking' appearance, exist in stark contrast with other statements about wellness, healthy lifestyle and disease reduction. Attention to the contradictions that exist between descriptions of health, the healthy appearance and the techniques employed to obtain it illustrates how the pursuit of a healthy-looking body can be paradoxical for women. It can involve participation in unhealthy or risky practices that result in ill health and which are often concealed or denied. The accounts of the women in this study indicate that the image of the so-called healthy body cannot be unhinged from the dominant feminine aesthetic.

> MB: Why is having that fit, athletic body ... important to you?
> Pam: Because I need it for my sport, and for myself.
> MB: So it's functional?

Pam: Yeah, so it's healthy, yeah definitely. But that doesn't mean that I could be up two sizes and still be that same shape. I don't know if I'd be happy or not, but as long as I am still fit, fit and healthy.
MB: So you say that being fit and healthy is important. Some people would say

Pam: Ummm ... I'm smoking cigarettes.
MB: Yeah, that, but some people would say that the eating and the laxative use, and um ... the vomiting is not a healthy thing so how do you make that fit with the whole idea of being healthy is quite important?

Pam: Um ... It's quite contradictory isn't it? Oh God! Yeah, I put my foot in my mouth [laughing]. It doesn't fit in at all! Yeah it allows me, it probably allows me to cheat to stay that way [laughing]. Sorry but that's the only answer I can think of.

In this account being slender is constructed as indicating health without the experience of health necessarily being present. Raising this contradiction with Pam resulted in her attempting to manage the conflict between her justification for her weight loss attempts (to attain the healthy physique) and the unhealthy practices she engages in to this end. As a result of the inconsistency, Pam positioned herself as a 'cheat'. This subject position is produced within a gendered discourse discussed by Bordo (1993) in which women's bodies are constructed as potentially unruly and in need of management characterised by discipline and control. Such a construction imbues regulation and management as the good and moral way to a healthy/thin body and conversely constructs indulgence as weak. Through her practices Pam obtains the body that represents what White, Young and Gillet (1995) have described as a moral and regulated lifestyle and she therefore appears to demonstrate control over her potentially 'unruly' female body. However, her behaviours (smoking and purging) are far from regulated, controlled or health giving despite their contribution to this 'look'.

Interestingly, the physical outcomes of Pam's unhealthful behaviours cannot be seen because they are not written on her body (unlike 'overweight', which exists as a clinical 'sign' of compromised health). On the contrary, through the meticulous control of the energy that is absorbed into her body, Pam conforms to current aesthetic definitions of health. Contemporary constructions of the slender body as the ultimate sign of health therefore potentially provide the cultural conditions and motivations that support practices such as Pam's smoking, purging and laxative abuse to manage weight. This is possible because this construction of the body implies two types of 'bodies' to be regulated by 'healthiness'. One is 'internal' and refers to practices that contribute to well-being and experiential health. The other is 'external' and is a body subject to a normalising gaze and is therefore concerned with practices that produce the socially constructed 'healthy looking' body (see Featherstone, Hepworth & Turner, 1991). It is the latter (inevitably gendered image) that pervades popular Western culture and that interacts in potentially problematic ways with those obesity prevention initiatives advising weight control for experiential health. By emphasising external, quantifiable indices of health (e.g., BMIs), health promotion inadvertently reinforces gendered images of health and unintentionally endorses practices that might sacrifice 'real' health and well-being.

Energy regulation for healthy body management

Cultural context

> Obesity represents the consequences of a mismatch between energy intake and energy expenditure.
>
> (*Fit magazine*, 2001, p. 51)

> Your body and its metabolism are like a furnace. ... by exercising the right way and fuelling your furnace with the right food you will create a leaner, smaller, more toned body and because your furnace is more efficient and burning brighter than ever, your new look will be easier and healthier to maintain.
>
> (*Les Mills* [Gym] *News*, Auckland, 2001, p. 2)

Not only does Western culture provide a 'look' of health to strive for, it also provides and promotes the technologies or practices for achieving it. Techniques of body measurement and management have been produced within fields of knowledge (e.g., sports and nutritional science) that rely on biomedical constructions of the body. These fields objectify and quantify the body as a plastic and malleable material within a discursive framework of 'metabolics, energy, and measurable force' (Bray & Colebrook, 1998, p. 62). Discourses of bodily quantification and management reduce bodies to mechanistic devices, ignoring their social meanings and their lived experience. This objectification of bodies has arguably interacted with the slenderness imperative for women and been assimilated into Western cultural landscapes, into the food, fitness and fashion industries and into mass media where it informs popular techniques of body regulation (Turner, 1982, 1991). Meticulous bodily surveillance and regulation is exemplified by various body monitoring products. For example, The Weight Watchers Bonus Buddy is 'a specialised, personalised pedometer that measures your every movement in "steps" which you can convert to Bonus Points – so the more you move, the more you are rewarded' (Weight Watchers, 2001a, p. 2). Likewise the MioSensor watch 'not only records the kilojoules you burn while training, but keeps a tally of the kilojoules you eat during the day, then compares the number burnt and the number eaten with your daily target' (*Cosmopolitan*, 2001, p. 177).

Healthy living prescriptions such as these are concerned with maintaining equilibrium between calorific intake and expenditure and as such support obsessive attention to energy intake, exercise and dietary restriction. This focus on the energy that is ingested and exerted and the rate that the body is able to perform this function is a feature of current strategies aimed at both weight loss (dieting) and at health promotion in public health as well as in popular cultural sites. The New Zealand Health Strategy on obesity argues that in order to promote healthy weights, we must 'reduce the consumption of high fat, high sugar foods and promote habitual physical activity' (Ministry of Health, 2001, p. 14). This population-wide message fails to take into account that many women are already caught in a cycle of compulsive exercising and strict dietary management to achieve the 'beautiful' (rather than 'healthful') slender ideal.

Women's talk

The following sections illustrate that the practices we might identify as 'bulimic' can be understood within a discourse of health, as modes of body regulation that are continuous with other methods of 'healthy' caloric management. This analysis suggests that 'bulimic' behaviours can be conceptualised as a series of culturally available and interconnected practices or techniques that might converge with the production of a healthy body/self. Potentially, the practices of restriction, binge eating and compensating along with their attendant behaviours of ongoing weighing, calculating and measuring the body, and the food (energy) that passes between internal and external boundaries, are locatable within the domain of health. Here, slenderness is health embodied and practices of regulation and scrupulous body management are key to its attainment (Austin, 1999a). As such 'bulimic' practices share discursive space with other more 'normative' practices of body management including dieting and exercising for body shaping. The 'bulimic' practices that a woman enacts therefore are less simply 'situated' within her as a symptom of disorder but have a rationality within sociocultural contexts that support such behaviours.

In the next sections, we will consider body-management practices concerned with the regulation of energy into and out of the body. The subsections are divided into those practices constructed as 'healthy' and those considered indicative of 'bulimia'. Exercise is difficult to categorise in this way due to its simultaneous representation as a healthy activity and as deviant when combined with binge eating or when engaged in to 'excess'.

Regulatory practices deemed 'healthy'

> Toni: ... I started learning more about it and how weight training increases muscle mass and I learnt that putting on muscle mass at the same time as working your diet to decrease fat, works [for weight loss]. Muscle burns more fat than fat, more energy than fat. Like, I think it's about nine times more. It burns nine grams of energy whereas fat burns one gram in your body.

> Lara: I try and do different things whereas when I first started exercising, I was doing all high impact until I found out that high impact is ok for building your fitness up but it's not a good fat burner, you've gotta keep your heart rate down.

Within these accounts, fat is constructed in negative ways as a sign of disequilibrium and inefficiency in the body and as something that must be 'burned up'. Toni and Lara both report participating in specifically 'fat burning' exercises rather than participating in the activities to increase cardiovascular fitness (a more appropriate index of health). In these excerpts, the body and its energy (fat) burning qualities are quantified in numerical terms as grams and heart rates. Such descriptions overlap with widespread contemporary discourses of health that vilify fat and construct it (on the body and in the diet) as a potential health threat (Austin, 1999b). They are deployed in health-promotion material, weight-loss literature, in the fitness industry and in advertising for foods and exercise products.

Of course exercising is easily deployed in the construction of a healthy self despite its entanglement in discourses of slenderness and beauty for women. Magazines containing healthy-living advice suggest that 'the role of exercise in creating and maintaining good health is well known. It helps to control our weight, to stay fit, and look youthful, and is a proven factor in preventing illnesses such as diabetes and heart disease' (Knight, 2001, p. 91). Power is shown to operate on women's bodies through the healthy weight discourse once again however, when we consider that some of the women in the present study reported exercising for up to 20 hours a week, not for health, but to compensate for the food they had ingested. Although there is truth to the claim that exercise contributes to health and well-being, it is also firmly imbricated in a discursive mix where it exists as an effective 'compensatory' practice concerned with eradicating unwanted calories.

Regulatory practices deemed 'bulimic'

Western cultural concerns with body regulation, healthy eating, exercise and obesity prevention, combined with a construction of female bodies as requiring measurement and management, cannot be disarticulated from the host of new obsessions, anxieties and questionable practices that have emerged for many women around eating and embodiment. Consider in isolation the practices associated with 'bulimia': they include attempts to embody what is a culturally admired 'healthy physique' by participating in 'healthy' attempts to regulate and restrict dietary intake as prescribed in many sites of health promotion. Binge eating or unregulated consumption often follows food restriction and has been demonstrated to be a predictable outcome of dieting (see French & Jeffrey, 1994). Finally, 'bulimia' is characterised by compensatory behaviours aimed at redressing the calorific imbalance that has occurred. Although some of these compensatory behaviours exist outside 'normal' body-management regimes, they are practices that are concerned with the restoration of energy equilibrium in the body and therefore they share discursive space with a discourse of healthy weight:

> If I get up in the morning and exercise then it's good I can have breakfast, I can eat normal breakfast and not think about what I'm eating and then if I exercise at the end of the day it like – then justifies having dinner as well and you don't have to stress about it.
>
> (Jo)

> Bonus Points let you trade in physical activity for food – a brisk half-hour walk could mean an extra couple of slices of bread or a sweet treat.
>
> (Weight Watchers International Inc., 1999, p. 12)

> Well [vomiting's] helpful in the way that ... You might ... undo the damage you've done by eating too much ... So instead of having or

letting all my food in my tummy you can take it out and like you say 'back at square one'.

(Frances)

Bonus Points are also great if you have a party or special occasion coming up – move more, bank a few points and you'll have more to spend! Or if you blow your points one day, you can undo the damage by getting a little exercise the next.

(Weight Watchers International Inc., 1999, p. 12)

The points referred to in these extracts represent Weight Watcher's numerical classification of various foods according to their caloric properties. A diet club, Weight Watchers increasingly markets its products by appealing to healthy weight discourse and exploits the popular notion that health is dependent on a certain size and weight and on regulation. Clearly the body, energy and food are quantified and manipulated through adherence to the 'points' technology. Consumption is similarly represented or constructed by both Weight Watchers and by women with 'bulimia' as 'damage' or as something that must be earned. This trope of balance demonstrates that meticulous calculation of the transformations of the body are not specific to women who are described as 'bulimic' but are part of a wider management of the body via dietetic (and health) regimens in general in Westernised cultures. In short, a compensatory or 'bulimic' rationale is revealed as a normative social phenomenon. Practices of restricting, bingeing, purging and continual weighing are continuous with the same discourse that enables the 'healthy' practices of dieting and exercising with their attendant practices of weighing, measuring and record-keeping. Remember the function of the Miosensor watch described earlier? It constantly keeps track of energy consumption and expenditure resonating eerily with Naomi's reports of her continuous regulatory (bingeing, vomiting and weighing) practices:

I mean there was [sic] days when you couldn't, couldn't be sick. Um ... and, and you'd weigh yourself every, you know whenever you eat, before you binge, after you purge just to see how much weight you've lost. Um ... and it's continuous.

In the following extract Alison deploys what Turner (1992) has referred to as a 'rational calculation over the body' (p. 192) when she describes the practices she uses to compensate for her 'sluggish' metabolism.

Well, I think through my exercise I control how much fat's going into my body. Also, I think I have a – not a slow metabolism, but a slow bowel you know like ... if I don't eat enough bran, I just don't go at all and so by vomiting some of it, I'm getting rid of it. Like my husband spends all day on the toilet, you know. I said to him, 'I'm just doing what you do but I'm doing it from the other end' [laughing]. So I just feel like I'm just helping to get rid of some of the food that my body doesn't really need.

Here excess fat or weight is accounted for by a discourse of healthy metabolism that produces fatness as a sign of disequilibrium between consumption and expenditure. Fat is paradoxically constructed as both a personal responsibility and something that is difficult to avoid if one is unfortunate enough to have a sluggish metabolism. Although Alison does not mention any negative health implications of fat in the diet and on the body, this 'knowledge' is culturally pervasive (see Austin, 1999b). It legitimates Alison's desire to control the amount of fat that is absorbed by her body regardless of whether her motivation is health or the attainment of slenderness. Within this account a somewhat 'medicalised' discourse of regulation constructs Alison's body as inefficient and supports her active interventions to restore the balance by purging. The onus is on Alison to compensate for her ineffective body that does not rid itself of fat as efficiently as those with more effective metabolisms (like her husband's). Although vomiting is considered unhealthy and exists outside of what are considered normal body-management regimens, Alison's attempts to counteract her supposed sluggish metabolism are provided with a kind of coherence within a discourse of health wherein regulation and harmony between energy ingested and expended is central. Vomiting in order to maintain equilibrium therefore exists on a continuum with other more normative practices engaged in by Alison, such as exercising and eating bran to facilitate an efficient metabolism and restore balance.

Concluding comments

This chapter has discussed how contemporary healthy weight discourse forms a rationalising framework that is consistent with women's participation in health-risk practices. A discourse of healthy weight provides the cultural conditions that support, rationalise, and to some extent normalise, practices that are described as 'bulimic'. The reductionist focus on healthy weight that characterises public health and popular derivatives against obesity provides choices and opportunities that are profoundly gendered in terms of their meanings and salience. Health promotion in the field of weight, diet and exercise often fails to consider how existing cultural ideals of femininity and slenderness have produced women as self-surveilling subjects (Bartky, 1988; Bordo, 1993) already concerned with maintaining slenderness regardless of health outcomes. Indeed both 'bulimic' and 'healthy' female bodies are regulated by normalising discourses that derogate female amplitude and that promote engaging in regulatory practices designed to produce a slender body. Focusing on healthy weight rather than health per se is, therefore, paradoxically implicated in the shaping and production of subjectivities, practices and bodies for some women in ways that are antithetical to an overt health message. As such the practices derived from this discourse are not neutral practices but can be understood as one more technology of femininity involved in the production of the 'ideal' slender body.

References

Agencies for Nutrition Action. (2001). *Healthy weight New Zealand/Tumaha Tika Aotearoa*. New Zealand: Agencies for Nutrition Action.
American Psychiatric Association. (1994). *Diagnostic and statistical manual of mental disorders*, revised 4th edn. Washington, DC: APA.
Aronne, L. (2001). Epidemiology, morbidity, and treatment of overweight and obesity. *Journal of Clinical Psychiatry*, 62(23), 13–22.
Austin, S. B. (1999a). Fat, loathing and public health: The complicity of science in a culture of disordered eating. *Culture, Medicine and Psychiatry*, 23, 245–68.
Austin, S. B. (1999b). Commodity knowledge in consumer culture. In J. Sobal & D. Maurer (Eds), *Weighty issues: Fatness and thinness as social problems* (pp. 159–81). New York: Walter de Gruyter.
Austin, S. B. (2001). Population-based prevention of eating disorders: An application of the Rose prevention model. *Preventive Medicine*, 32, 268–83.
Bartky, S. L. (1988). Foucault, femininity and the modernisation of patriarchal power. In I. Diamond & L. Quinby (Eds), *Feminism and Foucault: Reflections on resistance* (pp. 61–86). Boston, MA: Northeastern University Press.
Berg, F. (1999). Health risks associated with weight loss and obesity treatment programs. *Journal of Social Issues*, 55(2), 277–97.
Bordo, S. (1993). *Unbearable weight: Feminism, western culture and the body*. Berkeley, CA: University of California Press.
Bray, A. & Colebrook, C. (1998). The haunted flesh: Corporeal feminism and the politics of (dis)embodiment. *Signs*, 24(1), 35–67.
Burns, M. (2004). Eating like an ox: Femininity and dualistic constructions of bulimia and anorexia. *Feminism & Psychology*, 14(2), 269–95.
Burns, M. (2006). Bodies that speak: Examining the dialogues in research interactions. *Qualitative Research in Psychology*, 3(1), 3–18.

Burns, M. & Gavey, N. (2004). Healthy weight at what cost? Bulimia and a discourse of weight control. *Journal of Health Psychology*, 9(4), 549–65.
Chapman, G. E. (1999). From 'dieting to healthy eating': An exploration of shifting constructions of eating for weight control. In J. Sobal & D. Maurer (Eds), *Interpreting weight: The social management of fatness and thinness* (pp. 73–88). New York: Walter de Gruyter.
Cogan, J. C. (1999). Re-evaluating the weight-centred approach towards health: The need for a paradigm shift. In J. Sobal & D. Maurer (Eds), *Interpreting weight: The social management of fatness and thinness* (pp. 229–53). New York: Walter de Gruyter.
Cosmopolitan. (2001). Cosmo body love. Sydney: Hearst/ACP. October, p. 177.
Davies, D. (1998). Health and the discourse of weight control. In A. Petersen & C. Waddell (Eds), *Health matters: A sociology of illness, prevention, and care* (pp. 141–55). Buckingham: Open University Press.
Featherstone, M., Hepworth, M. & Turner, B. S. (Eds). (1991). *The body: Social process and cultural theory*. London: Sage Publications.
Fit. (2001). Words from the man, the legend, the former surgeon general. New York: Goodman Media Group. April, p. 51.
French, S. A., & Jeffrey, R. W. (1994). Consequences of dieting to lose weight: Effects on physical and mental health. *Health Psychology*, 13, 195–212.
Germov, J. & Williams, L. (1996). The epidemic of dieting women: The need for a sociological approach to food and nutrition. *Appetite*, 27, 97–108.
Gillespie, J. (Executive Producer). (2000). *Generation XXXL* (television broadcast). Auckland: TVNZTVOne.
Hepworth, J. (1999). *The social construction of anorexia nervosa*. London: Sage Publications.
Knight, C. (2001). Heavenly bodies. *Good medicine: Health and beauty*. Sydney: ACP Publishing Pty Ltd. April, pp. 90–2.
Les Mills News, Auckland. (2001). Fat loss vs weight loss. What's happening and who's doing it at Les Mills world of fitness. March, p. 2.
Lupton, D. (1996). *Food, the body and the self*. London: Sage Publications.
Malson, H. (1998). *The thin woman: Feminism, poststructuralism and the social psychology of anorexia nervosa*. London: Routledge.
Malson, H. & Burns, M. (forthcoming). *Critical perspectives on eating dis/orders: An international reader*. London: Psychology Press.
McFarlane, T., Polivy, J. & McCabe, R. (1999). Help, not harm: Psychological foundation for a nondieting approach toward health. *Journal of Social Issues*, 55, 261–76.
Ministry of Health. (2001). *New Zealand Health Strategy. DHB Toolkit: Obesity*. Edition 1.
Neumark-Sztainer, D. & Story, M. (1998). Dieting and binge eating among adolescents: What do they really mean? *Journal of the American Dietetic Association*, 98, 446–50.
Noonan, J. (2001). Girl on the move. *Who Weekly*. NSW: Time Inc. Magazine Company Limited. 12 November, p. 1.
Rodin, J., Silberstein, L. & Streigal-Moore, R. (1985). Women and weight: A normative discontent. In T. Sonderegger (Ed.), *Psychology and gender: Nebraska symposium on motivation* (pp. 267–307). Lincoln, NE: University of Nebraska Press.

Ryan, K. & Carryer, J. (2000). The discursive construction of obesity. *Women's Studies Journal*, 16(1), 32–48.

Spitzack, C. (1990). *Confessing excess: Women and the politics of body reduction*. New York: State University of New York Press.

Swinburn, B., Ashton, T., Gillespie, J., Cox, B., Menon, A., Simmons, D. & Birkbeck, J. (1997). Health care costs of obesity in New Zealand. *International Journal of Obesity*, 21, 891–96.

Turner, B. (1982). The government of the body, medical regimes, and the rationalisation of diet. *British Journal of Sociology*, 33(2), 252–69.

Turner, B. (1991). The discourse of diet. In M. Featherstone, M. Hepworth & B. S. Turner (Eds), *The body: Social process and cultural theory* (pp. 157–69). London: Sage Publications.

Turner, B. (1992). Regulating bodies: Essays in medical sociology. London: Routledge.

Visscher, T. & Seidell, J. (2001). The public health impact of obesity. *Annual Review of Public Health*, 22, 355–75.

Weight Watchers. (2001a). Congratulations for choosing 1,2,3 Success 2000 the points diet that really works! Available from Weight Watchers New Zealand Ltd., PO Box 22403, Christchurch, New Zealand.

Weight Watchers. (2001b). The ultimate slimming and lifestyle magazine. New South Wales: Pacific Client Publishing, March/April.

Weight Watchers International Inc. (1999). *123 Success: 2000 and beyond. Week 1: Getting started*. Australia.

White, P., Young, K. & Gillet, J. (1995). Bodywork as a moral imperative: Some critical notes on health and fitness. *Loisir et Societe/Society and Leisure*, 18(1), 159–82.

8
Sustaining Imbalance – Evidence of Neglect in the Pursuit of Nutritional Health

Lucy Aphramor and Jacqui Gingras

Introduction – taking on energy balance

> I mean the moment when it seems most plain
> is the moment when you must begin again.
> (MacEwen, 1996, p. 70)

As dietetic students, we learnt of a category of patients who presented with 'simple obesity'. Notwithstanding the notoriously high failure rates of treatment, it was these patients who were (and often still are) deemed most suitable for students to advise when first on placement. The advice given would be underpinned by the so-called energy balance equation. This holds that body weight is a function of the amount of calories consumed minus the amount of calories expended. A diet that gives a daily 600-calorie deficit would be typical of the sort of calculations we were trained to undertake, planning individualised meal plans designed to achieve a 'safe' and sustainable weight loss of 1–2lb a week. Granted some fat people might have an Eating Disorder, but the majority needed to be told (how) to eat less calories and/or exercise more: it really was that simple. Failure might arise from an individual's lack of adherence but the effectiveness of the approach itself needed no scrutiny: assuming someone stuck to the prescribed regime, weight loss was deemed to be possible, predictable and profitable for health.

As part of our professional education and socialisation we were familiar with the pitfalls of 'non-compliance' and understood that willpower, moral turpitude and ignorance were particularly relevant to prognosis in weight management. In fact, as we were to discover, our efforts failed (with) patient after patient. Instead of marking steady regular weight loss we heard repeated stories of dieting 'success' followed by weight gain, guilt, depression and a pervasive sense of lives-on-hold. We were adept purveyors of the energy balance metaphor, yet something didn't add up. On balance, no one really seemed much healthier, let alone happier. It wasn't as if we were bad dietitians having both excelled in our dietetic exams and placements. Our clients were characterised by determination, fortitude, faith in us and a good working knowledge of energy balance. Their narratives produced a widening sense of experiential/theoretical disconnect creating an unease that we gradually came to trust and explore.

In this chapter we look at reasons for this disconnect, re-examining the effectiveness, and the effects, of health practitioners' practices concerning fatness by bringing into the foreground some of the hidden ideological assumptions our work embodies around fatness, science, health, ethnicity, class, language, patriarchy and power.

Trained in similar intellectual traditions as dietitians in England and Canada we recognise that ours is always going to be a somewhat parochial view. Our hope is that this chapter encourages constructive scepticism and collective activism concerning any deficiencies in dietetic practice and theory, seeding the way for a socially integrated feminist science and more respectful, ethical and effective interventions in the name of public health nutrition.

On balance: Clinical practice versus the evidence base

> ... basic scientific ideas are protected by taboo reactions which are no weaker than are the taboo reactions in so-called primitive societies ... the similarities between science and myth are indeed astonishing.
> (Feyerband as quoted in Beer, 1999, p. 200)

What seems remarkable is that the evidence base from which the 'energy balance approach' is taught strongly demonstrates that ours were not isolated experiences. It has been consistently shown that interventions designed to produce weight loss by encouraging change in lifestyle choices (dietary restraint and/or exercise) are not effective in their primary aim, as acknowledged in UK clinical guidelines on 'obesity' (BMJ, 2000). In fact, Jain (2006), discussing her synthesis of systematic reviews of 'obesity treatment and prevention', writes: 'Rather than showing what does work for preventing and treating obesity, research to date shows us clearly what does not' (p. 1389). Moreover, Jain continues: 'Although these were the best studies available according to the principles of evidence based medicine, many did not fulfil its requirements ... These flaws bias the results and can exaggerate the effects' (pp. 1388–89). Similarly, *The Manual of Dietetic Practice* (2003), a regularly revised comprehensive textbook for dietitians in the UK, reports 'a dearth of long-term prospective studies in which weight has been successfully lost and maintained alongside data in relation to health outcomes' (p. 464). That said, there follow several pages outlining assessment and treatment protocols aimed at realising this very impossibility: 'to improve health through the achievement and maintenance of a healthy weight' (p. 466).

The point is that diets don't work. We're not suggesting that nobody ever loses weight, but clarify that it is currently impossible to make a case recommending weight loss based on studies of clinical effectiveness (the extent to which an intervention improves the outcome for patients in practice) because the evidence clearly and consistently shows that the vast majority of people who engage in weight-loss behaviour are very unsuccessful. True, there is a USA national registry of people who have successfully lost weight, yet the numbers of registrants as a percentage of the total number of people who engage in weight-loss behaviour helps illustrate the emperor's nakedness. Solovay (2000, p. 192) questions the lack of rigour for inclusion, unusual among scientific databases, and suggests that this leads to over-inflated numbers – 3000 registrants in a population of over 300 million people where $50 billion is spent annually on weight-loss products. The myth of the energy balance equation as an effective, scientifically legitimate means of prescribing weight loss is a hallmark of dietetic theory and practice sustained by obedience to biomedical historicity that flies in the face of practical reasoning and evidence-based practice.

All of this hangs a question mark over the ethics of current practice. Simply put, one logic pathway justifying weight-loss interventions assumes that (a) fatness arises primarily from rational lifestyle choices (b) fatness is always detrimental to health (c) encouraging weight loss is effective and promotes health. And although (c) is deductively valid, despite sound argument, this conclusion – the conclusion underpinning dietetic anti-obesity campaigns – is a false one.

Measuring health: Fitness outweighs fatness

> The data linking overweight and death, as well as the data showing the beneficial effects of weight loss, are limited, fragmentary and often ambiguous.
> (Kassirer & Angell, 1998, p. 54)

Contemporary dietetic education seeks to address the high failure rates of weight reduction interventions by improving students' behaviour change skills. This response concretises the myth of energy balance as effective for weight control and skirts engagement with the fundamental issues debated in this book and elsewhere. First, good listening skills taught as part of a behaviour change toolbox are an oxymoron. Fiumara (1990) argues that the operationalisation of listening mitigates against us hearing anything that we are not already tuned into

> ... for as long as we move in a noosphere that is saturated with both scientific and intellectual discourses constantly reaching out to inform, permeate and mould, the process of listening can never be more than a minimal philosophical aspiration or the concern of a minority.
>
> (p. 19)

In her discussion of the implications of a logocratic culture she explains:

> The expansion of a kind of knowledge that is capable of moulding but not of generative listening appears to be linked with an underlying strategy of *fac et excusa* (first do and then justify) transposed onto the epistemic level.
>
> (p. 22)

Fiumara (1990) also avers that a tradition of reductive reasoning, the template of masculinist science, not only promotes a non-listening rationality but also rational suppression. For the same reasons it is futile in the long term to turn to psychology for motivational strategies while we neglect to educate ourselves about practices for a critical liberation psychology (Moane, 2003). Instead, as we have discussed elsewhere (Aphramor & Gingras, in press), 'normal science' would have us seeking 'the behavioural equivalents of protease inhibitors' (Buchanan, 2000, p. 46). As Kelly and Charlton note (as quoted in Popay, Williams, Thomas & Gatrell, 1998), striving to draw maps that integrate the subjective experiences of individuals and the influence of structures of power and control in which they are embedded from an interactionist perspective prevents us from reducing people to system outcomes: 'Such dynamic and reciprocal analysis of the individual set into context ought to be at the heart of health promotion ... Developing this, and making it work, is the task ahead' (p. 90). Second, and expanding on the above, in upholding a focus on weight, the response lends credence to the notion of fatness *per se*, measured as body mass index (BMI) or waist circumference, as a static reliable indicator of health status. Yet the BMI category 'obese' is historically and culturally specific. It's not only that the measurements used to define who is diagnosed as 'obese' vary across time (and in response to corporate pressure [Moynihan, 2006]) but that particular defining intersections of knowledge and power construct fatness as if it were unitary, timeless and universal, which of course it isn't. And focusing on reducing fatness/BMI also implies that all fat people are unhealthy because they are fat. It's a bit like saying all old people are unhealthy because they are old. It would be easier to argue the latter if we viewed older people as a homogenous group and restricted our studies to older people seeking medical advice, and discounted any effects of ageism, poverty, isolation, elder abuse and the results of the Masters Games (an international sporting event for older athletes), but it wouldn't be scientifically valid. Readers unfamiliar with critical fat studies may be surprised to learn that the framing of fatness as pathology, a framing which is constantly reinforced every time we use the words 'obesity' or 'overweight', is persuasively contested within the established scientific community. We provide a few key examples by way of disrupting received conceptual maps to enhance engagement with our argument.

Fitness, for example, is classically invoked as a parameter to illustrate fat bias. Thus, studies over many years involving several thousands of adults (mostly white, non-smoking people) conclude that men and women classified as 'overweight' or 'obese' who exercise regularly have lower all-cause death rates than thin men and women who do not exercise and are unfit. In one study of 21,000 men of varying body sizes, Barlow and colleagues (1995) found that unfit lean men with BMIs of ≤ 25 had twice the risk of mortality from all causes than fit men with BMIs of 27.8 and greater. Blair and colleagues (1996) found that cardiorespiratory fitness was predictive of reduced risk for cardiovascular disease and all-cause mortality across all weight categories. The American Dietetic Association's (ADA's) position statement on weight loss (ADA, 2002) acknowledges that fat, fit people have lower all-cause morbidity and mortality risk than lean sedentary people. Here, if we're looking for a single determinant that impacts on health outcomes, it's fitness, not fatness. Consider also the American study of over 15,000 adults which concluded that diabetes, not fatness, increases risk of death in middle age (Slynkova, Mannino, Martin, Morehead & Doherty, 2006).

The associated assumption that unhealthy fat people need to lose weight to improve health is also refuted. The Scottish Intercollegiate Guidelines on Obesity report (SIGN, 1996), used to support weight loss in the UK, states that a healthy diet and exercise have marked health benefits for fat people independent of weight loss and the ADA guidelines mentioned above note that there is strong evidence that physical activity increases fitness with or without weight loss. Switching from a low to a high fruit-and-vegetable intake (unless contraindicated) is conducive to good health whatever your weight. *The Manual of Dietetic Practice* (2003) tells us that 'improvements in cholesterol profile have been shown to be more directly related to improved dietary habits than to amount of weight lost' (p. 479).

Behind the advice to cut energy intake is another belief that fatness primarily results from behavioural dysregulation of calorie consumption – that is, all fat people eat too much. This makes for a tidy 'energy balance' metaphor but in so doing eclipses pertinent research on the effects of foetal nutrition, sleep deprivation, childhood circumstances and inter-generational health on adult body weight and health (Aphramor, 2005; Wadsworth, Kuh, Richards & Hardy, 2006).

The cornerstone assumption that weight loss is healthy is also strongly debated. For example, Sørensen, Rissanen, Korkeila & Kaprio (2005) argue that '[d]eliberate weight loss in overweight [sic] individuals without known co-morbidities may be hazardous in the long term' (p. 3). So too, weight cycling, or yo-yo dieting, which the UK National Centre for Clinical Excellence recognises as an almost inevitable consequence of weight loss behaviour (BMJ, 2000), is associated with all-cause mortality and coronary mortality in particular (British Nutrition Foundation, 1999). Hardly a recipe for health.

The energy balance conceit perpetuates the notion of fatness/BMI as something constructively indicative of health, eclipsing people's lived realities as gendered, situated bodies in an inequitable – and fat-phobic – world. It dissolves power. Energy balance is a compact house with little room to introduce clutter. That said, given the serious attention now being given to abdominal adiposity as a risk indicator, it behoves us to mention the research (albeit a single study and apparently not repeated) linking women's experience of racism with unhealthy fat storage independent of weight (Butler , Tull, Chambers & Taylor, 2002). And imagine, despite the very strong link in the public, and medical, imagination between fatness and several disease conditions, a study of 8000 adults and 4000 children in England from Black Caribbean, Black African, Pakistani, Indian, Bangladeshi, Chinese and Irish groups found that among the groups surveyed 'obesity [sic] does not seem to have a clear association with' diabetes, coronary heart disease and stroke (Anon, 2006). Perhaps, then, neither energy metabolism nor dietetic theorising on fatness happens in splendid isolation.

The outcomes of dietetic health promotion

> The lived reality of fatness is a socially contingent phenomenon rather than a measurable biological fact.
>
> (Monaghan, under review)

If not weight loss, what do we achieve by our interventions? Figure 8.1 is typical of both the dietetic and more general health promotion resources developed to 'tackle' fatness. The intended message, reiterated in campaign literature, is to encourage men to make dietary and

Figure 8.1 'Size Matters' Leaflet (BDA, 2004)

(unidentified) lifestyle changes depicted as highly likely to lead to a substantial change in their appearance. They have authoratively and repeatedly been told that this change, that is, thinness, is necessary for health in relation to heart disease, stroke, diabetes and self-esteem. Thinness is presented as synonymous with health and as well within reach. The overarching message of 'size matters' indulges a discursive obsession with the mechanics of (hetero)sexual performativity, seamlessly contributing to the anxieties generated around the body and risk in consumerist culture.

Red, amber, green: prescriptive injunctions for a marketplace approach to health. Fat people are slovenly, they greedily spill food, they mostly eat chips and burgers, they grab takeaways, they don't care about their personal appearance. They don't care. Or perhaps they don't get it. If only they would wise up and take personal responsibility for food choices and controlling their appetites they could be thin – and they could fit in. Red, don't go there: fatness disparaged, self-esteem denied, the fat person cruelly stereotyped as a matter of course. Health is about will power, individual responsibility, thinness. Thinness makes a man more upright. It is a sign of civilisation, something to aspire to, says the aesthete, wiping his lips with no food in sight as he steps righteously into the shoes of *homo sapiens* away from the shadow of his fat evolutionary ancestor. Intended or unintended, the unarticulated references to intelligence, civilised norms and developmental position have alarming resonances with a colonial mentality. Fatness is Othered. Respect and trust in health care, identified as essential to empowerment (Ekpé, 2001), are given short shrift. Here, comically oversimplifying fatness has real and painful consequences. Green: a naive reading of health promotion that we can no longer realistically stick to.

In its mechanistic simplicity the 'energy balance mind-set' is a metonym for much of the limitations of public health nutrition practices dealing with fatness. It sustains a partial cartoon-like view of individual and societal nutritional health by obscuring the interconnectedness of science/people/the social body. Vividly portraying the myth in action, this type of 'before and after' diet representation, promulgated and encouraged by nutrition professionals (Gardner, 2005), escalates size prejudice (Geier, Schwartz & Brownell, 2003). Dovetailing with healthist ideologies media representations reassure us of the power of the individuals to return themselves to health. Never mind that '[often] it seems we have [weight-loss] policy looking for an evidence base' (Anderson, 2005). *Fac et excusa*.

Dietitians, personal responsibility and anti-healthist approaches

> Watch your waist size; it's time to deflate those spare tyres to reduce your health risk.
>
> (BDA, 2004)

> It's about making you feel bad about yourself. That cannot be about anything else than saying 'at the moment you are not acceptable' can it?
>
> (Research participant's response to above, Aphramor, under review)

When public health focuses primarily on interventions to change an individual's behaviour, the outcomes are healthist. Healthism as defined by Crawford (1980) is '... the preoccupation with personal health as a primary – often *the* primary – focus for the definition and achievement of well-being; a goal which is to be attained primarily through the modification of life styles, with or without therapeutic help. The aetiology of disease may be seen as complex, but healthism treats individual behaviour, attitudes, and emotions as the relevant symptoms needing attention' (1980, p. 368, italics in the original). A single-minded focus on treating an individual's health through reliance on the energy-balance equation leads practitioners to develop expectations of that individual that are unrealistic and healthist. For individuals, the discrepancy between expectations and actual experience is in itself detrimental to health (Freund & McGuire, 1995) and the overall iatrogenic consequences of encouraging weight loss are far-reaching (Aphramor, 2005).

This is an individualist project. As Roy (2004) claims: 'The discourse of healthism places responsibility squarely on the individual who is encouraged to exercise self-control, personal determination, and self-denial in all aspects of life' (p. 28). When we recognise health as socially constituted, we see that health cannot be 'achieved' without acknowledging the context in which we live; a context that is complex and presents contradictions to health-achieving behaviours. As concerned with a functional and respectful approach to health promotion practice, we can not accept healthist approaches, much like we can not accept sexist, heterosexist, ageist, racist, ableist or sizeist approaches. Working in healthist structures can lead to distrust and scepticism on the part of those who seek our support. Nyquist-Potter (2002) reminds us that '[given] current societal conditions, where power, privilege, and oppression are realities of our political and social lives, trust is something few of us can afford to offer innocently and unreflectively' (p. 10). Lack of social trust, arising from all forms of power abuse, including size discrimination, has long been associated with higher rates of most major causes of death, including coronary heart disease, malignant neoplasms, strokes and infant mortality (Kawachi, 1997). Trust is central to the relational encounter we work to establish in dietetic practice, and when we persist in promoting weight loss as the path to health despite the evidence to the contrary, we risk disappointing self and Other (Gingras, 2005).

Viewing the attainment and maintenance of health as a personal responsibility may well be politically expedient in capitalist societies but it's hard to see how relying on measures of the commodified body as if it was in solitary confinement is going to advance our understanding of real lives and well-being.

Coronary heart disease (CHD), a condition popularly linked with poor health behaviours and fatness (BDA, 2004), shows a marked social gradient. Controlling for health behaviours reduces the gradient by only 16 percent (Chandola, Brunner & Marmot, 2006). The biomedical literature elucidates some of the other 84 percent as pathways that link inflammatory changes arising from care-giver burden (Vitaliano, Scanlon, Zhang, Savage, Hirsch & Siegler, 2002), air pollution (Pope, Burnett, Thurston, Thun, Calle, Krewski & Godleski, 2004), loneliness (Steptoe, Owen, Kunz-Ebrecht & Bryson, 2004), control at work (Chandola et al., 2006) and sleep deprivation (Van Cauter & Spiegel, 1999) with CHD. Focusing on fatness, food and fitness collapses complexity and works to disqualify other verities. In this way it can create a circular argument that demonises fatness as it discursively dismisses the influence of class, control, gender and relationships in an unproblematised rally against lifestyle imbalance.

Fugelli (2006) extols: 'Like medical crusaders, we invade the lives of the heathens and hedonists armed with the health belief model, the theory of reasoned action, the social cognitive theory, the stages of change model, the diffusion of innovation theory – with these Bibles we try to convert the hedonists into healthy souls and sound bodies' (p. 271). The purpose of these models is to change health behaviour, yet in the absence of reflexivity, our motivations go unchecked and the consequences of our oppressive practices go unattended. We faced similar ethical dilemmas when we began to confront racism as a society (although we have more work to do in dietetics regarding racism, sexism, heterosexism etc). It is now time to confront our ever-fanatical reliance on well-intentioned shaming, blaming and guilting to get populations to eat more vegetables and to move their bodies. As Fugelli (2006) urges: 'We must be alert to a medico-moralistic police state silently emerging, hidden behind the holy mantra: health' (p. 271). It is disingenuous to construct ourselves as influential experts on fatness on the one hand and distance ourselves from the most damaging aspects of an anti-fat culture on the other.

Exposing deception, reconfiguring health

> The biggest contribution government could make to improving future health and reducing inequalities would be to make gender-equitable parenting and socialisation the top national political priority.
> (McDonald & Scott-Samuel, 2004, p. 12)

The statement of principles known at the Ottawa Charter for Health Promotion is internationally accepted as the guiding framework for health promotion activity. It describes five approaches: building healthy public policy, creating supportive environments, strengthening community action, developing personal skills and reorienting health services (Speller, Learmonth & Harrison, 1997). Despite authorative calls to refocus interventions 'upstream', dietetics' anti-obesity strategies focus on the individual. Policy level interventions often mention the environment but only with regard to altering energy balance. Maternal nutrition and poverty are less frequently included and even then the goal is thinness. We have argued that anti-obesity behaviour is itself unnecessary, unethical, ineffective and dangerous. It also functions strongly against a reorientation of health services.

A recent internationally focused edition of the journal *Health at Every Size* (HAES, 2006) presents an overview of responses to the problem of weight-centred thinking. HAES is a philosophy which is based on the belief that healthy bodies come in all shapes and sizes, and that good health is more a function of social, physical and emotional well-being than of being a certain weight. It holds with the tenets of size acceptance that accept helping people feel good about their bodies as an end in itself with the knock-on effect that it is likely to enable health-promoting behaviour. The journal exists to further 'the search for truth and understanding. ... Recognizing that weight is an easily-exploitable health and social concern HAES is also committed to exposing deception, reshaping detrimental social attitudes, and promoting good health for people of every size and shape' (HAES, 2006, inside page).

Aspects of the HAES approach are alluded to in *The Manual of Dietetic Practice* (2003) in a section called 'the evolution of a new weight paradigm' (pp. 479–81) which is seen as encompassing two main movements: size acceptance and non-dieting. Filtered through the lens of mainstream anti-fat rhetoric there's nothing new about the end result: weight loss goals are modified but remain prioritised, attention to emotional wellbeing becomes about managing 'the psychological consequences of obesity [*sic*] ... so that patients can sustain the continuous effort needed for treatment success' (p. 481). HAES, seen as another weight-loss tool, becomes a blunderbuss.

This resistance to health-promoting paradigms varies between dietitians and within dietetic organisations. It is worrying that mainstream dietetics, although not unusual in being fat-phobic (Aphramor, 2006), is professionally charged with intervening in the health of fat people. Efforts by individual and small groups of dietitians to raise awareness of size discrimination and (the need for) alternative approaches (Gingras, 2000; Ikeda, Hayes, Satter, Parham, Kratina, Woolsey, Lowey, & Tribole, 1999) have yet to receive the profession's support. In a 'stages of change' reading dietetics as a profession is pre-contemplative and readily able to rationalise the contradictions that keep us stuck. Collective docility and denial of our clinical experiences might keep us a conditional place at the top table but it doesn't transform.

Bodies of knowledge

> I had no special training and my own training was against me.
> (Rich, 1994, p. 145)

At no time during our four-year course did it ever occur to us to question the diagnosis, treatment or terminology around 'obesity'. Our educators passed on their unquestioned acceptance of the appropriateness of energy balance, the effectiveness of dieting and the value/s of positivistic science more generally. It would have been off the horizon to consider that ideological prejudices influenced biomedical narratives on fatness. This philosophy also immunised dietetic practice from scrutiny of risk and erased issues of collective professional accountability.

Given the lack of critical awareness and the absence of conceptual or scientific rigour that continue to characterise our weight-loss campaigns, it is somewhat ironic that, at least in England, some dietitians have sought 'to maintain a medical mystique that distinguishes dietitians as the authority on food and distances them from the general public or other professionals' (Scott, Verne & Fox, 2005, p. 251). We contend that this fear and insularity is part of a bigger problem that we locate in the unquestioning allegiance to a masculinist science and the patriarchal professional mores that keep out unwanted insights.

Everyday dietitians sit with people who have not lost weight despite intervention; who have tried laxatives, diuretics, vomiting and smoking to lose weight; who are ashamed of their fat and not-so-fat bodies; who feel a failure because they have 'no willpower'; who have lost weight only to inevitably regain – and then some – who know someone who lost weight and kept it off which proves anyone can do it, and whose doctor or consultant, partner or teacher has told them to get thin out of concern for their health. (How) do we hear, or honour, these stories?

Against a current trend for patient involvement, the narratives of fat people in health care seem to fall on stony ground (Aphramor, under review). Yet quality care requires a body of knowledge that reflects the experiences of marginalised populations. It means paying attention to the extent that people are 'stereotyped, rendered voiceless, silenced, not taken seriously, peripheralized, homogenized, ignored, dehumanized and ordered around' (Meleis & Im, 1999, p. 96). Challenges to convention have met with accusations of organisational insubordination and professional irresponsibility (Gingras, 2005). We are encouraged to be silent about the extent of silencing. In other words, '... [dietetic associations have] learned not to bite the hand that feeds [them]' (Rampton & Stauber, 2001, p. 165). The irony of this current dilemma is that Dietitians of Canada promotes dietitians as the most *trusted* source of information on food and nutrition (Dietitians of Canada, 1997, emphasis added). Our credibility is contingent on our trustworthiness. If we cannot be trusted, our *raison d'être* is compromised.

When we instruct clients to follow cognitive appraisals of 'need to eat' rather than re-educating them to trust visceral cues of hunger, we distance the client from the knowledge contained in the bodyself. We teach them that their own body as a source of knowledge is inherently unreliable. Undermining self-trust catalyses a hierarchical, disempowering dependence on expert knowledge.

At what cost?

> Obesity, the result of private actions by individuals, imposes [avoidable] costs on others through higher taxes, or higher insurance premia, and, given the ever-present waiting list for hospital

care, through increased pain and suffering on others arising from delays in treatment.
(The Report of the National Taskforce on Obesity, 2005, p. 57)

Deservingness and financial culpability feature regularly in health promotions' moral subtext on fatness, which given the socially stratified realities of fatness is confusedly misleading. Cost comes into other health equations. Malnutrition costs the UK twice the amount that fatness does (BAPEN, 2005) but typically the call is for the re-allocation of resources, invoking empathy for a marginalised group. The UK costs of mental ill health are now approaching £100 billion a year – an amount far in excess of fatness' budget. It is a concern that '[m]any explanations have been offered for this trend – from globalisation and changes in economic stability to changing social trends and diminishing interpersonal networks' (*Feeding Minds*, 2006, p. 5). Here we have healthcare demonstrating commitment to a situated, integrated and compassionate understanding, a perspective reflected later on in a discussion of the links between food and mental well-being.

Even restricting ourselves to the growing body of research that illustrates the relationship between our diet and our feelings and behaviours, it becomes obvious that what we eat is affected by why and how we eat, both of which may also have an impact on our mental health. For example, if we see food purely as a means of 're-fuelling', our meal times will affect us differently than if we see food as a vital source of nourishment for our body and mind. Similarly, if we eat alone, the psychosocial benefits of food may be different than if we eat with others (*Feeding Minds*, 2006, p. 17).

Mental health operates as much within market-driven forces as nutritional public health and yet this is science in a different voice. It sounds potentially less destructive and seems to arise from a more robust and reliable premise. Revisioning the particularities and needs of people who are frequently belittled or blamed can open a window onto creative possibilities and change what can be accomplished. Rather than uncoupling the contemporaneous rise in fatness and mental health problems, reframing questions away from weight loss to improved social and personal well-being might help uncover common pathways and effective solutions.

The obesogenic environment is often presented as fact, when in fact its presuppositions are uncorroborated. For example, recreational physical activity may have increased in step with claims for increasing fatness (Gard, 2004). Moving away from the metaphorical power of this unsubstantiated construct could lead to more effective health-promoting interventions: alternative mindsets are available as 'healthy neighbourhoods

(Cummins & Macintyre, 2006), mindful practitioners (Reason, 1988; Aphramor & Gingras, in press), Health at Every Size informed practice (Gingras, 2006), the interactive biopsychosocial model (Tessler, Laumann, Levinson, & Waite, 2003) and engagement with coherent critical pedagogy for community empowerment (Ledwith, 1997). Rather than concealing, or even exacerbating social divisions, working within these frameworks may enable effective and anti-oppressive dietetic and health promotion interventions.

A view from the Edgelands

> One must be willing 'to begin an argument', and so formulate questions that will redefine the context, displace the terms of the metaphors and make up new ones.
> (de Lauretis as quoted in Spanier, 1995, p. 9)

Where does this leave us? In the UK and Canada, as in many other countries, it may be that some groups of people, but not all, are getting fatter. Concomitantly the incidence of non-communicable diseases such as heart disease, diabetes, stroke and depression remains high, alongside eating distress and health inequalities. Current interventions targeting fatness as culprit are notoriously unsuccessful and even counterproductive. A rich source of new insight, interprofessional exchange and dialogue may further integrate, and hence enhance, approaches to the theory and practice of nutritional health promotion. So a prerequisite to effective health-promoting practice concerning (fat and thin) bodies is a renegotiation of what counts as valid knowledge and learning communities at the level of the profession. This maintains a commitment to evidence-based practice that openly acknowledges controversy about the construct of knowledge, the power of ideology and the role of the non-rational or unarticulated – emotions, imagination, creativity, personal and professional vulnerabilities – in guiding our inquiries (Avis & Freshwater, 2006). Using a transformative education paradigm, MacDonald (2002) highlights the limited recognition of 'unlearning' in the health professions, arguing the value of safe and discerning 'communities of unlearning'. Within a healthist framework the individual dietitian would be held responsible for changing his/her department and ultimately the profession. While personal change may result in more health affirmative client–therapist interactions, we contend that sustainable professional change requires transformation at a systemic level in organisational knowledge creation where, as a 'knowing organization' (Choo, 1998), dietetics mobilises the expertise of its members to induce innovation and creativity effectively integrating sense making, knowledge creation and decision making.

How can dietetics achieve a practice that recognises and challenges ideological norms rather than entrenching them? What will enable us to move beyond our penchant for decontextualised data towards a stronger reliance on integrated evidence and more critical appraisal? Throughout we have foregrounded how the energy balance metaphor constrains our thinking and the research questions we pose. Instituted as the perfect yardstick of understanding its clipped logic is easily accepted because it obtains immediate resonance with the cognitive structures that produced it, in which case, reflexive analysis is evidently called for (Wacquant & Bourdieu, 1992, p. 168). Other suitably unsuitable metaphors enter nutritional discourse equally unremarked: the arena is filled with battling, tackling, fighting talk in the war on 'obesity'. How a militaristic approach is going to help anyone make peace with their bodies or food is unclear. Meanwhile, the societies we refer to in this chapter abhor fatness and interdependence. They value streamlined, lean, firm, visibly efficient, rational, independent and self-contained businesses, bodies and data sets. Nutritional discourse speaks this realist, materialist, capitalist, healthist position on fatness and disseminates it in its perception of possible research directions. More particularly, the permeable, leaky, messy, emotional – female – body is despised and feared as incalculable and non-controllable (Shildrick, 1997). It is acknowledging the power of this symbolic imposition of gender-polarised and fat-phobic schemata that we highlight as being crucial to altered directions in fat-bashing. Perhaps it is partly the unconscious lure of this metaphor that impedes interdisciplinary dialogue. Either way, it is a deep unconscious part of the force field in which our practice evolves. The reality is that the language we choose incarnates our preconceptions and prefigures possibility. As poets, as well as dietitians, we would like to add this complication.

> others have dreamt of this vastness
> I know I am not alone, diffident still I try hard to believe it
> (Aphramor, 2005a)

References

American Dietetic Association (ADA). (2002). Weight management: position paper. *Journal of the American Dietetic Association*, 102, 1145–55.

Anderson, A. (2005). Obesity prevention and management – evidence and policy. *Journal of Human Nutrition and Dietetics*, 18, 1–2.

Anon. (2006). Health survey for England 2004: Health of ethnic minorities – full report. Retrieved 1 November 2006 from http://www.ic.nhs.uk/pubs/health-survey2004ethnicfull

Aphramor, L. (2005) Is a weight-centred health framework salutogenic? Some thoughts on unhinging certain dietary ideologies. *Social Theory and Health*, 3(4), 315–40.

Aphramor, L. (2005a). *An audience with uncertainty*. IAQS, (Directed by P. Allender) Ellen Terry Building, Coventry University. 25 November.

Aphramor, L. (2006). A report on size discrimination in employment and in society. Commissioned by the Welsh Development Agency SME Equality Project. Unpublished.

Aphramor, L. (under review). Size discrimination affects health and health-seeking behaviour. *Journal of Human Nutrition and Dietetics*.

Aphramor, L. & Gingras, J. R. (in press). That remains to be said: Disappeared feminist discourses on fat in dietetic theory and practice. In S. Solovay & E. Rothblum (Eds), *The fat studies reader* CA, USA: The University of California Press.

Avis, M. & Freshwater, D. (2006). Evidence for practice, epistemology, and critical reflection. *Nursing Philosophy*, 7, 216–24.

BAPEN. (2005). The cost of disease-related malnutrition in the UK and economic considerations for the use of oral nutritional supplements (ONS) in adults. M. Elia, (Chairman and editor) R. Stratton, C. Russell, C. Green, F. Pan. BAPEN, UK. www.bapen.org.uk

Barlow, C. E., Kohl, H. W., Gibbons, L. W. & Blair S. W. (1995). Physical fitness, mortality and obesity. *International Journal of Obesity*, 19 (Suppl.), S41–S44.

Beer, G. (1999). *Open fields. Science in cultural encounter*. London: Open University Press.

Blair, S. N., Kampert, J. B., Kohl, H. W. III., Barlow, C. E., Macera, C. A., Paffenbarger, R. S. Jr., Gibbons, L. W. (1996). Influences of cardiorespiratory fitness and other precursors on cardiovascular disease and all-cause mortality in men and women. *Journal of the American Medical Association*, 276, 205–10.

British Dietetic Association (BDA). (2004). *Size matters campaign literature*. London: BDA.

British Medical Journal. (2000). Clinical evidence. Concise version. London: British Medical Journal Publishing Group.

British Nutrition Foundation. (1999). *Obesity*. The Report of the British Nutrition Foundation Task Force. London: Blackwell Science.

Buchanan, D. (2000). *An ethic for health promotion: Rethinking the sources of human well-being*. Oxford: Oxford University Press.

Butler, C., Tull, E. S., Chambers, E. C. & Taylor, J. (2002). Internalized racism, body fat distribution, and abnormal fasting glucose among African-Caribbean women in Dominica, West Indies. *Journal of the National Medical Association*, 94(3), 143–8.

Chandola, T., Brunner, E. & Marmot, M. (2006). Chronic stress at work and the metabolic syndrome: Prospective study. *British Medical Journal*, 332, 521–5.

Choo, C. W. (1998). *The knowing organization: How organizations use information to construct meaning, create knowledge, and make decisions*. New York: Oxford University Press.

Crawford, R. (1980). Healthism and the medicalization of everyday life. *International Journal of Health Services*, 10(3), 365–88.

Cummins, S. & Macintyre, S. (2006). Food environments and obesity – neighbourhood or nation? *International Journal of Epidemiology*, 35(1), 100–4.

Dietitians of Canada. (1997). *DC corporate profile*. Retrieved 10 February 2004 from http://www.dietitians.ca/dc/index.html

Ekpé, H. (2001). Empowerment for adults with chronic mental health problems and obesity. *Nursing Standard*. 15(39) 37–42.

Feeding Minds. (2006). The impact of food on mental health. London: Mental Health Foundation.

Fiumara, G. (1990). *The other side of language. A philosophy of listening*. Translated by C. Lambert. Routledge: London.

Freund, P. & McGuire, M. (1995). *Health, illness and the social body: A critical sociology*. New Jersey, NY: Prentice Hall.

Fugelli, P. (2006). The zero-vision: Potential side effects of communicating health perfection and zero risk. *Patient Education and Counseling*, 60, 267–71.

Gard, M. (2004). An elephant in the room and a bridge too far, or physical education and the 'obesity epidemic'. In J. Evans, B. Davies & J. Wright (Eds), *Body knowledge and control. Studies in the sociology of physical education and health* (pp. 66–82). London: Routledge.

Gardner, E. (2005). British Dietetic Association food first 2005 – Weight Wise@Work Campaign evaluation report. Retrieved 20 November 2006 from http://www.bda.uk.com/weightwise.html

Geier, A. B., Schwartz, M. B. & Brownell, K. D. (2003). 'Before and after' diet advertisements escalate weight stigma. *Eating and Weight Disorders*, 8, 282–8.

Gingras, J. R. (2000). From self-awareness to size acceptance: Deepening your experience with health-centred philosophy. *Practice – A Supplement to the Canadian Journal of Dietetic Practice and Research*, 12, 6–7.

Gingras, J. R. (2005). Evoking trust in the nutrition counsellor: Why should we be trusted? *Journal of Agricultural and Environmental Ethics*, 18, 57–74.

Gingras, J. R. (2006). Throwing their weight around: Canadians take on health at every size. *Health at Every Size Journal*, 19(4), 195–206.

Health at Every Size (HAES). (2006). HAES around the world. *Health at Every Size Journal*, 19, 4, inside page.

Ikeda, J., Hayes, D., Satter, E., Parham, E. S., Kratina, K., Woolsey, M., Lowey, M. & Tribole, E. (1999). A commentary on the new obesity guidelines from NIH. *Journal of the American Dietetic Association*, 99, 918–20.

Jain, A. (2006). Treating obesity in individuals and populations. *British Medical Journal*, 331, 1387–90.

Kassirer, J. P. & Angell, M. (1998). Losing weight – An ill-fated new year's resolution. *New England Journal of Medicine*, 338(1), 52–4.

Kawachi, (1997). *Community action for mental health*. London: Health Education Authority.

Ledwith, M. (1997). *Participating in transformation: Towards a working model of community empowerment*. Birmingham: Venture Press.

MacDonald, G. (2002). Transformative unlearning: Safety, discernment and communities of learning. *Nursing Inquiry*, 9(3), 170–8.

MacEwen, G. (1996). *Selected poetry of Gwendolyn MacEwen*. Virago: London.

McDonald, R., & Scott-Samuel, A. (2004, 24 May). Missed opportunities? Wanless and the white paper. *Public Health News*, 10–12.

Manual of Dietetic Practice. (2003). B. Thomas (Ed.), 3rd edition. Oxford: Blackwell Publishing.

Meleis, A. I. & Im, E. (1999). Transcending marginalization in knowledge development. *Nursing Inquiry*, 6, 94–102.

Moane, G. (2003). Bridging the personal and the political: Practices for a liberation psychology. *American Journal of Community Psychology*, 31(1/2), 91–101.

Monaghan, L. (under review). Everyday bigness, fitness and sport: Physical activity and the questionability of anti-obesity campaigns.

Moynihan, R. (2006). Obesity task force linked to WHO takes 'millions' from drug firms. *British Medical Journal*, 332, 1412.

Nyquist-Potter, N. (2002). *How can I be trusted? A virtue theory of trustworthiness*. Lanham, MY: Rowman and Littlefield Publishers.

Obesity: The policy challenges – The report of the national taskforce on obesity. (2005) Department of Health and Children. Ireland.

Popay, J., Williams, G., Thomas, C. & Gatrell, A. (1998). Theorising inequalities in health: The place of lay knowledge. In M. Bartley, D. Blane & G. D. Smith (Eds), *The sociology of health inequalities* (pp. 59–84). London: Blackwell Publishers.

Pope, C. A., Burnett, R. T., Thurston, G. D., Thun, M. J., Calle, E. E., Krewski, D. & Godleski, J. J. (2004). Cardiovascular mortality and long-term exposure to particulate air pollution: Epidemiological evidence of general pathophysiological pathways of disease. *Circulation*, 109(1), 71–7.

Rampton, S. & Stauber, J. (2001). *Trust us, we're experts! How industry manipulates science and gambles with your future*. New York: Penguin Putnam.

Reason, P. (1988). *Human inquiry in action*. Sage: London.

Rich, A. (1994). *The fact of a doorframe. Poems selected and new 1950–1984*. New York: WW Norton & Company.

Roy, S. C. (2004). 'Fifty-two easy steps to great health': Rrepresentations of health in English–Canadian women's magazines. Unpublished doctoral dissertation. OISE, University of Toronto.

Scott, P., Verne, J. & Fox, C. (2005). Promoting better nutrition: The role of dietitians. In A. Scriven (Ed.), *Health promoting practice: The contribution of nurses and allied health professionals* (pp. 247–60). Basingstoke: Palgrave Macmillan.

Shildrick, M. (1997). *Leaky bodies and boundaries: Feminism, postmodernism and (bio) ethics*. London: Routledge.

SIGN. (1996). Integrating prevention with weight management: A national clinical guideline recommended for use in Scotland by the Scottish Intercollegiate Guidelines Network. SIGN Publication Number 8, Edinburgh, Scotland. www.sign.ac.uk/pdf/sign8.pdf

Slynkova, K., Mannino, D. M., Martin, G. S., Morehead, R. S. & Doherty, D. E. (2006). The role of body mass index and diabetes in the development of acute organ failure and subsequent mortality in an observational cohort. *Critical Care*, 10(5), R137.

Solovay, S. (2000). *Tipping the scales of justice: Fighting weight-based discrimination*. New York: Prometheus Books.

Sørensen, T. I. A., Rissanen, A., Korkeila, M. & Kaprio, J. (2005). Intention to lose weight, weight changes, and 18-y mortality in overweight individuals without co-morbidities. *PLoS Medicine*, 2(6), e171 OP.

Spanier, B. (1995). *Im/partial science: Gender ideology in molecular biology*. Bloomington, Indiana: University Press.

Speller, V., Learmonth, A. & Harrison, D. (1997). The search for evidence of effective health promotion. *British Medical Journal*, 315, 361–3.

Steptoe, A., Owen. N., Kunz-Ebrecht, S. R. & Brydon, L. (2004). Loneliness and neuroendocrine, cardiovascular, and inflammatory stress responses in middle-aged men and women. *Psychoneuroendocrinology*, 29(5), 593–611.

Tessler, L. S., Laumann, E. O., Levinson, W. & Waite, L. (2003). Synthesis of scientific disciplines in pursuit of health: The interactive biopsychosocial model. *Perspectives in biology and medicine*, 46(3), S74–S86.

Van Cauter, E. & Spiegel, K. (1999). Sleep as a mediator of the relationship between socioeconomic status and health: A hypothesis. *Annals New York Academy of Sciences*, 896, 254–61.

Vitaliano, P. P., Scanlon, J. M., Zhang, J., Savage, M. V., Hirsch, I. B. & Siegler, I. C. (2002). A path model of chronic stress, the metabolic syndrome, and coronary heart disease. *Psychosomatic Medicine*, 64, 418–35.

Wacquant, L. & Bourdieu, P. (1992). *An invitation to reflexive sociology*. University of Chicago: Polity Press.

Wadsworth, M., Kuh, D., Richards, M. & Hardy, R. (2006). Cohort profile: The 1946 national birth cohort (MRC national survey of health and development). *International Journal of Epidemiology*, 35, 49–54.

9
Older and Younger Women's Experiences of Commercial Weight Loss

Debra Gimlin

Introduction

In light of the UK's rising rates of obesity and public concerns about their implications for the nation's health and medical resources, it is not surprising that the weight-loss market is growing, with its estimated value predicted to reach £11.2 billion by 2007 (Truby et al., 2006). Commercial weight-management groups, including Weight Watchers, Rosemary Conley's Eat Yourself Slim, Slimming World and many others, account for a large segment of the marketplace. As the sector leader in the UK, Weight Watchers takes in approximately £1 million each week from members' fees alone, in addition to its profitable business of selling various diet accessories, such as snack foods, recipe books, CDs and calorie-counting calculators (*BBC News Online*, 15 January 2002).

Such groups reflect the broader processes of consumer culture, which encourages the purchase of body-related goods and services by fostering a sense of personal responsibility for appearance (Featherstone, 1991). Many of these messages target women, instructing them that slenderness is synonymous with self-control, health, beauty and success (Hurd Clarke, 2002a; Oberg & Tornstam, 1999). At the same time, social scientists have pointed to the active ways that individuals respond to such messages (Croteau & Hoynes, 2000; Joanisse & Synott, 1999) and to the resources which groups and institutions provide for such responses (Martin, 2002). Indeed, some organisations – like the National Association to Advance Fat Acceptance in the US – attempt to empower their members by challenging negative cultural constructions of fatness (Gimlin, 2002; Sobal, 1999). Yet it would be overly simplistic to suggest that understandings of the body and its alteration are negotiated only within politically oriented groups. Rather, any setting where individuals come together to discuss their bodies and embodied experiences is necessarily a sight in which the meanings of both are constructed (Lester, 1999; Martin, 2002). Drawing upon participant-observation and interview data, this chapter examines such processes as they are played out in a commercial weight-loss group.

Women and dieting culture

Compared to men, women are more likely to diet and to use drastic weight-loss measures, including diet pills, laxatives and surgery (Garner, 1997; Wardle & Johnson, 2002). Such efforts are understandable, given that women pay particularly high social costs – in terms of marriage, income, education and divorce – for being overweight (Cash & Roy, 1999; Gortmaker et al., 1993; Rodin, 1992; Sargent & Blanchflower, 1994). Feminists have characterised the social sanctions for female fatness as a reflection of the 'tyranny of slenderness' that equates a woman's social value with her physical appearance (Chernin, 1981) and engenders female competition, jealousy and conflict (Brownmiller, 1984; Wolf, 1991). Feminist writers have also pointed out that many women's struggles with food and body size are complicated by the demands of partnership and motherhood (Charles & Kerr, 1988; DeVault, 1991). That is, while they are expected to provide nutritious and appetising meals for their families, women frequently feel obliged to deny themselves this food (also see Heenan, this volume). Moreover, numerous studies indicate that restrictive dieting is associated with a range of negative emotional and physiological effects, including depression and low self-esteem (Ackard et al., 2002; Pesa, 1999), reduced cognitive functioning (Green & Rogers, 1995, 1998; Vreugdenburg et al., 2003) and elevated stress response (Johnstone et al., 2004). Such findings are particularly striking in light of research which shows that limiting food intake rarely produces long-term weight loss (Aphramor & Gingras, this volume; Hesse-Biber, 1996), the implication being that most women who try to reduce weight are left feeling not only dissatisfied with their bodies but also ashamed of their presumed lack of self-control (Rodin, 1992).

At the same time, such claims do not apply equally to all females, given that women's investment in physical appearance has been shown to vary according to factors such as class (McLaren & Kuh, 2004; Wardle & Griffith, 2001), 'race'/ethnicity (Altabe, 1998; Molloy & Gerzberger, 1998) and sexual orientation (Beren et al., 1996; Bergeron & Senn, 1998). So too, there is growing evidence to suggest that body dissatisfaction is less significant among females in the later stages of the life course (Hetherington & Burnett, 1994). For instance, older women tend to view a wider range of body shapes and sizes as acceptable (Hurd Clark, 2002b) and to have more realistic weight-loss goals than their younger counterparts (Allaz et al., 1998). Research has shown, moreover, that older females frequently consider weight gain to be an 'unavoidable consequence' of the physical deterioration associated with ageing, rather than a marker of personal failure (Tunaley et al., 1999, p. 755). Thus, because constructions of ageing allow the older woman to see body size as beyond her control, they seemingly absolve her of responsibility for being overweight.

Organised slimming

Like age, the social context of dieting too shapes women's experiences of their body and weight management (Martin, 2002). While far from the only weight-loss approach available today, group slimming has grown increasingly popular over the last two decades (*BBC News Online*, 5 February 2003), particularly among women. In a recent survey of nearly 2000 adult Britons, 18.1 per cent of females reported joining a slimming club during the past three years; only 1.6 per cent of men reported doing so (Wardle & Johnson, 2002). Compared to other popular weight-loss techniques (such as meal replacements, books like *The Atkins Diet* and Internet slimming), group dieting is surpassed in popularity only by self-designed programmes, although its usage decreases with increasing weight. For example, among women categorised as 'obese' (indicated by a body mass index [BMI] of 30 or more), just under 44 per cent had joined a slimming group within the preceding three years, while 48 per cent had followed a diet of their own design; for women deemed 'overweight' (BMI = 25 to 29), the comparable figures were 30 per cent and 51 per cent, respectively (Wardle & Johnson, 2002). In Britain, Weight Watchers alone holds 7000 meetings every week, each with approximately 40 members of whom 85 per cent are women (*The Independent*, 3 August 2006).

Like dieting culture more generally, slimming organisations (whether commercial or not) have been criticised on a number of grounds. Quoted in the *BBC News Online* (5 February 2003), Susie Orbach has accused Weight Watchers of offering members false hopes of weight loss in the interest of profits. She says: 'Weight Watchers ... has to fail, otherwise how would it make money?' Spitzack (1990) focused instead on the confessional aspects of group weight management. She argued that a 'demand on the individual' to recount to others her personal transgressions 'of excess' and 'indulgence' is central to contemporary weight-loss discourses; this aspect of group slimming, in turn, reinforces broader cultural constructions of the female as 'insatiable' and the female body as uncontrollable, as well as women's own feelings of bodily alienation (Spitzack 1990, p. 18; also see Rich & Evans, this volume, for a discussion on the female body as imperfect). Millman (1981) raises several related points in her analysis of Overeaters Anonymous (OA), a not-for-profit weight-management group modelled after 12-step programmes like Alcoholics Anonymous. OA offers its members a means of overcoming the 'disease' of compulsive overeating, achieved by admitting their powerlessness over the condition. According to Millman (1981, p. 33), recovery requires that the member surrenders 'her "will" to a force beyond or larger than herself' and acknowledge that she is not in control. In so doing, the member also relinquishes her individual power, turning it over to the 'community' of self-proclaimed food addicts, who actively police one another's behaviour.

Such criticisms draw attention to the power of weight-loss discourses and the surveillance inherent in organised slimming, but they ignore many of the complexities involved in women's experiences of group dieting. On the one hand, weight-management companies shape members' perceptions. Their characteristics (e.g., formal structures, informal hierarchies and commercial interests), their rhetoric about the causes of weight loss and gain, and the emotional labour performed by personnel are all reflected in the vocabularies that members use to understand and describe the body and its management (Martin, 2000). On the other hand, individuals enter slimming groups with their own embodied perceptions and beliefs about weight and dieting; these too come into play as members make sense of their feelings and practices (Stinson, 2001). Existing criticisms of commercial slimming also neglect the degree to which women's experiences differ according to factors such as age. As the present research shows, organisational features (including processes of surveillance and vocabularies about the body and dieting) and resources (e.g., the opportunities provided for social interaction and support) vary in their meaning and significance for different age groups of women. Such variations are fuelled in part by broader cultural discourses around ageing, appearance and femininity, which are themselves incorporated into organisational teachings and approaches to weight management.

Research methods

The data for this study are drawn from six months of participant-observation in weekly meetings of a multinational weight-management corporation and in-depth interviews with a sample of its members. The sessions were held near Aberdeen, Scotland's largest shopping district and attracted a clientele that was diverse in age, employment background and education. After attending the meeting for two months and obtaining permission from the leader, I asked the approximately 40 (all female) members to participate in the study. Twenty women were interviewed: 15 aged 55–76 years and 5 aged 18–25 years.[1] All of the respondents were white and all lived in the Aberdeen area at the time of the interview; 15 had resided in Scotland throughout their lives. Fourteen of the women had been or were currently employed, part- or full-time; four of the five younger ones were students. Among the older respondents, all were or had been married and four were widowed. None of the younger women was married but one had previously cohabitated with a male partner. The older women had been members of the group for slightly longer than the younger ones and were more likely to have dieted in the past. Six older respondents had attended the meeting previously, dropped out and rejoined prior to the study.

The interviews addressed topics such as the respondents' motivations for joining the group, the influence of others upon their decision to lose weight and the challenges they had faced. They also collected basic information on employment, children and marriage. All but three of the one-hour interviews were conducted in the woman's home. In eight cases, I asked follow-up questions by telephone. The interviews were audiotaped and transcribed; respondents were invited to review the transcriptions but none did so. Thematic analysis of the interview and observational data was carried out according to the basic principles of the 'grounded theory' approach (Strauss & Corbin, 1998). Specifically, I read and re-read transcripts and notes and coded them according to themes such as 'age', 'beauty ideals', 'health', 'resistance' and 'organisational rhetoric'. I then examined the relationships among these themes across the sample (e.g., references to age-specific beauty ideals) and the differences and similarities in both themes and their relationships between and within the two age groups.

The project was motivated in part by my own experiences of 'fatness' and 'thinness' and my sense that neither feminist nor biomedical perspectives on weight management fully capture the complex nature of the practice or its variations by age, gender, class and ethnicity. Over the past 20 years, I have joined slimming groups several times and so entered the research site with certain expectations about what I would find. Those expectations were in turn shaped by feminist politics that incline me to be critical of beauty ideals and practices like dieting (including my own), to strive to 'hear' women's words and to acknowledge their potential to resist cultural imperatives. Numerous authors have stressed the importance of acknowledging one's involvement in the research process, not least because our respondents' narratives are themselves shaped by the research relationship (Cotterill & Letherby, 1993). In hopes of minimising inequalities of power and control in that context, I endeavoured throughout the study to 'make myself vulnerable' to participants (Stanley & Wise, 1993). I did so both by situating myself personally, politically and intellectually and by taking part in the group's activities, including the slimming programme itself, rather than simply conducting observations and interviews. Yet, I am different from my respondents in many socially important ways: I am American rather than Scottish, a middle-class academic and smaller than most members of the group; I am decades younger than the older women I interviewed and decades older than the younger ones. Such differences surely influenced my interactions with respondents, the accounts they provided and my understanding of their narratives.

Findings and discussion

Meanings that respondents attached to dieting coalesced around three discourses: ageing; previous embodied experiences and their historical contexts and interactions with others both within and outside the group. While such factors fostered a sense of personal responsibility for body size and a commitment to weight loss, they also provided study participants with a (greater or lesser) capacity to reflect upon that commitment and to forgive themselves their deviation from appearance ideals.

Motivations for weight loss

Although existing studies of organised dieting suggest that women of all ages attribute their participation to concerns about appearance (Martin, 2002), such accounts figured prominently only in the narratives of my younger respondents. For example, Sarah[2] (aged 22) said that she joined the organisation because she was '... tired of never looking good, never being able to wear the clothes that my friends can wear'. Other young women characterised the ability to wear small-sized clothing as a sort of 'yardstick' against which they measured their body's acceptability. Emily (aged 21) described this process of self-assessment:

> When you look in the magazine it's all size eight or ten and here's me a size 20. You know what I mean, I'd like ... to be able to go into a shop and pick up even a size 12 and have it fit.

Attention from males also served as grounds for the negative self-appraisals that motivated younger respondents' dieting. Karen (aged 18) remarked, 'My friends ... they all have boyfriends but I never did ... We'd go out and guys would chat them up. They'd only talk to me because I was standing there'. Maddy (aged 25) voiced apprehension about her marriage prospects. She said, 'My sister got married last month. I couldn't help thinking that if I don't lose weight, it'll never be my turn'.

Although the younger women cited other reasons (such as improving their physical fitness) for trying to lose weight, they did so only after repeated probes about their decision to join the group. In contrast, most older members attributed their dieting first and foremost to concerns about the health implications of being overweight. For example, Mary (aged 66) said,

> Whenever I go to the doctor's surgery, he says that I need to lose weight ... I know it's true because I'm not able to do the things I used to without losing my air ... It'd also be nice to look a bit smarter in my clothes.

While Mary's narrative begins by focusing on health, it eventually turns to the topic of physical appearance. The language Mary used, however, differentiates her motivations from those of my younger respondents: when she said that she wants to look smart in *her own* clothes, she implied that she does not feel compelled to look nice in all clothes, including styles designed for younger women. Cassie (aged 67) made a similar point, 'Maybe it's easier because I'm not a young girl. You see them in town wearing the wee tops and trousers ... Those clothes aren't really right for someone my age'. By Cassie's account, age reduces the pressure she might otherwise feel to display her body in revealing clothing: 'wee tops and trousers' may be appropriate for young girls, but not for a woman in her mid 60s.

Older respondents also commonly de-emphasised the relevance of appearance for their relationships with men. Cassie said, 'I don't think ... [my weight] really matters to ... [my husband]. We've been married nearly 40 years and he knows by now I'm never gonna be slim'. Similarly, Caroline (aged 70) contrasted her situation to that of a young, single woman 'going on dates'. She said, 'I suppose then I might be more self-conscious about my appearance'. The older women's tendency to minimise the role of male approval in their dieting likely derives in part from the fact that many were involved in a long-term relationship and so did not feel that finding or keeping a male partner depended on their achieving a slim body. At the same time, this tendency also reflects the notion that older women need not be overly concerned about their physical attractiveness and that attractiveness is related to slimness. Such assumptions were reproduced in the participants' talk. For instance, Cassie described how her husband might react if she cheated on her diet: 'He might say, "Do you think your doctor would want you eating that?" But he'd never say, "Don't eat that or you'll look fat."' Although Cassie was imagining her partner's remarks, this 'active voicing' produces an understanding that fatness is not attractive and that needing to be physical attractive to her husband is not essential in her marriage.

Experiences in the group

A central feature of weekly meetings was the 'weigh-in', in which every member's progress (or lack thereof) was measured and recorded by the leader. The weigh-in caused considerable anxiety for the members, including myself; at one time or another, most voiced apprehension at the prospect of having failed to lose – or even having gained – weight. This anxiety was based in part on the common perception of weight loss as unpredictable and even irrational. For example, after learning that she had gained a pound during the previous week, Marjory (aged 55) exclaimed, 'It can't be true! These scales can't be right!' The leader responded by reassuring Marjory that the scales were accurate. She then proposed other possible reasons for Marjory's lack of success, asking if she had eaten salty food recently or consumed a large quantity of water before weighing. Marjory said that she had done neither. The leader probed further: had Marjory eaten all of the food she was permitted? When Marjory answered in the negative, the leader said, 'That's probably it. Lots of people tell me that if they don't eat everything, they don't lose'. After my own first week of dieting, the scales showed that I had lost only half of a pound. Noting my disappointing performance, the leader remarked, 'Don't worry. Some people have to wait a week before they start losing'.

Such exchanges served important functions for both members and the organisation. For the latter, they reinforced company rhetoric which centres around the idea that weight loss requires nothing more than careful planning and reasoned eating (see Aphramor & Gingras, and Burns & Gavey, this volume for further discussions regarding the 'energy-balance' literature). Among members, they helped to infuse a seemingly illogical practice with some degree of order and alleviated the guilt associated with a failure to meet weight-loss expectations. However, even as organisational discourse emphasised the predictability of weight loss, many members apparently doubted their ability to control the process. This doubt was manifest in a variety of ritualistic practices preceding the weigh-in. I observed members of all ages crossing their fingers prior to stepping on the scales, wearing exactly the same outfit each week, avoiding the tea and coffee on offer until after weighing, and removing belts, watches and as much clothing as decency permitted (for similar findings, see Stinson, 2001). At the same time that they engaged in such behaviours, the members also made light of them. Mary (aged 66) joked, 'I'm on a roll these days. I'd hate to ruin my luck!'

Yet despite such similarities in the women's practices, there were significant differences in the ways that younger and older respondents talked about – and apparently thought about – the weigh-in experience. In particular, young women were considerably more likely to refer to the potential public shame associated with a failure to reduce. Emily (aged 21) explained,

> You try to lose weight because of the scales ... You have to go on them and you might be really embarrassed because someone else sees how you've done. They know if you've been bad.

Other young respondents related the weigh-in to body monitoring experienced outside the group. Catriona (aged 23) said, 'It's like going to the GP when you're young. You're put on the scale and the person weighing you goes "tsk, tsk"'.

The older women rarely associated the weigh-in with past experiences of body-related censure, even though many of them recalled being heavy in childhood and adolescence. In fact, older respondents generally recounted either positive or indifferent reactions to their youthful plumpness. Margaret (aged 69) said, 'Oh, I was a round wee'un. Back then, they thought it was healthy for children to have a bit of meat on their bones'. The apparently divergent experiences of younger and older members are attributable in part to the different historical contexts in which the two groups were raised. That is, as youths in the post-WWII period of relative food scarcity, the older women are unlikely to have faced the same degree of anti-size bias in childhood that arguably characterised the final decades of the 20th century. Accordingly, they commonly told me that they had become concerned about weight only in adulthood. Linda (aged 58) recalled, 'I gained three stone with my third child. I guess that's when I started tryin' to lose'. In contrast, younger respondents often remembered seeing themselves as 'fat' and 'ugly' even as children.

Despite such differences, the fact that the participants of my study had joined a weight-loss programme implies that both younger and older ones viewed their bodies as unacceptable. However, the experiences that drew these groups to the organisation apparently differed, as did the meanings they attached to the weight-loss process. For example, in speaking about the weigh-in, older women tended to focus on the usefulness of the practice rather than on its humiliating potential. Mary (aged 66) said, 'No one really *looks forward* to being weighed, but it's the only way to know if you're doing things properly' (her emphasis). Like Mary, many of the older respondents described the weigh-in as a moderately unpleasant, but essential, part of dieting – i.e., as 'the only way' to ensure that one is 'doing things properly'.

Older women also discounted the potential shame associated with a failure to lose weight, in part by emphasising the shared experiences (and common disappointments) of organised slimming. According to Rhoda (aged 69), that very commonality alleviates the embarrassment that might otherwise be associated with dieting setbacks. She said, 'If you have put on, it's not the end of the world ... [The other members] don't look down at you because they've been there'. Some older women even made light of their failure to comply with weight-loss expectations. For example, Caroline (aged 70) told me about her most recent weigh-in: 'I dinna lose weight, but it stops me from getting even huger ... You want to do it for [the leader] if not for yourself. I just haven't got round to doing it [laughs]'. Caroline's quote speaks to many of the complexities of older women's experiences of organised dieting. That is, it reflects Caroline's desire to lose weight (or at least not to gain), both as part of the group's project and in response to broader cultural standards for female appearance. It also evinces the interpersonal element of organised weight management, insofar as Caroline characterised her motivations for dieting in terms of wanting 'to do it for' the leader. And yet, Caroline's light-hearted attitude about her inability to reduce suggests that despite being committed to weight loss, she experienced little of the embarrassment described by younger members of the group. A later quote shed light on how Caroline avoids such emotions. She said, 'I would like to be slimmer, but then I think, "I've worked hard all my life ... what's the harm in a few sweeties?"' In effect, Caroline equates the 'work' of dieting to other forms of labour she has performed. Caroline may wish to be thinner, but a lifetime of hard work qualifies her for self-indulgence (at least with 'sweeties') during old age.

Older women's ability to evade the self-blame and -criticism experienced by younger dieters was encouraged by the organisation, insofar as it was personified by the group leader. That is, during several of the weekly lectures, the leader referred to the unique 'challenges' that many older women face when trying to slim down, including 'slow metabolism', hormonal changes and the difficulty of exercising after illness or surgery. Notably, such explanations do not release older members from the responsibility for losing weight, but they do provide them with age-specific, physiological justifications for any setbacks. So too, these explanations reinforce the notion that 'older women' constitute a distinct category of female, with bodily experiences, practices and goals that may differ from those of other women. Such notions were reflected in the older members' discussions of physical changes over the life course. Kate (aged 68) told me, 'When I was in my 30s and 40s, I could lose weight without really trying, but now ... over time, your body just, um, slows down. It gets harder and harder'.

Like the group leader's comments, the older members' behaviour also helped to define them as a sub-group of meeting participants. Specifically, the older women often sat together in discussions, chatted during the weigh-in and even socialised outside of class. Janice (aged 76) described their interactions: 'It's quite a nice group ... especially the wee group [of older women] that goes for coffee after [meetings]. Everybody's very friendly. It's nice, we all chat and have a good laugh'. In effect, the older members created a circle of friendship, or at least of acquaintanceship, from their involvement in the dieting programme. Although Janice's remarks fail to indicate whether or not the women's camaraderie was based in a shared sense of themselves as a distinct age group, they do suggest that the older members' interactions and affective attachments helped to foster support and encouragement among them.

The social and emotional meanings of food and feeding

Although writers like Brownmiller (1984) and Wolf (1991) argue that dieting undermines women's relationships by encouraging competition and resentment, the older respondents in this study seemed to benefit from the social resources provided by organised weight management. Such was not the case among younger members, who did not join in the older women's activities. Younger members also frequently described feeling excluded from social interactions with outsiders. For example, Emily (aged 21) said that she and her friends

> ... used to go out clubbing and we'd drink quite a lot, so obviously I can't do that now. ... Some of my friends think I'm avoiding them, but I don't want them knowing I'm going to [the group], at least not until I've lost a bit of weight.

Emily's dieting was problematic for her social relationships because it limited her participation in activities with her friends, to whom she was unwilling to confess her involvement in the weight-management programme. Like Emily, other young respondents indicated that they had both concealed their participation from outsiders and been forced to forego social interactions in order to follow the diet. Regarding the latter point, Maddy (aged 25) told the group about her recent decision to stop socialising with work colleagues. She said, 'I used to go to the pub with my workmates two or three times a week ... but I stopped going because I wasn't losing any weight'. In response to her announcement, the other dieters congratulated Maddy on her commitment to the programme.

Although the group's unanimously positive reaction to Maddy's decision suggests that it failed to recognise the interpersonal significance of eating with others, the organisation was apparently aware of at least some of the social aspects of food consumption. That is, both the company's literature and the group leader offered participants a range of strategies for maintaining their diet while sharing meals, such as becoming familiar with restaurant menus and planning choices in advance in order to avoid impulsive eating. These recommendations were typical of the organisation's overall approach, insofar as it emphasised the individual's capacity to alter weight through effective strategising. At the same time, however, the organisation also paid at least some attention to the emotional aspects of dieting. In fact, a considerable portion of class time was devoted to the exchange of support and encouragement among participants, most commonly in response to reports of successful weight loss. I recorded one such experience in my field notes: '[The leader] asked me to tell how much I'd lost that week. When I told them seven pounds, one of the older women said, "Now that deserves a round of applause" and they all clapped with great enthusiasm. I was embarrassed, blushing, feeling both ridiculous and proud'. Outside of such encounters, though, the organisation rarely acknowledged the emotional significance of food consumption and preparation.

Numerous studies show that cooking for others is closely connected to feminine identity and forms of caring (Fürst, 1997; Lupton, 1996). Women are not only responsible for meal preparation in most families, but also use the act of giving food to demonstrate caring and kinship bonds (DeVault, 1991). However, neither organisational literature nor the group leader addressed the gendered meanings of food and feeding or how those meanings might vary across the female life course. Because age is linked to family roles and responsibilities, older and younger women are positioned differently in relation to food-related practices and meanings within the family. Among the respondents in this study, all but one younger woman still resided full- or part-time with their family of birth, in which many meals were prepared by a female head of household. In that context, rejecting food was akin to rejecting affection and so problematic for familial relationships. Karen (aged 18) said,

> My mum is good when I first start dieting, but after two weeks, she's back to cooking the fatty things she knows I like. If I don't eat it, she gets upset. That's where the downfall starts.

Karen's eating is not simply a matter of rationality and education, as company rhetoric would imply. Instead, it involves choices that are produced and constrained by social relationships that imbue food with symbolic significance.

Because the organisation tended to assume that members are the primary food providers within their family, its recommendations were generally more relevant to the experiences of my older respondents, most of whom lived with and cooked for others. These women tended to prepare separate evening meals for themselves and their family members, largely because the latter resisted changes in their eating patterns. Cathy (aged 56) said, 'I wouldn't even try to get them to eat the foods I'm eating lately. Especially my husband, he'll hardly touch vegetables. I make his usual dinner ... he likes gammon steak, pork chops ... And I eat mine with him'. Strikingly, the burden associated with this added work was never addressed in meetings and the older women I interviewed generally viewed it as an undesirable but manageable part of their weight-loss efforts. Conversely, for the four older respondents who were widowed and living alone, participation in the programme seemed to instil cooking with a new significance. Although research shows that the value of food as an expression of caring is largely lost to women after their partner's death (Fieldhouse, 1995), such processes were in some ways reversed by the women's involvement in the slimming group. That is, preparing food according to the novel guidelines and requirements of the diet often constituted the first time that these women had cooked to suit (what they at least perceived to be) their own preferences. Barbara (aged 73) described this experience, 'You know, I've never cooked for myself before, but now I do! It's quite nice to eat the food I want ... rather than what someone else wants'. Food preparation may have lost its value as a way of caring for others. However, for women like Barbara, it took on a new significance as a means of caring for one's self.

Conclusions

This project highlights the importance of both organisational factors and social categories like age in shaping women's embodied experiences, self-perceptions and body-related goals. Specifically, the slimming group under study provided its members with resources (e.g., strategies for sharing meals while following the programme and legitimised explanations for dieting setbacks) and opportunities (for emotional support, social interaction and the like), which were informed in part by cultural understandings of the ageing process and, ultimately, served to reinforce those understandings. For example, the organisation presented older respondents with an age-specific vocabulary for excusing (at least temporary) failure to lose weight and so helped them to avoid the feelings of guilt that such failure might have engendered. At the same time, insofar as company rhetoric drew upon discourses about physical decline across the life course, it also contributed to social constructions of 'older women' as a group with unique body-related experiences and expectations. When played out in the setting of commercial slimming, such discourses were themselves mediated by company interests aimed at maintaining members' commitment to dieting and their sense of responsibility for body size. Thus, notions about the physical changes of ageing did not so much diminish older respondents' desire to lose weight as enable them to forgive their departures from normative bodily control and their deviation from (what they saw as) the more exacting appearance standards of youth, including those pertaining to slimness. Moreover, while such constructions may have benefited the older women by counteracting their potential self-reproach, they left unquestioned important assumptions about older females' sexual neutrality and disinterest in physical attractiveness.

Women's beliefs about appearance and weight loss are shaped not only by organisational processes and discourses of ageing, but also by individual life trajectories, personal relationships and historical circumstance. Each group of respondents in this study matured into early adulthood in a social environment characterised by particular appearance norms, gender relations and eating practices. In the latter decades of the 20th century, the proliferation of idealised human images, food abundance and the increasing availability of technologies for rationalising the body have all contributed to the body's status as a moral project (Shilling, 2003). In that context, younger respondents' understanding of the (unacceptable) body as a marker of (undesirable) selfhood is not surprising. Furthermore, being in their late teens and twenties and without the socially valued accomplishments of motherhood, employment and romantic partnership, younger members arguably had access to fewer resources for identity construction than were available to the older women. Seeing weight loss as a means of increasing their social value and attractiveness to others, the younger respondents' dieting may or may not have brought their body into line with contemporary standards for female appearance. In either case, though, because organised weight management problematised their relationships with outsiders, the young women's efforts to meet those standards seemingly came at considerable personal cost.

If measured by the organisation's standards (i.e., weight loss and its maintenance) the older dieters in this study were the more 'successful'. On average, they lost more weight than did the younger women, with five of the older (but none of the younger) dieters reaching and maintaining their pre-set 'goal weight' during my participant-observation. Arguably, the greater success of the older women is to be expected, given that their lives more easily accommodated the programme's assumptions and recommendations. However, even the younger members lost some weight and all were enormously pleased about having done so. In light of the improved self-perception that they professed, the fact that this weight loss can be considered an improvement to their health (all of my respondents met the organisation's minimum weight requirements of being 10 or more pounds over their 'healthy' weight and could therefore be classified as overweight and in a risk of developing health problems) and the social opportunities gained by older members, it is difficult to be entirely critical of commercial slimming like that studied here, despite the organisation's inattention to many important aspects of women's relationship to food. Cultural constructions that limit women's ability to accept their body – independent of its weight – rather than slimming groups per se are perhaps the more appropriate target for critique, given that (as any number of feminist authors have argued) such constructions lie at the heart not only of women's dieting, but perhaps also of their being overweight.

This study was limited by the small sample size and its focus on a single weight-loss setting. Additional research on other weight-management companies, non-profit dieting groups and government-funded slimming programmes would provide greater insight into older and younger women's experiences of organised weight loss. More emphasis on variables such as class, 'race'/ethnicity and sexual orientation would also elucidate the relationship between age and thinness norms, and the literature on women's body management has to date paid far too little attention to cohort effects. Despite a growing literature on older women's embodiment, longitudinal studies addressing the impact of changing social values on women's body (dis)satisfaction across the life course are sorely lacking. Such research would contribute greatly to social scientific understanding of the themes examined here, including women's attachment to beauty ideals and the ways that their negotiation of those ideals is both provided for and limited by cultural constructions of ageing, group processes and organisational structures.

Notes

1. Throughout the article, these groups are described as 'older' and 'younger' women respectively.
2. All names are pseudonyms.

References

Ackard, D.M., Croll, J.K. & Kearney-Cooke, A. (2002). Dieting frequency among college females: Association with disordered eating, body image and related psychological problems. *Journal of Psychosomatic Research*, 52, 129–36.

Allaz, A.F., Bernstein, M., Rouget, P., Archinard, M. & Morabia, A. (1998). Body weight preoccupation in middle-age and ageing women: A general population survey. *International Journal of Eating Disorders*, 23, 287–94.

Altabe, M. (1998). Ethnicity and body image: Quantitative and qualitative analysis. *International Journal of Eating Disorders*, 23, 153–9.

Aphramor, L. & Gingras, J. (2007). Sustaining imbalance – Evidence of neglect in the pursuit of nutritional health. In S. Riley, M. Burns, H. Frith, S. Wiggins & P. Markula (Eds), *Critical bodies: Representations, identities and practices of weight and body management*. Basingstoke: Palgrave Macmillan.

BBC News Online. 15 January 2002. Cashing in on slimmer ambitions. Retrieved 23 November 2006 from http://news.bbc.co.uk/1/hi/business/1759223.stm

BBC News Online. 5 February 2003. The diet business: Banking on failure. Retrieved 23 November 2006 from http://news.bbc.co.uk/1/hi/business/2725943.stm

Beren, S.E., Hayden, H.A., Wilfley, D.E. & Grilo, C.M. (1996). The influence of sexual orientation on body dissatisfaction in adult men and women. *International Journal of Eating Disorders*, 20, 135–41.

Bergeron, S.M. & Senn, C.Y. (1998). Body image and sociocultural norms: A comparison of heterosexual and lesbian women. *Psychology of Women Quarterly*, 22, 385–401.

Brownmiller, S. (1984). *Femininity*. New York: Linden Press.

Burns, M. & Gavey, N. (2007). Dis/Orders of weight control: Bulimic and/or 'healthy weight' practices. In S. Riley, M. Burns, H. Frith, S. Wiggins & P. Markula (Eds), *Critical bodies: Representations, identities and practices of weight and body management*. Basingstoke: Palgrave Macmillan.

Cash, T.F. & Roy, R.R. (1999). Pounds of flesh: Weight, gender and body images. In J. Sobal & D. Maurer (Eds), *Interpreting weight: The social management of fatness and thinness* (pp. 209–28). New York: Aldine de Gruyter.

Charles, N. & Kerr, M. (1988). *Women, food and families*. Manchester: Manchester University Press.
Chernin, K. (1981). *The obsession: Reflections on the tyranny of slenderness*. New York: Harper and Row.
Cotterill, P. & Letherby, G. (1993). Weaving stories: Personal auto/biographies in feminist research. *Sociology*, 27(4), 22737.
Croteau, D. & Hoynes, W. (2000). *Media/Society: Industries, images and audiences*. Thousand Oaks, CA: Pine Forge Press.
DeVault, M. (1991). *Feeding the family: The social organization of caring as gendered work* Chicago: University of Chicago Press.
Featherstone, M. (1991). The body in consumer culture. In M. Featherstone, M. Hepworth & B.S. Turner (Eds), *The body: Social process and cultural theory* (pp. 170–96). London: Sage.
Fieldhouse, P. (1995). *Food and nutrition: Customs and culture* (2nd Edn). London: Chapman & Hall.
Fürst, E. (1997). Cooking and femininity. *Women's Studies International Forum*, 20, 441–9.
Garner, D.M. (1997). The 1997 body image survey results. *Psychology Today*, 30, 30–44, 75–84.
Gimlin, D. (2002). *Body work: Beauty and self-image in American culture*. Berkeley, CA: University of California Press.
Gortmaker, S.L., Must, A., Perrin, J.M., Sobol, A.M. & Dietz, W.H. (1993). Social and economic consequences of overweight in adolescence and young adulthood. *New England Journal of Medicine*, 329, 1008–12.
Green, M.W. & Rogers, P.J. (1995). Impaired cognitive function in spontaneous dieting. *Psychological Medicine*, 25, 1003–10.
Green, M.W. & Rogers, P.J. (1998). Impairments in working memory associated with spontaneous dieting behaviour. *Psychological Medicine*, 28, 1063–70.
Hesse-Biber, S. (1996). *Am I thin enough yet? The cult of thinness and the commercialisation of identity*. New York: Oxford.
Hetherington, M.M. & Burnett, L. (1994). Ageing and the pursuit of slimness: Dieting restraint and weight satisfaction in elderly women. *British Journal of Clinical Psychology*, 33, 391–400.
Hurd Clarke, L. (2002a). Older women's perceptions of ideal body weights: The tensions between health and appearance motivations for weight loss. *Ageing & Society*, 22(6), 751–73.
Hurd Clarke, L. (2002b). Beauty in later life: Older women's perceptions of physical attractiveness. *Canadian Journal on Ageing*, 21(3), 429–42.
Joanisse, L. & Synott, A. (1999). Fighting back: Reactions and resistance to the stigma of obesity. In J. Sobal & D. Maurer (Eds), *Interpreting weight: The social management of fatness and thinness* (pp. 49–72). New York: Aldine de Gruyter.
Johnstone, A.M., Faber, P. & Andrew, P. (2004). Influence of short-term dietary weight loss on cortisol secretion and metabolism in obese men. *European Journal of Endocrinology*, 150, 185–94.
Lester, R.J. (1999). Let go and let God: Religion and the politics of surrender in Overeaters Anonymous. In J. Sobal & D. Maurer (Eds), *Interpreting weight: The social management of fatness and thinness* (pp. 139–64). New York: Aldine de Gruyter.
Lupton, D. (1996). *Food, the body and the self*. London: Sage.
Martin, D. (2000). Organizational approaches to shame: Management, avowal, and contestation. *Sociological Quarterly*, 41, 125–50.

Martin, D. (2002). From appearance tales to oppression tales: Frame alignment and organizational identity. *Journal of Contemporary Ethnography*, 31(2), 158–206.

McLaren, L. & Kuh, D. (2004). Women's body dissatisfaction, social class, and social mobility. *Social Science and Medicine*, 58, 1575–84.

Millman, M. 1981. *Such a pretty face*. New York: Berkley Books.

Molloy, B.L. & Gerzberger, S.D. (1998). Body image and self-esteem: A comparison of African-American and Caucasian women. *Sex Roles*, 38(7/8), 631–43.

Oberg, P. and Tornstam, L. 1999. Body images among men and women of different ages. *Ageing & Society*, 19, 5, 629–44.

Pesa, J. (1999). Psychological factors associated with dieting behaviours among female adolescents. *Journal of School Health*, 69, 196–201.

Rich, E & Evans, J (this volume). Learning to be healthy, dying to be thin: The representation of weight via body perfection codes in schools. In S. Riley, H. Burns, H. Frita, S. Wiggins, & P. Markula (Eds), *Critical bodies: Representations, identities, and practices of weight and body management*. Basingstoke: Palgrave Macmillan.

Rodin, J. (1992). *Body Traps*. New York: William Morrow.

Sargent, J.D. & Blanchflower, D.G. (1994). Obesity and stature in adolescence and earnings in young adulthood. *Archives of Paediatric and Adolescent Medicine*, 148(7), 681–7.

Shilling, C. (2003). *The body and social theory* (2nd edn). London: Sage.

Sobal, J. (1999). The size acceptance movement and the social construction of body weight. In J. Sobal & D. Maurer (Eds), *Interpreting weight: The social management of fatness and thinness* (pp. 29–47). New York: Aldine de Gruyter.

Spitzack, C. (1990). *Confessing excess: Women and the politics of body reduction*. SUNY series in gender and society. Stony Brook, NY: State University of New York Press.

Stanley, L. & Wise, S. (1993). *Breaking out again: Feminist ontology and epistemology*. London: Routledge.

Stinson, K. (2001). *Women and dieting culture: Insi de a commercial weight loss group*. New Brunswick, NJ: Rutgers University Press.

Strauss, A. & Corbin, J. (1998). *Basics of qualitative research: Grounded theory procedures and techniques* (2nd edn). Newbury Park, CA: Sage.

The Independent, 3 August 2006. Weight Watchers feels the pinch from rival diets. Retrieved 23 November 2006 from http://news.independent.co.uk/uk/health_medical/article1211286.ece

Truby, H., Baic, S, deLooy, A., Fox, K.R., Livingstone, B.E., Logan, C.M., Macdonald, I.A., Morgan, L.M., Taylor, M.A. & Millward, D.J. (2006). Randomised controlled trial of four commercial weight loss programmes in the UK: Initial findings from the BBC 'diet trials'. *British Medical Journal*, 332, 1309–14 (Electronic version).

Tunaley, J.R., Walsh, S. & Nicolson, P. (1999). 'I'm not bad for my age': The meaning of body size and eating in the lives of older women. *Ageing and Society*, 19, 741–59.

Vreugdenburg, L., Bryan, J. & Kemps, E. (2003). The effect of self initiated weight-loss dieting on working memory: The role of preoccupying cognitions. *Appetite*, 41, 291–300.

Wardle, J. & Griffith, J. (2001). Socioeconomic status and weight control practices in British adults. *Journal of Epidemiology and Community Health*, 55, 185–90.

Wardle, J. & Johnson, F. (2002). Weight and dieting: Examining levels of weight concern in British adults. *International Journal of Obesity*, 26, 1144–9 (accessed online).

Wolf, N. (1991). *The beauty myth*. New York: William Morrow.

Critical Bodies: Discourses of Health, Gender and Consumption

Sarah Riley, Hannah Frith, Sally Wiggins, Pirkko Markula and Maree Burns

The aim of *Critical Bodies* has been to demonstrate an understanding of body weight and body management as always political and intertwined with a multiplicity of discourses including health, medicine and identity. Consequently, the meanings attached to weight are dynamic, fluid and context dependent. The authors in this book wanted to challenge conventional understandings about weight and body management as individual problems. The chapters in *Critical Bodies* showcase work that represents a range of critical, post-structuralist and social constructionist research to examine meaning making around body weight as a social, rather than a private, process.

While the chapters in this book use different methodologies from a variety of theoretical approaches, they share a concern over how weight management practices are constructed in contemporary discursive contexts. They argue for a framework that constructs food, weight and body management as discursive and for analyses that locate meanings in context. In so doing, the chapters have explored some of the complex relationships between representation, subjectivity and practices in relation to weight and body management, problematising unified health ideals and/or body practices. In this concluding chapter, we draw together some of the overarching themes addressed by the contributors and then discuss areas of future research and how critical and constructionist research may be applied.

The disciplined body

In the introduction to *Critical Bodies* we discussed how powerful discourses discipline bodies through 'correct' body management practices. The work in this book highlights particularly the roles of health-related discourses, gender-related discourses and discourses of consumption in relation to body weight.

Health-related discourses

As many of the contributors note, the construction of obesity as a diseased state and an apparent increase in this 'condition' has become a concern for governments throughout the industrial world. This has provided the impetus for the 'war on obesity' rhetoric that provides the discursive backdrop to this book. This rhetoric has been generalised into a concern about weight that has come to characterise early twenty-first century healthcare policies, creating an unprecedented coupling of weight with health, which is then (re)produced in a plethora of contexts including schools (Rich & Evans), magazines (Burns & Gavey, Malson), commercial weight-loss literatures (Burns & Gavey, Gimlin), eating disorder treatment clinics (Malson) and dietetic advice to the overweight (Aphramor & Gingras). Body size has become such a 'key determinant' of health that it often excludes from consideration other factors that may be considered (Aphramore & Gingras, Burns & Gavey, Malson).

As we discussed in the introduction, 'war on obesity' rhetoric invariably draws on the bio-medical model to describe the processes of weight gain or loss. The bio-medical model produces techniques of body measurement and management that rely on mechanistic constructions of the body that focus on 'energy balance'. These produce public health discourses that call on people to maintain a 'healthy weight' through meticulous regulation of the body's energy intake. As many of the contributors to *Critical Bodies* note, there are problems with this understanding of weight and body management.

First, mechanistic views of the body ignore the social and cultural status of food, eating and body management, absenting the complex and subtle, socially meaningful contexts in which exercise is undertaken and food is consumed, such as the associations between food and love (Gimlin). This mechanistic view of food and eating can be understood as potentially enabling a variety of negative outcomes, such as attributing blame or failure to the individual who does not achieve a culturally ideal body (Aphramor & Gingras) or eating disorder treatment practices that themselves (re)produce fixations on food and reify certain body measurements as 'healthy' (Malson, Saukko).

Second, a bio-medical perspective creates the context in which it makes sense to understand those with problematic eating as pathological. Such deficiency models, often employed in popular, clinical, psychiatric and even feminist discourses (Saukko), locate the causes of problematic eating within the individual, obscuring any overlaps between problematic eating/body management and wider cultural discourses. Instead, the authors in this book have argued that clear parallels can be identified between broader discourses of 'normal' weight management (such as those that equate slimness with health) and those employed by women (and men) experiencing so-called disordered eating (Burns & Gavey, Day & Keys, Gill, Heenan). This obfuscation can be so complete that those entrusted with the care of people in treatment may themselves be re-articulating discourses that underlie eating disorders (Heenan, Malson, Saukko). In contrast to the bio-medical model, work that takes a critical and/or constructionist approach to weight and body management examines how eating disordered practices share discursive space with other more 'normative' practices. From this perspective disordered eating can be understood as 'a "crystallization of culture", a distressingly intense amalgam of certain dimensions of the norm' (Malson, this volume).

Gender-related discourses

In the introduction to this book, we discussed how problems with weight management, particularly eating disorders, are closely associated with cultural constructions of femininity. The authors continue this discussion in their chapters by examining the links between discourses of the feminine body, ideal thinness and health. For example, Day and Key's internet discussants were able to associate extreme thinness with feminine virtue by drawing upon a gendered aesthetic of slimness, which has long been entrenched in the Western cultural requirements of femininity and heterosexual attractiveness. Associating slimness with 'good' femininity draws on a historical narrative of beauty, which as the research in this book demonstrates, is often reproduced in both public (e.g. media) and personal accounts of health and body size (Burns & Gavey, Malson).

Discourses of women's understandings and experiences of their bodies are simultaneously also bound up within Western cultural understandings of gender that associate femininity with being passive, weak and dependent and men as active, strong and autonomous. Women are then problematically located within cultures that value autonomy and independence, but which associate these culturally valued traits with masculinity. Day and Keys, Heenan and Saukko discuss how women may find embodied (but potentially 'toxic') solutions to these contradictions in the production of a thin body.

Discourses of consumerism

In exploring embodiment and identity some of the contributors also touched upon discourses around the politics of consumption. Cultural shifts have led to politics being increasingly understood through actions that can be considered individual and 'everyday' (e.g. understanding exercising to maintain one's health as an act of good citizenship), rather than collective and official (for example, belonging to a political party) (Maffesoli, 1996; McRobbie, 2007; Walkerdine, 2003). In this context, consumption and everyday political identities become confabulated within postmodernist meaning making that values surface/aesthetics in their own right (and not as part of a system of vertical representation in which symbols represent some 'deeper' or 'inner' truth) (Featherstone, 1991; Lyotard, 1984). For example, Gill describes how her male participants drew on notions of rebellion to explain their clothing choices, even if there was 'little substantive evidence of revolutionary attitudes' (this volume). Burns and Gavey examined how women who engaged in bulimic practices were able to use external indices of health to argue that they were attaining a healthy *looking* body even if they had to engage in unhealthy behaviours to achieve it. In equating a healthy-looking body with being healthy, these women could then locate their body-management practices as forms of 'everyday' politics, since good citizens work to keep their bodies healthy (looking).

The politics of consumption were also drawn upon by Days and Key's internet correspondents, who described an anorexia-related identity constructed in terms of resistance to gluttony and over consumption, a powerful critique of capitalism given the un-sustainability of much of Western consumption. A topic also addressed by Heenan, who, in describing consumer culture as 'toxic' for women because it leads to self-blame when the goods consumed inevitably fail to fulfil desires and needs, suggests the use of a feminist-informed psychotherapy to find alternative constructions of self.

Negotiating individuality

In the introduction to *Critical Bodies* we noted that from a social constructionist perspective, bodies and subjectivities are understood as constituted by and within complex and multiple gendered discourses. For example, in one way or another, all the chapters in this volume describe contexts in which weight management is coupled with health, and weight/health with beauty, 'worthiness' and morality. The association between health, weight and goodness is reinforced by notions of neoliberal subjectivity, which positions the body and self as a project to be worked on. As we noted in the introduction, neoliberalism constructs an understanding of personhood that is rational, 'choiceful', responsible, independent and risk managing (Featherstone, 1991; Giddens, 1992; Rose, 1999; see also Heenan and Gill, this volume). Thus, as the contributors to this book identify (e.g. Aphramor & Gingras, Burns & Gavey, Gill, Malson, Rich & Evans), the 'ability' to have body with a 'healthy weight' becomes read as not only signifying health, but also a sign of achieving (or failing to achieve) appropriate personhood and citizenship. As Malson (this volume) argues:

> It might be hard to imagine how body-weight could be made to signify more ... it is already more than familiar as a fictive index of one's personality, moral character and aesthetic value; one's un/successful embodiment of femininity (or, increasingly, masculinity) and one's ability to properly conduct a self-directed life; one's health and, as a consequence of all this one might imagine, one's entire life.

Many authors observe the relationships between body size and morality and the consequent construction of cultures that encourage self-vigilance and the surveillance of others. For example, Rich and Evans describe how school girls are taught to associate thinness with health and morality though body perfection codes in which the body is understood as imperfect, in need of constant work and as a way of gaining recognition in a competitive school culture. In addition, Day and Keys discuss the way food and consumption are bound up in discourses of morality that associate certain foods with sin, debauchery, weakness and gluttony, which then enables women to position self-starvation as an act of (feminine) virtue and strength.

While professional discourses (e.g. psychiatric, medical, dietetic) and institutional influence (e.g. commercial dieting or schooling) discipline individuals, individuals also participate in the structuring of these discourses by reworking and creating new representations and practices or adapting the current practices to their own needs. For example, Burns & Gavey, Day & Keys, Gill, Gimlin, Malson & Saukko, all demonstrate how individuals shape/interpret the cultural images of slenderness to create understandings and practices of body management. For example, women negotiate cultural understandings of personhood that value both autonomy and dependence (Heenan, Day & Keys, Saukko); unhealthy behaviour (e.g. purging) can be used to produce a healthy (looking) body (Burns & Gavey); and health mandates in schools can create the contexts for some young women to develop eating disorders (Rich & Evans). Gill (this volume) examines how the association of masculinity with autonomy can become internalised and experienced as part of oneself 'that is, *really, truly our own*, not experienced as impositions or as socially constructed, but felt to flow from individual convictions, from uniquely personal choices'.

Day & Keys, Heenan, Gill, and Malson, all identify discourses of autonomy and 'choice' as ways of making sense of oneself in relation to weight and body management. For example, Day and Keys examined the employment of 'choice' rhetoric by young self-starving women, to resist psychiatric discourses. In several very different contexts (e.g. on-line pro-ana groups, psychodynamic analysis of gender development and consumer culture, men's talk on appearance and eating disorder treatment programmes) four chapters problematise the rhetoric of choice. They show how the rhetoric functions to mask the ways social contexts make available particular types of choices and promote a notion of free 'choice' that is anything but.

In addition, the authors in this volume regard identities as dynamic, complex and contradictory. For example, Day and Keys show how eating disorders can offer a variety of identities (such as virtuous femininity or a rejection of Western over-consumption) which are conceptualised as fluid, in constant negotiation, development and produced in interaction. These authors demonstrate, therefore, that there is no 'anorexic self' that is a unitary, pre-existing one-dimensional entity separable from the social context. Indeed, Saukko argues that discourses may be inherently contradictory because they 'echo the complex social struggles of their time' (this volume) and are thus always 'double-sided', being often simultaneously empowering and disempowering (Foucault, 1982).

To summarise, the authors in *Critical Bodies* emphasise that while weight management practices are part of a larger social context, individuals are not considered to be passive recipients for health, nutrition or exercise advice. On the contrary, they actively participate in the construction of their identities and practices within a given cultural context, albeit utilising the frameworks of knowledge that exist there. The chapters in this book show how representations of bodies/weight are negotiable and contested arenas, identity management as, thus, an active, fluid and relational process that occurs from moment-to-moment when people engage with identity construction, with one another and with the meanings found in their particular sociocultural context. For instance, Gimlin's chapter demonstrates how participants reported wanting to lose weight for the 'leader' as well as for themselves. Weight loss became, then, an element of the social activity in the groups just as it was part of communicative interaction on the 'pro-ana' websites examined by Day and Keys.

Researchers must therefore examine not only the broader sociocultural contexts that provide the conditions of possibility for the ways that people make sense of themselves and their actions (for example, how the rise in 'obesity epidemic' rhetoric has facilitated an association between health and weight) but also how discourses are deployed in moment-to-moment interaction, since different accounts can be used by the same people, almost in the same breath (see Gill for examples), and the same account can have multiple and contradictory meanings (e.g. Day & Keys, Saukko).

Where next?

It is noticeable that most of the empirical chapters in this book focus on those with so-called disordered eating (Burns & Gavey, Day & Keys, Malson, Rich & Evans, Saukko) or those who are actively trying to lose weight (Gimlin). In addition, the majority of chapters examine women's weight concerns. In this regard, *Critical Bodies* follows a well-established tradition in feminist research that focuses on the consequences of the cultural promulgation of female thinness (Yancey, Lesley & Abel, 2006). Setting up the 'obesity epidemic' rhetoric as the backdrop for our book, we have focused on how it informs the conditions of possibility that enable distressed eating, for example, in the construction of anorexic identities or bulimic practices. What we have not focused on are the issues regarding body weight, eating and health concerns of those who would be considered to be 'obese'. Aphramor and Gingras begin this work with their critical account of the 'fat bias' in dietetic and health promotion interventions, which reproduce negative stereotypes about the personal characteristics of 'over weight' people. This work could be developed further to explore the impact of 'obesity epidemic' rhetoric on the subjectivities and health-related practices of those with larger bodies.

A second area we identify for future research are issues of racialisation and ethnicity in relation to weight and body management. Several contributors comment on the impact of white, Eurocentric thinking in research on the body (Day & Keys, Gill, Heenan). For example, Heenan notes that while the beauty myth (Wolf, 1991) may have negative consequences for women, white women are at least invited to participate in this cultural ideal of femininity. The contributors call on us to explore the complex and subtle ways that subjectivities, including those orienting around ethnicity, as well as class, sexuality and able-bodiedness, interact with and impact on weight issues.

The third area we highlight for further focus is reflexivity, in particular the researchers' involvement(s) in the co-construction of participants' meaning making. Of all the contributors, only Gimlin discussed her own position in the research when she described her own body size and experiences of dieting that positioned her in important ways alongside her participants. Given that critical theory is generally critical of the pathologisation of individuals and the separation of some groups of women from others (see, for example, Heenan and Day & Keys), we suggest that future research more explicitly incorporates the researcher(s). We need to examine how the women we write about may be like ourselves, how we locate ourselves within the social construction of the body ideal and the practices that follow the logic of 'thin equals healthy'. After all, as women researchers do we not diet, have body concerns, and worry about weight gain and aging? We are further reminded by Saukko (this volume) that our analyses will have multiple and potentially contradictory meanings and thus to subject our own analyses to the same kind of rigorous critical eye that we apply to other discourses (see also Burns, 2006 for an example of this type of reflexive analysis).

Practical implications

Critical Bodies is part of a broader critical project within the social sciences that aims to explore the relationships between knowledge, power and action in order to provide analyses that examine the complex and subtle relationships between the self, body, eating/not eating and politics. The work presented here is critical of approaches that individualise concerns around body weight and size, in particular those that draw on neoliberal subjectivity, constructing (over, under and normal) weight as the outcome of a series of rational choices in relation to a mechanical body. Such approaches fail to incorporate or interrogate experiences of diet and exercise within their social contexts, creating health promotional activities that can, paradoxically, produce unhealthy behaviours and distressing outcomes.

Critical and constructionist approaches to weight and body management potentially have several practical applications including offering alternative ways of sense-making that can be used in therapeutic environments to overcome problematic ways of relating to food (see for example, Heenan, Malson, and Saukko). However, careful consideration is needed when thinking about how to apply our research. Psychology, in particular, has a history of reproducing dominant power relations either from self-interested or humanist motivations (for further discussion of this critique see, for example, Henriques, Hollway, Urwin, Venn & Walkerdine, 1984; Rose, 1996; Stainton Rogers, Stenner, Gleeson, 1996). We therefore need to consider carefully the role of the researcher in terms of suggesting 'alternative' or 'better' body practices: who do we empower, disempower, exclude or silence in our research practices?

When considering the 'application' or the utility of critical research, questions must be asked regarding how any of the findings might be applied and to whom this application might be aimed, particularly given the context in which policymakers often need 'hard facts' or generalisable claims to generate policy (see also Wiggins & Hepburn [2007] for a discussion on the issues surrounding the application of discursive psychological research).

The potential 'usefulness' of an approach is not something that can be measured in any straightforward way, nor would we wish to. Instead, taking a position that a critical stance on bodies and weight is already and inherently a practical approach, we might consider how, for instance, critical work may *already* be applied. For example, the work described by Rich and Evans on young women with eating disorders is an example of researchers working directly with young women to understand their ways of representing weight and eating practices. We might also consider how, instead of working with a cognitive model of talk/interaction as being separate from individual cognition and action, we can move towards a model where discursive practices of representation and identity are *always, already* intertwined with other social practices. That is, talk about weight (for example) *is part of* weight itself, since discursive and embodied practices are bound up with how we conceptualise and manage 'weight' as a thing in itself.

Therefore the potential for social change may already be incorporated within our research practice in a variety of ways (for example, employing co-operative inquiry and action research designs). This is not to argue that all research should engage with such active praxis, but there are a range of options for those who wish to move beyond academic research and theorising and who seek to implement critical work. For example, in this book, we have several researchers who are also practitioners: Aphramor and Gingras are dieticians whose work is informed by their critical thinking. Heenan is a psychotherapist who aims to actively change the therapist–client relationship based on critical reading of bodies in psychotherapeutic literature and Burns is the co-ordinator of the Eating Difficulties Education Network (EDEN). This is a feminist community agency in New Zealand that provides a range of support services for eating issues and works in the community to promote body satisfaction. EDEN's work is informed by an acknowledgement of the gendered socio-political context that contributes to disordered eating. There are other examples of 'practitioner-researchers' whose engagement with critical theory has directly informed their practice. For example, Blood (2005) uses her research on critical psychology to create different, more empowering language in her therapeutic work with clients with eating disorders.

Conclusion

Useful critical and constructionist research should produce novel solutions to their topic of study, and with them, new questions and problems (Potter & Wetherell, 1987). We hope *Critical Bodies* has met these criteria, providing the reader with alternative ways to understand weight and body management. In doing so, we hope this book has also raised a set of new concerns around how to engage with the complexity of bodily experiences in context. It is clear that much remains to be examined regarding the body and its location in a constantly changing discursive environment. We invite you to join in this project, to be another voice in the feminist tradition that seeks to enhance critical awareness in order to challenge oppressive gendered representations, identities and practices.

References

Aphramor, L. & Gingras, J. (2007). Sustaining imbalance – Evidence of neglect in the pursuit of nutritional health. In S. Riley, M. Burns, H. Frith, S. Wiggins & P. Markula (Eds), *Critical bodies: Representations, identities and practices of weight and body management*. Basingstoke: Palgrave Macmillan.

Blood, S. (2005). *Body work: The social construction of women's body image*. London: Routledge.

Burns, M. (2006). Bodies that speak: Examining the dialogues in research interactions. *Qualitative Research in Psychology*, 3(1), 3–18.

Burns, M. & Gavey, N. (2007). Dis/Orders of weight control: Bulimic and/or 'healthy weight' practices. In S. Riley, M. Burns, H. Frith, S. Wiggins & P. Markula (Eds), *Critical bodies: Representations, identities and practices of weight and body management*. Basingstoke: Palgrave Macmillan.

Day, K. & Keys, T. (2007). Starving in cyberspace: The construction of identity on 'pro-eating disorder' websites. In S. Riley, M. Burns, H. Frith, S. Wiggins & P. Markula (Eds), *Critical bodies: Representations, identities and practices*. Basingstoke: Palgrave Macmillan.

Featherstone, M. (1991). *Consumer culture and postmodernism*. London: Sage.

Foucault, M. (1982). Afterword: The subject and power. In H. Dreyfus & P. Rabinow (Eds) *Michel Foucault: Beyond structuralism and hermeneutics*. (pp. 208–26). Chicago, IL: University of Chicago Press.

Giddens, A. (1992). *Modernity and self-identity.* Cambridge, UK: Polity Press.
Gill, R. (2007). Body talk: Negotiating body image and masculinity. In S. Riley, M. Burns, H. Frith, S. Wiggins & P. Markula (Eds), *Critical bodies: Representations, identities and practices of weight and body management.* Basingstoke: Palgrave Macmillan.
Gimlin, D. (2007). Older and younger women's experiences of commercial weight loss. In S. Riley, M. Burns, H. Frith, S. Wiggins & P. Markula (Eds), *Critical bodies: Representations, identities and practices of weight and body management.* Basingstoke: Palgrave Macmillan.
Heenan, C. (2007). Feminist object relations theory and eating 'disorders'. In S. Riley, M. Burns, H. Frith, S. Wiggins & P. Markula (Eds), *Critical bodies: Representations, identities and practices of weight and body management.* Basingstoke: Palgrave Macmillan.
Henriques, J., Hollway, W., Urwin, C., Venn, C. & Walkerdine, V. (1984). *Changing the subject: Psychology, social regulation and subjectivity.* London: Methuen.
Lyotard, J. F. (1984). *The postmodern condition: A report on knowledge.* In G. Bennington and B. Massumi (trans). Minneapolis: University of Minnesota Press.
McRobbie, (2007). *Illegible rage: Young women's post-feminist disorders.* http://www.lse.ac.uk/collections/newFemininities/
Maffesoli, M. (1996). *The time of the tribes: The decline of individualism in mass society.* London: Sage.
Malson, H. (2007). Deconstructing un/healthy body-weight and weight management. In S. Riley, M. Burns, H. Frith, S. Wiggins & P. Markula (Eds), *Critical bodies: Representations, identities and practices of weight and body management.* Basingstoke: Palgrave Macmillan.
Potter, J. & Wetherell. M. (1987). *Discourse and social psychology: Beyond attitudes and behaviour.* London: Sage.
Rich, E. & Evans, J. (2007). Obesity discourse, education and identity. In S. Riley, M. Burns, H. Frith, S. Wiggins & P. Markula (Eds), *Critical bodies: Representations, identities and practices of weight and body management.* Basingstoke: Palgrave Macmillan.
Rose, N. (1996). *Inventing our selves: Psychology, power and personhood.* Cambridge: Cambridge University Press.
Rose, N. (1999). *Governing the soul: The shaping of the private self* (2nd edn). London: Free Association Books.
Saukko, P. (2007). 'I feel ridiculous about having had it' – Critical readings of lived and mediated stories on eating disorders. In S. Riley, M. Burns, H. Frith, S. Wiggins & P. Markula (Eds), *Critical bodies: Representations, identities and practices of weight and body management.* Basingstoke: Palgrave Macmillan.
Stainton Rogers, R., Stenner, P., Gleeson, K. & Stainton Rogers, W. (1996). *Social psychology: A critical agenda.* Cambridge: Polity Press.
Walkerdine, V. (2003). Reclassifying upward mobility: Femininity and the neo-liberal subject. *Gender & Education,* 15 (3), 237–48.
Wiggins, S. & Hepburn, A. (2007). *Discursive research in practice: New directions in psychology and everyday interaction.* Cambridge: Cambridge University Press.
Wolf, N. (1991). *The beauty myth.* London: Vintage.
Yancey, A. K., Leslie, J. & Abel, E. K. (2006). Obesity at the crossroads: Feminist and public health perspectives. *Signs,* 31, 425–43.

Index

A
Age/Aging 175–192
Agency 9, 46, 92–95, 117, 121, 123, 125–7
Anorexia Nervosa (see Eating Disorders)

B
Beauty 28–9, 35, 44–5, 56–7, 82, 129, 143, 148, 195, 196, 199
Biomedical model (see medical discourse)
Body image 5–7, 48, 81
   in men 102–4
Body management practices 16, 27–42, 139–154, 193–203
Bulimia Nervosa (see Eating Disorders)

C
Critical approaches 3–4, 8–17, 27, 30, 43–5, 77–80, 84, 158–9, 193–203
Class 49–52, 63, 69–70, 96, 101, 107, 111, 115, 128, 176, 199
Control 2, 34–9, 55–6, 66–7, 69, 73–4, 81–100, 113, 117–9, 121, 145
Consciousness raising 118
Consumer culture 16, 94, 102–4, 123–6, 175, 196

D
Dieticians/Dietetics 135–8, 155–74, 194, 197, 199, 201
Dieting 28–30, 60–73, 118, 124–6, 139–54, 155–6, 197, 200
Discursive approaches 3, 10–2, 23–6, 27–42, 43–6, 62–73, 139–54

E
Eating 65–72, 139–54
Eating disorders 27–42, 43–59, 60–3, 81–84, 103, 117–128, 139–154, 193–203

Anorexia Nervosa 27–42, 48–52, 62, 69, 73, 81–99, 103–4
   as individual pathology 30
   Bulimia Nervosa 52–56, 81–99, 139–154
   critique of medical/psychiatric categories 81–4, 119
   discourses of 43–59
   treatment programmes 31–42, 44–5, 62, 66, 193
   and femininity 43–59
   and psychoanalytic theory 118–119
Energy equation balance 136, 139–51, 155–174, 193
Exercise 29, 37, 65–6, 70–3, 142–52, 159, 194, 198, 200

F
Family 49–52
Fatness 4–5, 24–5, 27–30, 65–72, 101, 113–4, 155–74
   as antithetical to health/fitness 1, 89, 136, 139–41, 148, 157–159
   as related to morality 66–70
Fat burning 148–50
Femininity 9, 28–9, 33–6, 43–59, 88–92, 94–5, 124, 140, 152, 195–9
Feminist approaches 9, 27–31, 43–59, 81–84, 117–134, 141, 193–203
Fitness 24, 70–2, 146, 148, 157–62
Food and feeding 31–3, 50–5, 61–2, 66–8, 89–95, 120–123, 146–51, 168, 185–7
Foucauldian approaches 23–26, 27, 46–7, 56, 72

G
Gender (see also masculinity and femininity) 2–3, 27–39, 45–6, 51, 84–86, 118–20, 140, 145–6, 193–203
Gender development 120–23

H

Health 139–154 155–7, 193–203
  as personal responsibility 66, 164
  as conflated with appearance 2, 28–9, 34–5
Health promotion (see public health)

I

Identity 3, 16, 77–80, 81–99, 101, 116
Individualism 6, 30, 35–6, 39, 55–6, 60–1, 64, 66, 74, 83–4, 94–5, 104, 110–13, 193–199
Interviews 25, 43–59, 27–42, 62–3, 105–6, 141, 179–80

M

Masculinity 43–57, 101–116
Media 5–6, 30, 43–59, 60–1, 82, 101–116, 142
  as simplistic explanation for disordered eating 43–5, 57, 102–3
Medical discourse (see also energy equation balance) 4–7, 9–10, 64, 82–4, 93, 136–7, 143, 146, 150, 155–74, 194–5
Morality 23, 64–69, 73–4, 89–92, 114–5, 143–5, 155–74, 196–7
Muscularity 2, 34, 148

N

Normalisation 12–13, 25, 27–31, 66, 68, 71–3, 141, 149–52

O

Obesity (see also fatness) 60–1, 62–3, 66, 73, 136–7, 139–154, 155–174
'Obesity epidemic' 29–30, 35, 39, 61, 73, 90, 92, 137, 140, 194, 199
Object relations theory 117–134
Obsession 36–8, 53–6, 112–3, 140, 147, 149,

P

Participant observation 178–180
Passivity 31–3, 38–9, 41–52, 48–52, 85, 93–5, 195, 198
Pathologisation 4–7, 27–42, 93, 139, 140–1, 144, 200
Pedagogical discourse 24, 60–76, 155–74, 197

Perfectionism 34, 60–76, 82, 92–4, 107, 112–3, 197
Post modernism 138, 120, 123, 129–30
Post structuralism 9, 30–42, 141
Power 9–13, 25, 43–57, 74, 84–5, 91, 95, 129, 149, 193–203
Psychiatric discourse 4–7, 82–4, 93, 117–9, 168, 194, 197, 198
Psychodynamic approaches 117–134, 198
Psychotherapy 54, 56, 126–30, 196
Public health 3, 61, 89, 139–40, 155–74
Purging (see also vomiting) 140, 143, 145, 150–1

R

Race/ethnicity 101, 128, 176
Representations 16, 23–26, 86, 91, 96
  of eating disorders 25, 43–59
  of weight management practices 27–42
  of weight 60–76
  of male bodies 101–16

S

Schools (see pegagogic discourse)
Self 6–7, 44–48, 52, 77–80, 81–100, 117–134, 196–200
  critique of mainstream theories of self 81–84
  self-transformation 52–6
Sexual orientation 46, 105, 107–15, 174
Slenderness (see thinness)
Social constructionism 81–100, 194
Subject positions 85
Subjectivity 8, 12–5, 36, 77–80, 95, 120–127, 140, 196–200

T

Thinness 23–6, 27–42, 43–5, 94, 118, 128, 160, 195
  as socially valued 1, 2, 24, 82–6, 92, 94
  as conflated with health 24–5, 29, 64, 94, 137–8, 144–6

V

Vanity 52, 111–12
Vomiting (see also purging) 143–5, 149–50

W

Websites (pro-anorexia) 81–100
Weighed (Being weighed) 37, 71, 180–3
Weight control 139–54
Weight gain 31–3, 139, 142
Weight loss 61, 82, 118–9, 124–139, 142, 147–9, 155–7, 159–61, 166–7
and commercial organisations 135–8, 175–92
and 'healthy weight' 135, 139–54
Weight management practices 64–6, 193–203

9781349355433

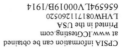

CPSIA information can be obtained
at www.ICGtesting.com
Printed in the USA
LVHW081711260520
656594LV00019B/1914